Great Britain

*A Concise Overview of The History of Great Britain –
Including the English History, Irish History, Welsh
History and Scottish History*

English History

A Concise Overview of the History of England from Start to End

Eric Brown

Text Copyright © Eric Brown

Legal & Disclaimer

The information contained in this book and its contents is not designed to replace or take the place of any form of medical or professional advice; and is not meant to replace the need for independent medical, financial, legal or other professional advice or services, as may be required. The content and information in this book has been provided for educational and entertainment purposes only.

The content and information contained in this book has been compiled from sources deemed reliable, and it is accurate to the best of the Author's knowledge, information, and belief. However, the Author cannot guarantee its accuracy and validity and cannot be held liable for any errors and/or omissions. Further, changes are periodically made to this book as and when needed. Where appropriate and/or necessary, you must consult a professional (including but not limited to your doctor, attorney, financial advisor or such other professional advisor) before using any of the suggested remedies, techniques, or information in this book.

Upon using the contents and information contained in this book, you agree to hold harmless the Author from and against any damages, costs, and expenses, including any legal fees potentially resulting from the application of any of the information provided by this book. This disclaimer applies to any loss, damages or injury caused by the use and application, whether directly or indirectly, of any advice or information presented, whether for breach of contract, tort, negligence, personal injury, criminal intent, or under any other cause of action.

You agree to accept all risks of using the information presented inside this book.

You agree that by continuing to read this book, where appropriate and/or necessary, you shall consult a professional (including but not limited to your doctor, attorney, or financial advisor or such other advisor as needed) before using any of the suggested remedies, techniques, or information in this book.

Table of Contents

Introduction

The history of England is just as interesting as its land and people. It's a long and winding summary of accounts relating to its centuries of struggle, turmoil, upheavals, and scandals. Although to an outsider, it's interesting to note that England's history was formed by a violent autocratic powerplay among long lines of dynasties and anarchy exhibiting their greed for power and bloodshed, still everything had helped formed what England is today.

Even what seems to be an unending battle of wills between the state and religion is another factor that's noteworthy along with the long lists of women who played significant roles in major events which had contributed much to the development of its culture.

The history of England, just like the history of any nations revealed to us the constant fight for supremacy among those in power which had not only sacrificed so many lives - especially of people born with less luck if not the lack of it.

It's sad to note that the authority given unto these people along with many lives that were put into their hands were exploited and rummaged while they go after their own personal whims and schemes. As history unfurls itself before our eyes, it showed us that even religion was only a tool for those who seek for power but was not lucky enough to take the throne. There's really no difference between these two superpowers. In fact, they share the same goal which is to rule the world at the expense of the land and people.

Regardless of the countless bloodsheds and sacrifices of many who were regarded as a pawn in their persistent powerplay, the constant struggle always leads to a change and it's this changes which brought humanity to where it is now.

Despite the many losses in the past, England remained to be a symbol of power and wealth. Even as England has become more diverse culturally, it continues to exert a strong cultural influence on the rest of the countries all over the world. English literature, arts, and culture are still enjoying a wide audience overseas, and the English language remains to be the preferred medium of communication in many parts of the globe especially in the world of business.

Chapter 1: Prehistory and Antiquity

The English prehistory includes massive spans of time, so archeologists at that time divide history into three major periods.

- Stone Age
- Bronze Age
- Iron Age

Each of these periods was further subdivided. Take for example the Stone Age which was further subdivided into:

- Paleolithic (Old)
- Mesolithic (Middle)
- Neolithic (New Stone Age)

Archeological findings and the use of cutting-edge technologies including DNA, Isotopic, and chemical analyses along with the new ways of interpreting carbon dating all helped in overturning old certainties while challenging long-held ideas and raising new questions about the fascinating pre-historical events in the history of England.

The Early Dwellers

The Ice Age

Some archeologists working in an area near Happisburgh in Norfolk were able to uncover flint tools dating back to about 900,000 years ago. These tools were used by hominoids who would periodically visit Britain during warmer eras between Ice Ages. At this time, Britain wasn't even an island but a peninsula of the Continent of Europe.

So far, the oldest human remain found in England dated back to 500,000 years ago of a six-foot-tall species of Homo Heidelbergensis. Based on archeological studies, the Neanderthals who were shorter and stockier visited Britain between 30,000-35,000 years ago. Following them were the direct ancestors of the modern human race.

The people during the Ice Age created the earliest known cave art in England about 13,000 years ago at Creswell Crags in Derbyshire.

The Stone Age

Hunters and Gatherers (9500-4000 B.C.)

As the climate improved at the end of the Ice Age, people in Britain were preoccupied with hunting and gathering of food. Although these people were generally nomadic, recent discoveries showed that some had settled lifestyle. Around 6500 B.C., the rising water level had buried the land bridge connecting to Europe leaving behind Britain as an island.

Over a thousand years ago, the first group of people that settled in England were from Europe. They were Stone Age hunters living all over Europe and the British Isles. It was around 2400 BC when a group of farmers arrived in England from Southern Europe. These people built the mysterious stone monuments including the Stonehenge.

In about 1700 B. C., another group of invaders came. These people were taller and stronger. They came from Germany and Holland and were using metal tools. Like all the settlers who came before them, they mixed and married with the natives.

First Farmers (4000 B. C.)

Farming was first introduced in England around 4000 B. C. by people from Europe who traveled by boat. They planted barley, wheat, and pulses, but people at that time still relied mainly on wild food and resources. Because Neolithic and Early Bronze Age people were used to hunting, instead of settling in one place, they moved around within territories. Such territories were focused on communal monuments. Some of these were gathering places while others were burial sites.

Sacred Landscapes (3500-2300)

During the Middle up to the late Neolithic era, there were new types of monuments which appeared including timber circles like Woodhenge at about 2300 B. C. Stone circles like Castlerigg in Cumbria appeared at around 3000 B. C. There were also earthwork henges like the Knowlton in Dorset. Sometimes, henges and circles are combined such as those stone circles at Avebury and Stone henge which were both estimated to be built about 2500 B. C.

In some other places, there are several types of monuments that were built in the same area over long periods like those sacred landscapes at Avery, Stonehenge, and Marden Henge. It is somewhere during this time when flint tools and weapons were first discovered at Grime's Graves in Norfolk.

Bronze Age

The first metal and jewelry reached Britain along with the new kind of pottery known as Beaker. When people died in the early days, these objects were buried along with them. Initially, metals used were made of copper but later - about 2200 B.C. bronze was introduced.

Iron Age

From the early - middle Iron Age, people began to make tools and weapons out of iron in addition to building bigger and elaborated hillforts like the Old Oswestry in Shropshire and Maiden Castle in hillforts. There were likewise many pieces of evidence recovered suggesting the dominance of a warrior aristocracy and emergence of tribal territories at that time.

It was during the late Iron Age that tribal centers were created and emerged such as Stanwick Iron Age Fortifications, North Yorkshire and Lexden Earthworks, Essex. It was also during this period that they deal with the Romans, and this became the beginning of the famous entry in English history as a result of their contacts with the Greeks and Romans. Famous among these accounts were those of Julius Caesar who raided Britain in 55-54 B.C. Accounts during this period include chariot warfare and the Druids - who were religious leaders who were said to have worshipped in oak graves and performed sacrifices. After a hundred years from the time of Caesar's raids, Emperor Claudius ordered for the invasion of the British territory.

The first metal and jewelry reached Britain along with the new kind of pottery known as Beaker.

The Celts

The Celts first step foot in England in about 800 B.C. They came from Germany and France. Another group of Celts who were fierce warriors came in the 4th century invading lands in the north of England and Ireland. They were the first group of the aristocracy to control a large part of Britain. They imposed the Gaelic language on the people which up to now are still used to some degree in Scotland, Ireland, and Wales.

The Romans

After the Celts were the Romans. They first came in 55 and 54 B. C. They lived peacefully in England for about 300 years and introduced a highly developed legal system - the system of taxation, engineering skills, the Latin language, and Roman architecture.

In the fourth century, Rome was converted to Christianity. To spread religion, Christian missionaries traveled to England. We call this period Celtic-Roman period because the two groups were able to live peacefully.

In the 4th century, at the time of the collapse of the Roman Empire, the Roman troops left England to go back to their place. There were disagreements among historians regarding the contributions of the Romans to the History of England. While others because their contributions were great, others believed it was indeed very minimal.

But after the Romans had left, the remaining Celtics were invaded by another group - the Anglo Saxons who played a significant role in English History.

Chapter 2: Medieval England

Norman Legacy

King Henry II became the King of England in December 1154 following anarchy and a Civil War of Stephen's reign. Though Stephen had sons that might succeed him, these sons were not able to reign in their father's stead. Eustace, Stephen's eldest son, died in 1153 while his younger son lived as count of Mortain. While primogeniture was not then established in England, Stephen acknowledged Henry II as his heir- designate to the throne of England.

Grandson of Henry I of England, young and vigorous Henry II became king on December 1154 and succeeded the civil war and anarchy of Stephen's sovereignty. Under him and his sons' (Richard I and John) kingship, Britain experienced fast uprising population, establishments of new towns, forest clearances for fields, and outward-looking crusading enthusiasm. Britain also attested to the 12th-century renaissance in arts and cultural festivals demonstrated by the Winchester Bible of c.1160 which was made from 300 calves' skins and extravagantly decorated with gold and lapis lazuli applied by a team of manuscript illuminators from continental Europe.1066 Norman invasion legacies remained.

Bruce, Balliol, and Wallace- families of French origin- that were dominant in Scottish medieval history became a minority that overlaid Scott population. Until after 1350, the aristocrats spoke French. For instance, the Saxon 'ox' and 'swine' were called 'boeuf' and 'porc' in French. England's north of Saxon (Sassenach) - normalized lowland of Scotland stayed disparate from the highlands where Gaelic flourished though both shared a common vernacular dialect with the north of Humber, England. Meanwhile, Ireland also was less dominated by the Normans. Despite Norman aristocracy and monarchy, majority of the indigenous regional culture still existed.

English Nationalism

There were external factors that contributed to making England more dissonant and inward-looking after 1200.

The Moslem recapture of Jerusalem in 1187 and the Battle of Hattin made a serious blow to Western hopes of international crusading ideals. Subsequent to this was also discouraging because in his campaign against Saladin, Richard I failed to recapture the city. In 1204, crusading ideals were fractured due to the siege and capture of Christian Constantinople led by a Venetian crusading force that was originally destined for infidel Egypt. Finally, crusading ideals were extinguished.

English barons declared anti-foreign attitudes as they became more conscious of their nationality. Soon after 1200, French lands were lost to John that frustrated and made England more country-conscious. As the population increased in the 1200s, many younger warrior sons looked for lands and glory. Primogeniture became more appealing and established.

Henry III (1216-1272)

King Henry III was not a militant king, and it was evident in his half-hearted campaigns in regaining lost lands in France by his father, King John. He conceded his claims to northern France and iconic Normandy by signing the Treaty of Paris in 1259 and secured remote Gascony. His reign induced closer links with France when Louis IX (St. Louis) became his brother-in-law. Thus, French culture was reverberated especially in Gothic architecture, in Britain.

Even though French names and manners were promulgated, English barons declared anti-foreign attitudes towards immigrant courtiers as they were increasingly conscious of their own nationality. In fact, the spare, simple Gothic architecture of the 13th century was also called

'Early English' by scholars, and the Salisbury Cathedral (built between 1220 and 1258) served as its epitome.

Edward I (1272-1307) and the English Government

During the 13th century, dominant English crusading continued. When the father of Edward I died in 1272, he was away crusading for two years.

Due to effective government administration in England, smooth transitions occurred. Centralized financial record keeping of the great roll of exchequer still functioned and remained unbroken early in the reign of Henry II. Indications of less dominant monarchy and tributes to growing institutions of the English government were accepted in this era:

Scotland recovered the Western Isle. England proved that expansionism was not the only way to preserve the country. Though absent for almost the entire period of his reign, Richard I realm was governed successfully.

Henry III succeeded his unpopular father at the early age of 9 and reigned for almost 10 years. The power transition from Henry III to Edward I while Edward I was gone for 2 years crusading.

Even though the financial organization was effective, some disadvantages also occurred.

- Peasant agriculture prospered.
- Urbanism grew.
- Rapid population growth.

These meant that during the 13th and 14th century, England could focus on Wales, Scotland and the lesser part of Ireland - its nearest neighbors.

When some parts of Wales were subdued by Edward I, he focused on building great castles in Wales by using his government's wealth. Through this, North Wales was put under his power.

On the other hand, the Western Isles were regained by Scotland from Scandinavian colonists subsequent to the Battle of Largs in 1263.

Another opportunity arose for England because of Alexander III of Scotland's untimely death due to a riding accident in 1289. This enabled England to get involved in the center of Scottish politics as Edward I was called to judge various claimants to the throne of Scotland.

His pre-eminence was shown in a contemporary manuscript illumination that portrayed him at the center of Prince Llewelyn of Wales (right) and Alexander, King of Scotland (left).

The Anglo-Saxons

It is said that the Roman Period in Britain ended in the year 410. It was during that time when the Roman Emperor Honorius told the Britons to look after their own defenses since the Roman Empire itself was suffering from constant attacks from the nearby barbarian kingdoms. Because of this, the Roman rule over the British land faltered, giving the nearby people from Northern Germany and Southern Scandinavia as well as the Vikings in the north the opportunity to dominate the entire territory. As of today, these immigrants became known as the Anglo-Saxons.

Known to be strong warriors, the Anglo-Saxons conquered southeast Britannia in year 450 and expanded their domain from there for over six centuries. During that time, England, as we know now, is still not in existence, though it is recorded that the one found by Anglo-Saxons was a heptarchy, meaning that the land is divided into seven petty kingdoms, each ruled by a different king. These seven petty kingdoms are the following: Wessex, Essex, Mercia, Northumbria,

Kent, Sussex and East Anglia. According to Henry of Huntingdon's Historia Anglorum, these kingdoms are medieval when it comes to historiographical traditions.

The rule of the seven petty kingdoms did not come without risks; however, In order to maintain it, they did lots of power struggles against the Vikings, who eventually defeated them through numerous territorial raids. This forced them to concede before the power of various Danish kings, most notably Canute (also known as Cnut or Knut), who managed to rule an empire in England as well as in Norway and Denmark, his own country.

During the ninth century, the country was divided between the Anglo-Saxons and Anglo-Danes through various Viking invasions, resulting in the rise of Old Norse language in provinces that were invaded. It was during the eleventh century that England became part of the Danish crown, which lasted until the Norman Invasion of the year 1066.

Origin

According to Bede, a Northumbrian monk who wrote about the tribe some centuries after wrote that the Anglo-Saxons were actually 'immigrants' from Southern Scandinavia and Northern Germany. Right after the fall of Roman Empire in Europe, the Celtic tribes resumed fighting against each other, making one of the local chieftains to hire help from those immigrants, which are composed of Angles, Saxons, and Jutes. However, when the war between Celts is over, the immigrants did not return to their homeland. Instead, they started claiming the entire territory for themselves, fighting and pushing the Celtic tribes north towards Scotland, west towards Ireland and south towards Wales.

On the other hand, the Frisians, Franks and the Batavi tribes traveled by boat to Britannia through the North Sea and the English Channel. Eventually, the occupied lands became known as England, meaning

'Land of the Angles.'

Once settled, the Anglo-Saxons merged together and formed their own towns, which eventually became kingdoms. By the 9th century, all territories in England except Scotland were unified into four different Anglo-Saxon kingdoms, namely: Wessex, East Anglia, Northumbria, and Mercia. The kingdoms of Essex, Sussex, and Kent were added to their number at a later date.

The Vikings (793 - 1066)

Also known as Norsemen, Osemen or simply Nords, the Vikings rose into power during the year 793 or late 8th century. Vikings are well-known for their ferocity as well as being battle-hardened warriors. The most memorable about Vikings, however, is none other than their raiding activities.

The primary target of these raids is monasteries since these places are rich with provisions, valuable treasures as well as potential slaves. The first-ever record of a monastery experiencing a Viking raid is during the year 793 when the Vikings raided the monastery in Lindisfarne, a place in the northeast coast of England.

Origin

Unlike the popular belief, the Vikings aren't a particular Scandinavian tribe. Instead, it is a collective name for a group that is usually composed of sons of Scandinavian and Northern Germanic royalty or nobility. Having inherited nothing from their parent's estate, these sons banded together with other fierce warriors like themselves and decided to leave their homeland. Known to be excellent sailors and traders, the Vikings usually raid places of value such as properties belonging to the Ecclesiastical community (e.g., Monasteries, Abbeys, and Churches) as well as towns, cities, and villages.

At first, the Viking raids only last for a few days or weeks per year before they return to their homelands to sell their booty. In addition to that, those raids are usually done by one or two longboats and a cargo vessel for carrying off booty. However, when the raids became known to be a very profitable business for Vikings, their activities also intensified and became widespread throughout Europe as well as in some parts of Asia. Eventually, their numbers increased to more than ten longboats and the raids last for months. Needless to say, the places the Vikings had raided during that time were literally 'shaved' from head to toe.

Culture

Since Saxons and Vikings came from the same places, they also happened to share similar traditions and beliefs despite their slight differences in language. Their gods happened to be the deities in Scandinavian or Norse Mythology, of whom Odin (for Vikings) or Wotan (for Saxons) or Woden (for Anglo-Saxons) is the chief. When it comes to technology, Vikings are unrivaled when it comes to their navy, as evident by their so-called 'longboats' and Knarr, their sea vessel for carrying off cargo.

Having reached its peak of development during the 9th century, the Viking Longboat is a shallow, long and narrow vessel. Optimized mainly for speed, the longboat is also capable of traveling rivers and coastal waters that can easily destroy other sea vessels. As a part of their custom, the longboats include finely-carved figureheads of mythological beasts in order to identify its owner or captain. In addition to that, the Viking longboat's keel and hull are reinforced with iron so that it can ram right into enemy ships with ease. They also use an instrument that is similar to astrolabe as well as caged crows. Pretty symbolic of the two crows that bring news to Odin, the Viking's caged crows are specially-trained to find land wherever they go.

The Normans (1066 - 1154)

Right after the Vikings, Normans, an ethnic group that originated from Normandy in Northern France, dominated England.

Origin

Even though the Normans that invaded England in the year 1066 came from Normandy, their origins can be traced back to Vikings from Scandinavia that raided the land until the 8th century. Unlike the other Vikings who usually terrorize coastlines and gathering profits from their collected booty, these 'Proto-Normans' decided to settle down and cultivate the land that they claimed for themselves. They also traded goods and shared knowledge with their neighbors peacefully until they eventually embraced their neighbors' traditions, which led them to abandon Paganism and embrace Christianity.

At the beginning of the 10th century, Charles the Simple of France decided to give some lands in Northern France to Rollo, a distinguished Viking Chief during that time. He did this since he thought that such a gesture would stop the Vikings from raiding French territory. By accepting the land, Charles the Simple hoped that the Vikings will join the feudal economy and will serve him in times of war. The land that he gave became known as Northmannia, which means "Land of the Northmen." It was then shortened to Normandy later.

By doing such thing, Charles the Simple managed to protect his own territory from the terror of the Vikings since these 'Proto-Normans' decided to initiate their raids elsewhere in respect for his goodwill. They also intermarried with the French, so they all became French-speaking Christians by the year 1000. However, they also started conquering territories in Italy in the year 1030. They were known to have taken over most of Southern Italy sixty-nine years later.

Culture

Well-known for being devout and pious Christians, Normans are remembered best for their achievements in the Crusades as well as displaying remarkable skill in governing territories, especially in Italy. They also established many churches, cathedrals, and monasteries for spreading Christianity as well as schools for education. After conquering England, the Normans also built many castles to defend their territory.

Chapter 3: Royal Turmoil and Successions

The Tudors are one of the most distinctive lineages in English history as Henry VII of Welsh origin significantly ended the Wars of Roses and established the House of Tudor. Henry VII and his children - his son Henry VIII, and his grandchildren Edward VI, Mary I, and Elizabeth I ruled for 118 eventful years.

It was the House of Tudor who took England's throne when he defeated Richard III - the last Plantagenet king. When King Henry defeated King Richard III of the Yorks at the Battle of Bosworth, it was the beginning of the Tudor era which lasted until the death of Queen Elizabeth I in 1603.

Henry VII, a Lancastrian laid the foundations of his dynasty and brought an end to the civil strife of the Wars of the Rosea. By his marriage to Yorkist heiress, Elizabeth of York, he was able to securely establish the Tudors to the throne of England.

During the reigns of three generations under the Tudor monarch, England underwent huge changes as Henry VIII ushered in a new state religion. The increasing confidence of the state goes along with the growth of an English culture distinct to them.

The English saw unprecedented upheaval during the Tudor era. The five Tudor kings and their queen introduced big changes that were brought down and were still with us until today.

The Reformation and Counter-Reformation

Henry VII (1485-1509)

Henry VII brought 85 years of civil war to a halt as he unified two factions - the Yorkists and the Lancasters and married Elizabeth, daughter of Edward IV and heiress of the York. Elizabeth bore him two sons, Arthur and Henry VIII. Callous and calculating, Henry secured his position by growing his financial base mostly at the expense of his people and controlling aristocratic powers.

Henry VIII

From the mid-1520s, the reign of King Henry was overshadowed by his need for a legitimate son to become the heir to the throne. He had a daughter by his first wife, Katherine of Aragon named Mary. Too desperate to have a son, he married Anne Boleyn but never got the papal consent for a divorce which made Henry decide to break ties with Rome. In 1533, he declared himself as the head of the Church of England and not the Pope. This decision led to the initiation of the Reformation of English religion, which was the most crucial event of the Tudor period which helped shape the history of England for centuries to come.

In line with the Reformation, Henry launched the Suppression or what was known as the Dissolution of Monasteries (1536-1940). The king and many favored subject were greatly enriched with the confiscated wealth of the monasteries.

Edward IV

With the accession of Edward VI, radical Protestant reform began as Edward himself is an enthusiastic Protestant. Despite the rising against the new Protestant Book of Common (1949) by a West Country, still, the reform intensified under Edward's Lord Protector, the ambitious Duke of Northumberland.

Crowned at the age of nine, Edward VI was the first king to be raised as a Protestant. His parents were Henry VIII and Jane Seymour. Edward was the King of England and Ireland from 1547 - 1553.

Because the former King Henry VIII had broken ties with Rome, Edward was educated by a Protestant tutor. His uncle who was his constant companion and also a Protestant encouraged the boy to make radical changes on the present. All these consequently led to his decision of dissolving chantries and seizing all their treasures. Such action was an attack on the Catholic's belief in Purgatory along with saying prayers for the dead.

Other changes as declared by the state included:

Priests were allowed to marry. However, this was opposed by the Catholics strengthening the rule of celibacy among Catholic priests and forbade them to marry. (1549)

- A new Prayer Book was introduced (1552)
- Abolition of altars and replacing them with simple tables
- Priests should not wear elaborate clothing
- Instead of the Mass, it was replaced by the Holy Communion.
- Predestination or the belief that it was already decided if you are bound for heaven or hell was accepted.
- Money can't buy you a place in heaven, good deeds, saying prayers or donating money to the church.

In 1553, Edward VI died at the age of 15. Before this Edward became ill, he bequeathed the Crown to Lady Jane Grey, a great-granddaughter of Henry Vii and Northumberland's teenage daughter-in-law. However, she managed to reign only for nine days as she was ousted by a group of enthusiasts yearning to install Mary as the legitimate heir to the throne.

Mary, the eldest daughter of Henry VIII, will be the next in line for the throne as indicated in King Henry's will. However, Sir John Dudley – the Duke of Northumberland wanted to prevent the succession of the Catholic Monarchs and announce that both Mary and Elizabeth could not take them through as they were both illegitimate and therefore chose Lady Jane Grey, the granddaughter of King Henry VIII youngest sister. And to have full control, Northumberland arranged a marriage for his son, Guildford and Lady Jane.

Lady Jane was able to serve for only nine days as Mary raise her claim to the throne. With the people on her side, she was able to take her position on the 19th of July 1553. Northumberland, Guillard, and Lady Jane were executed in 115 for treason.

Queen Mary I

Mary I was the daughter of Henry VIII and Catherine of Aragon who was called and remembered by many as "Bloody Mary." Nicknamed as such, Mary was hated by many for burning Protestants throughout the land in her bid to restore Catholicism to England.

It was in 1553 when Mary became Queen following the death of her brother Edwards and after Jane Grey was deposed. As soon as Mary was put to power, being a loyal Catholic, she immediately reversed the Reformation efforts of her father and brother before her. She executed many Protestants. Catholic fixtures and images were immediately restored, and the Parliament set the Heresy laws in 1955 proclaiming it a crime to be a Protestant and all Protestants who refused to recant their religion and be converted to Catholicism were burnt.

The first to be executed was John Rogers who was responsible for translating the Tynedale's Bible into English. Soon after, there were more who died for the sake of Protestantism including The Bishops,

Hugh Latimer, Thomas Cranmer, and Nicholas Ridley. Queen Mary was responsible for burning 227 men and 56 women – mostly in the South East of England.

Mary was married to Phillip II of Spain in 1554. Phillip has joined Queen Mary in her bid to restore England to Catholicism. However, the majority of the English people were not in favor of the marriage as they have no desire to be governed by a foreigner resulting in racial tension between the Spanish and English merchants in London. About 3,000 men led by Thomas Wyatt marched in protest against the marriage of the Queen and her anti-Protestant policies from Rochester in Kent to London.

In 1555, Mary's pregnancy which was supposed to be due in the month of June was announced, but many believed it to be a phantom pregnancy which came out to be right since Mary had cancer of the womb. Mary I who was also known as "Bloody Mary" had no child and neither was her death mourned.

It was her belief that unless Catholicism was restored in England, all her subjects would go to hell. Therefore, it was Mary's primary goal to restore Catholicism in the whole of England. The land was divided into those who favored her decision and those who were against it.

Through the persuasion of Philip, Mary declared war on France, but the move proved to be disastrous for both Mary and England. It was during this war that the French invaded and was able to reclaim Calais. Calais was the last possession England had in France. This decision of Mary proves to be the last straw as the people were fed up of paying higher taxes just to finance the war that was committed to help Spain.

After her, Elizabeth I, her half-sister succeeded Mary I.

Elizabeth I

Shortly after Elizabeth was declared a successor to the throne of England in 1559, a peace treaty was signed unifying England, Spain, and France which brought peace to Europe.

Without the cost of the war to pay for, England became prosperous, and in 1568, Elizabeth chose to spend funds for the development of the navy. New ships that were faster and easier to steer were built. By the end of the year when these ships were built, the English navy seized a treasure ship of Spain bound for the Netherlands. This angered King Philip II of Spain and hurting the relationship between these two countries.

King Philip was quite annoyed with Elizabeth when she restored Protestantism in England, and his anger was further aggravated after Elizabeth made Francis Drakes as one of the knights. Among the countries of Europe, there existed an agreement at that time that there would be free trade, yet Drake referred to trade in private. When Elizabeth gave him the knighthood, Phillip saw this as an insult to the free trade agreement and therefore prepare for war.

When William of Orange, the Protestant leader of Netherlands was assassinated, Elizabeth provided Drake with 25 ships of navy with a mission to harass Spanish ships. Drake followed Elizabeth order and took possessions from Colombia and Florida. In retaliation, Phillip seized all English shops in Spanish ports.

England allied with the Protestant Dutch states that yearned for freedom from Spain and sent them the English army. Philip in return blocked the Channel and allowed the Duke of Parma to invade England.

In 1587, Elizabeth ordered for the execution of Mary Queen of Scots and Phillip planned the England invasion. However, the plan was against foiled by Drake who managed to enter Spanish waters and burn a large number of Spanish ships bound for England.

On May 28, Phillips Armada set sail from Lisbon but was forced to dock to the port Corunna when it encountered a storm. Repairs were made, and in July of 1588, the Armada was ready to set sail again.

Mary Queen of Scots (1542-1587)

Mary Queen of Scots, daughter of James V of Scotland and Mary of Guise inherited the throne when his father died at the Battle of Solway Moss. Mary was supposed to marry Edward, the only son of Henry VIII but the Scots decided to have an alliance with France which broke the marriage arrangement. In 1558, Mary married Francis, an heir to the throne and in 1559; the couple became king and queen of France.

However, their happy times together ended when Francis died in 1560. Mary refused to stay in France and therefore returned to Scotland. During her stay in France, Scotland became a Protestant country and did not want Mary who is a Catholic to have an influence.

In 1565, Mary married her cousin, Henry Stuart, Lord of Darnley, also an heir to the throne. This time, Mary's married life wasn't a happy one as Darnley was always jealous of Mary's closeness with her secretary, David Rizzio and he had him killed before Mary in 1566. Mary was then six-months pregnant with James I.

Darnley had made enemies with many Scottish nobles that in 1567, his house was blown up and his body was found strangled inside. Three months after the incident, Mary married the Earl of Bothwell who was the major suspect in the death of his former husband. This angered the Scottish that they turned against her. To escape the people, she fled to England after being removed from the throne. She appealed to Elizabeth I of England for support. Suspicious that she would raise Catholic support to take the throne of England, Elizabeth kept Mary a prisoner for 18 years. It was in 1586 that letters sent to Mary by a certain Thomas Babington, a Catholic was found revealing a plot to kill Elizabeth and replaced her with Mary. With this evidence on hand, Elizabeth could do nothing else but signed Mary's death warrant. Mary Queen of Scots was then beheaded on February 8, 1957, at the Fotheringay Castle.

With the Armada under the control of Medina Sidonia, the Spaniards approached the English Channel putting the English navy ready for defense. The defending fleet under the command of Lord Howard of Effingham included sips of Drake, Hawkins, and Frobisher. Drake captained "The Revenge while Effingham" sailed in the "Ark Royal" which was built in 1581 for Raleigh.

However, Effingham stationed a large contingent at Plymouth in the protection of the south-west coast from a direct landing instead of concentrating all his resources on the straits of Dunkirk as Phillip had known. According to some version of the history, at this point, Drake was playing a game of bowls when their troop sighted the Armada, and he chose to finish the game before setting sail.

Most of the Armada's Captains want to conduct a direct assault on England, but they were strictly forbidden by the strict order of Medina Sidonia. So, the fleet sailed on from the Lizard to Calais to meet the Duke of Parma, but the Duke of Parma was not around. So, the Armada dropped anchor to await his arrival.

At midnight of August 1588, Howard sent eight fire ships to the congested Spanish ranks sending them scampering while trying to get away from the flame only to be exposed to the waiting gunfire of the enemies. It was unlucky on the part of the Spanish that their firepower is not as powerful as those of the English troops. Added to this, nature seemed to favor the English navy as a change of wind blew the Armada North out of the firing range of the English fire. The Spanish troops were then driven further to the North by a gale, and many were dashed on the Northern rocks. Those who were left of the Spanish troops were forced to make their way around the Orkneys and down the Irish coast. What remains of the proud Armada sailed back to Spain.

Armada may not have been defeated due to English superiority as according to some findings, cannon balls found at the bottom of the North Sea has shown that Spanish cannonballs were of different sizes. There is a great possibility that the cannonballs used by the Spaniards were not of the right size; hence they were not able to fire back at the English troops and cause them to retreat.

Lady Jane Grey

Lady Jane Grey was the daughter of Henry Grey and Frances Brandon (daughter of Mary who is the youngest sister of Henry VIII) who was born in October 1537. Lady Jane was well educated and a devout Protestant. She was sent to the Court at the age of nine under the protection of Katherine Parr until the death of Henry VIII. She joined Katherine's household when Katherine married Thomas Seymour. She became Thomas ward following the death of Katherine in 1548. Seymour tried to arrange a marriage between Jane and Prince Edward but failed.

Finally, Thomas was executed for treason in 1549 when he tried to murder Edward and Jane became the ward of John Dudley. In 1551, John Dudley became the Duke of Northumberland and the chief counselor of Edward VI.

By 1552, it was apparent that Edward illness was getting worse. John Dudley realized that if either Mary or Elizabeth would succeed the Throne, his position would be in danger and since both of the ladies were declared illegitimate, Jane Grey can have a claim on the throne. Dudley then arranged a marriage for Jane and his son, Guildford.

When Edward died in 1553, he proclaimed Jane Grey as his

successor which overruled the Third Succession Act of 1543 restoring Mary and Elizabeth to the line of succession. Dudley tried to keep the news of Edwards's death in his attempt to capture Mary and prevent her from gathering support for the throne, but the people believe that Mary had the right to the throne. However, prior to Mary accession to the throne, Jane Grey was officially proclaimed Queen and officially served her function for nine days before Mary was put in place. Although Dudley attempted to overthrow Mary, her support was great, and she was formally claimed Queen on the 19th of July of the same year. Jane Grey and her husband were imprisoned in the Tower of London along with John Dudley who was finally executed on August 21, 1553.

In 1954, when Thomas Wyatt led a rebellion protesting against the marriage of Queen Mary to Phillip II of Spain, many nobles supported the rebellion calling for the restoration of Jane Grey as Queen. This forced Mary to authorize the execution of Lady Jane Grey to abort and prevent further acts of rebellion.

The Tudor Ladies – Six Wives of Henry VIII

Here are some of the women who played significant roles in England history during the Tudor era being wives of Henry VIII.

Catherine of Aragon

Catherine of Aragon was King Henry VIII first wife who was also the mother of Mary I. She was the youngest among the daughters of Ferdinand and Isabella of Spain and at the age of 16, she came to England in 1501 to marry Arthur, the eldest son of Henry II and heir to the throne. Catherine was formerly the Queen of Wales when she was the wife of Henry's elder brother who was then the Prince of Wales. She was only three years old when betrothed to her first husband.

Five months after their marriage, Arthur died, and Catherine subsequently married his husband's younger brother. She served as regent of England while Henry VIII won France and the English won the Battle of Flodden.

When Catherine failed to bear a child for Henry, this created serious doubts in him about his marriage. He believed that God was punishing him for having married his brother's wife and this idea was backed up by a certain passage he found in the Bible.

At this time, he had also fallen in love with Anne Boleyn, the daughter of Thomas Boleyn who recently returned to England from France. Henry was not able to divorce Catherine because she refused to grant him his wish, so Henry instead began the Reformation of England so that he could marry Anne Boleyn even without the Pope's permission. Catherine was finally divorced by Henry in 1533 and died in 1536.

Anne Boleyn

Anne Boleyn was the mother of Elizabeth and second wife of Henry VIII.

Anne, at the age of 14, along with her sister, Mary, was sent to the French court as a maid to Queen Claude. In 1522, they returned to England. Anne attracted many admirers while her sister became mistress to the King. In 1526, the King also asked Anne to be his mistress, but Anne firmly declined. This makes King Henry more determined to divorce Catherine so he can marry Anne. In 1533, they married secretly after Anne became pregnant. The king's marriage to Anne was never popular with the people as many believed she was a witch who cast in alliance with Germany a spell on the King.

When Anne's baby turned out to be a daughter, Henry was not happy with that, and that's when they started having frequent arguments. Anne became pregnant twice after the birth of Elizabeth, but both were stillborn. Wanting to get rid of Anne, Henry planted evidence showing Anne had been unfaithful and had plotted for the king's death. This led to Anne's execution in May 1536.

Jane Seymour

Henry's third wife was the mother of Edward VI. Henry became attracted to Jane who was a quiet, shy girl and was a contrast to his two previous wives. Henry married Jane eleven days after Anne Boleyn's death; he was 45 years old, and Jane was 28 years old. Henry got concerned when it took long for Jane to get pregnant but was quite happy when she gave him a son in 1538. A month later, Jane died. Before King Henry's death, his last request was to be buried next to Jane.

Anne of Cleves

Anne of Cleves was Henry VIII fourth wife. Henry mourned Jane's loss for two years. His son Edward happened to be sickly.

Having no ties with Rome, England was isolated from the rest of Europe in 1530. Henry advisers suggested that it would be a good idea for him to marry a German princess to create an alliance with Germany – another Protestant nation in Europe. Henry chose the older of the two daughters of the Duke of Cleves to be his fourth wife. The German Princess arrived in England in December 1539, but Henry was too horrified when he met her that she demanded a way out of the marriage. Unfortunately, he could not. The couple got a divorce six months after their marriage. However, Anne was well provided for during her stay in England. She died in 1557.

Kathryn Howard

Kathryn was Henry's 5th wife who was executed for adultery two years after their marriage. Henry had already chosen her before his divorce with Anne. Kathryn Howard was the daughter of Edmund Howard and cousin of Anne Boleyn. She was barely 15 years old when she was married to Henry who was 49. At that time Henry was overweight and unable to walk due to his obesity along with an injury that refused to heal.

Because Kathryn was very young and flirtatious, having an old husband bored her that she made friends among the courtiers. Unfortunately, one of the courtiers named Francis Dereham had known her affairs before her marriage to the King and blackmailed her into giving a good position in the court. This led her to be accused of adultery and subsequently to her execution in 1542.

Katherine Parr

Henry 6th wife outlived him and died in 1548. Henry married again in 1543 to Katherine Parr who has been widowed twice. She was kind and was a good stepmother to his three children and took good care of the King. After the death of her husband, she became the wife of Thomas Seymour, Edward's uncle. In 1548, Katherine died in childbirth.

Chapter 4: The Late Medieval Wars

Despite the fact that most of England had been united during the late medieval period, wars simply didn't end. Now that the country demands one single ruler over all, the members of the royal family, the nobility as well as others who want the crown for themselves continue to wage war against each other. This kind of 'politics' not only involved their own family but the populace and their entire territory as well. All in all, the wars during this time can be summed up to this one short statement: The victor takes it all.

Capetian-Plantagenet Rivalry

Also known as the First Hundred Years War and Angevin-Capetian Struggle, the Capetian-Plantagenet Rivalry is a series of disputes between the House of Capet, which rules the Kingdom of France, and the House of Plantagenet, which rules the Kingdom of England. Having lasted for a hundred years (1159-1259), this rivalry seeks to undermine and suppress the power of the Angevin Empire, which is controlled by the Plantagenet (also known as the House of Anjou).

Even if the French Sovereign is the overlord of the English during that time, the latter's continental possessions are far greater than their own. This is the main reason why the Capetian wants to control England for themselves.

Henry II (1133-1189)

Henry II (or Henry Plantagenet) founded the Angevin Empire. Being the son of Geoffrey, the Count of Anjou and Empress Matilda of England, Henry was known for having good fortune in addition to his ambition. Through the help of Treaty of Winchester (which also happened to end the anarchy during King Stephen's reign) and demand of the Church, Henry became the undisputed successor to the English throne for over a century.

39

By the year 1154, Henry was already a powerful king in Europe. Having married Eleanor of Aquitaine, a divorced wife of King Louis VII of France, he managed to double his territory while cutting Louis' dominion into half at the same time. In addition to that, Eleanor also bore him four sons compared to the French king's two daughters (during that time, a Queen is considered a failure and eligible for divorce if she failed to bear sons for her husband).

For two decades, Henry's reign became very fruitful. Having re-established royal authority and order in England, he became free in pursuing his ambitions for expansion. By 1173, he became the overlord of Toulouse, Vexin and Brittany, which became places of strategic importance for the country. He also made alliances with the Duke of Saxony, with Lombardy as well as Navarre and subdued Ireland.

In the mid-1160s, his political authority increased because of Assizes of Clarendon and the Constitution, whose aim is to lessen the Church influence when it comes to governing the country. This political move became a double-edged sword for him since, even though he had obtained greater authority, the Church, as well as the populace supporting the Ecclesiastical community, showed discontentment to his governance. In addition to that, his most loyal knights assassinated Thomas Becket, the Archbishop of Canterbury in the year 1170 to show him their support to his cause. However, instead of getting the populace's favor back, this only made things worse, having his own family added to the list of those who hated him.

Three years after that, Henry's sons allied themselves with the King of Scotland and some nobles along with the aid of their mother and King Louis. Their rebellion, however, was quelled due to their lack of coordination with one another. Because of this, Henry managed to overcome the threat by defeating his sons in battle. After that, he imprisoned Eleanor (for being one of the masterminds) during the rest of his reign.

His share of troubles never ended with that. In the year 1183, a sibling rivalry arose with the young Henry III and Geoffrey against their own brother Richard. With the help of the new French King Philip II, the two threatened the empire's political structure. However, the danger was abated through the death of young Henry from dysentery. Because of this, the two sons' lands became Richard's.

Three years after that, Geoffrey attempted to disrupt the throne again but was accidentally killed during a joust in a local tournament. This left the division of throne between Richard, his most gifted son, and John, his youngest and most favored one.

The sibling rivalry simply didn't end there. When war broke out between Henry and Philip of France, Richard saw his unfairness when it comes to treatment towards him and his brother John during the war with the French. Due to the fear for his life and King Philip's dubious encouragement as well as rights of inheriting his father's throne, Richard decided to go against his father. Because of this, Henry loses control of Touraine and Le Mans, eventually resulting in his agreement with Richard and Philip's terms in the month of July, the year 1189. Two days after that, Henry died because of his wounds as well as heartache.

Richard I (1157-1199)

Richard I, also known as Richard the Lionheart, was born on September 8, 1157, in Oxford, England. The third but was known to be an illegitimate son; he succeeded the throne right after the death of his father Henry II. It was then that the dispute between the houses of Capetian and Plantagenet was brought to life once again. Despite the fact that England and France had joined forces in the Third Crusade (the year 1190-1192), this only happened because King Philip of France wanted to learn Richard's techniques when it comes to warfare. After doing this, Philip returned to France early, using the excuse of having an illness. The truth is that he wanted to exploit the opportunity of Richard's absence in order to lay claim of Flanders, which was originally a French territory.

Most people adored Richard for his chivalry. However, historical pieces of evidence showed that, despite that quality, he was nonetheless a selfish ruler, a bad husband and a bad father, which is evidence of his spending the throne for a few months and leaving his kingdom just to take part in wars, neglecting his royal duties and making his treasury suffer. The only saving grace during his time is that he happened to have a great royal minister in the personality of Archbishop Hubert Walter, who effectively led the country during his absence. On the other hand, nothing good comes from his family, which is evident from his brother John's cooperation with the French king himself.

After the Angevin-Capetian Rivalry, the war between the English and French went on, this time in the form of a Hundred Years War. Started from the year 1337 and ended by the year 1453, the Hundred Years' War is a series of conflicts between the House of Valois of France and the House of Plantagenet of England. Five generations of kings from these two dynasties emerged and fought against each other, making it one of the most notable conflicts during medieval times.

The conflict started during the time the women were denied the right of succession to the French throne. When Charles IV of France died in 1328, he left no heirs, technically making Edward III of England his closest male relative. However, due to the fact that he's English, he was denied this right, making his mother and Charles IV's sister, Isabella of France to claim the French throne on his behalf. Because of this, political sentiment arose, favoring a natural-born French citizen against foreigners and man against woman. This is the reason why the French throne was given to Count Philip of Valois (later Philip VI of France), which happened to be Charles IV's cousin from his father's side.

At first, the English did not pay much attention to the matter, given the fact that their territories are much more valuable. However, their disagreements led to Philip confiscating French lands belonging to Edward. This made him decide to eventually reassert his claim to the French throne as a whole.

The battles in Crecy, Poitiers, and Agincourt declared the English as victors, convincing them to continue pouring their manpower as well as resources on the war for decades. However, the French are known to have greater resources despite having a considerably smaller land area. Because of this, the battles in Orleans, Formigny, Patay, and Castillon became a decisive victory in favor of the French, making the English lose most of their possessions on the continent permanently. These incurred losses, as well as the fact that the English invested greatly in the century-long war, became the primary causes leading to the Wars of the Roses.

The Hundred Years War

The Hundred Years War started in 1937 and lasted until 1453. It was a series of turmoil and turbulence fought between England and France over the succession of the throne. It lasted for around 116 years with many major battles - from the Battle of Crecy in 1346 to the Battle of Agincourt in 1415 was the English completely defeated by the French. Here are some major facts covered in the Hundred Years War.

After the death of Charles IV in 1328 and without a son to succeed him, the throne was left to his cousin King Phillip VI. However, there are some groups who believed that Edward III of England, being the nearest male kin of the king had stronger claim over the matter of the throne.

Edward III pressed his claim to the French throne when Phillip VI confiscated the duchy of Aquitaine from England in 1337. It was the start of the Hundred Years War.

During the medieval times, there were legalities that one king could be the vassal of another if the first had inherited titles outside his own kingdom. This was the case with the English Kings since the time William I, the Duke of Normandy conquered England in 1328.

Edward III of England was also the Duke of Guyenne which is a part of Aquitaine in southwestern France and count of Ponthieu on the English Channel. Another thing, his mother was the sister of Charles IV and that when Charles IV left no heir to the throne, Edward III considered himself to be the legitimate successor. There was another claimant though, the Count of Valois, a grandson of King Phillip III of France.

To settle the issue, a French assembly was called. It decided in favor of Phillip VI who accepted the decision. However, afraid of another king's power in his realm, he maneuvered to confiscate Guyenne in 1337. This time, Edward III once again asserted his claim to the French throne and brought an army to Flanders.

In 1346, Edward the Black Prince, son of Edward III managed to capture John II at the victory of Poitiers. Edward III was given full sovereignty over lands he formerly held while a vassal of Philip through the Treaties of Calais.

When John who was held in captivity died, awaiting the fulfillment of all provisions of the cities, his son as the crowned Charles the V refused to recognize the treaties which cause the troubling to rise once again. This time, it was the French who were on the advantage until Charles V died in 1380 which stopped progress in the reduction of the English territory.

Both countries faced internal conflicts and power struggles after 1380 which provided them uncertain peace although the possession of Flanders remained an unsettled issue. Eventually, Richard Ii who was a grandson of Edward III was deposed by another grandson - Henry II.

While in France, siblings of Charles V fought over who would be in charge of Charles VI's affairs, who became mentally ill causing him to vacate the throne.

King Henry V of England who succeeds his father after his death in 1413 took advantage of the discord which was ongoing in France at the time. He campaigned for the English claims on the French crown. Henry V found an alley in Philip the Good who is the son of John the Fearless who was assassinated by the Armagnacs. By 1942, Aquitaine and all of France north of the Loire was controlled by the Anglo-Burgundian alliance.

Everything changed for the English when King Henry died leaving behind an infant child. It was only a few weeks later when Charles Vi died which allowed his son to have the French throne as Charles VII. The turning point for the war came in 1429 which forced the English to raise its siege of Orleans by a relief force led by Joan of Arc. This led to the capture of Joan by the Burgundians and was sold to the English and executed for heresy. Philip the Good, with his firm belief that the English could never assert their authority over France which is not small without the support of native nobility, he decides to switch side in 1435, so Paris once again came under the rule of France. Charles VII was able to conquer Normandy and the whole Aquitaine in 1453 after taking advantage of the internal dynasty upheavals connected with the Wars of Rose. England was only able to retain Calais which it later relinquished in 1558.

The Hundred Years War was considered by historians as a major milestone in the development of national consciousness among those living in Europe. After a long time of successions bringing along failures and frustrations, the English finally ceased their continental intervention and instead focus on issues related to internal development.

War of the Roses

From 1455 - 1485, the House of Lancaster and the House of York engaged in a series of battles. These wars were names Wars of Roses based on their badges. The Lancastrians used the red rose as their symbol while the Yorks used the white rose.

These two groups were in constant conflict due to the following:

- Both houses - Lancaster and Yorks were both direct descendants of King Edward III
- King Henry VI, the ruling Lancastrian king, was surrounded with unpopular nobles
- There was civil unrest by the majority of the population
- Many powerful Lords established their own private armies
- The untimely mental sickness of Henry VI

When Richard III who was the last king of the Yorkists was defeated at the battle of Bosworth, only then was the Wars of the Roses put to a stop. It was Henry Tudor of the House of Tudor who finally defeated him.

Origins of the Wars

It was in 1411 when Anne Mortimer brought forth a son - Richard Plantagenet for Richard V who was the 5th Earl of Cambridge. He was the son of Edmund who was the first Duke of York and the 4th son of Edward III. Richard would have been the crowned King of England if Henry the VI died before 1453, the year when Edward, the Prince of Wales was born.

Married to the ambitious French princess Margaret of Anjou, the Plantagenet King Henry VI was a weak king. During the time, there were complex issues of rivalries and jealousies among powerful noble aristocrat. The Queen, along with her circle of nobles was identified with the Lancaster. Henry belongs to the Lancaster family. Nobles who are against the Queen and the Lancasters led by Richard, the Duke of York are Henry's cousin, also a descendant of King Edward the III who likewise had a claim to the throne of England. Their group was the Yorkists.

Henry VI suffered from periods of insanity. It was during one of these periods that Richard of York was appointed to be the Protector of the Realm which gave him the opportunity to dismiss the advisors of the Queen. Upon the King's recovery, he was summarily dismissed from office.

King Henry was not able to stop the growing conflict between the Queen's party and that of the York's Earl of Warwick. Both groups started to recruit troops and prepare them for the war. Since many of these soldiers just came back from the Hundred Years War, recruiting them was easy. These two groups then choose a badge - Red Rose for Lancaster and White Rose for York, hence the wars that came after was names Wars of the Roses.

Two years after the Hundred Years War ceased, came this dynastic civil war. There were tremendous killings and bloodshed as defeated soldiers regardless on which sides were brutally killed.

Chapter 5: Renaissance Period (16th Century)

Generally, *Renaissance* marks the point of transition from the Middle Ages (or *medieval period*) heading to the modern era. The movement started in Italy at around 1300s with the decline of the Roman Catholic doctrine and the rise of interest in the classical Greek and Roman thoughts. However, the Renaissance took place at different times in various countries as it took time for other European countries to adapt its idea and concept.

Renaissance is described as a period of economic, political, and religious changes that resonates into the areas of philosophy, science, architecture, arts, and literature. Every field of life was explored, aiming for perfection. This endeavor served as a driving force to make today's era truly modern.

Education became a crucial factor in this movement as the number of schools and universities increased. The holistic concept of a humanistic curriculum focused on classical humanities subjects like poetry, history, philosophy, and drama was readily adopted in contrast with the traditional Christian theological texts. In England, humanism was accepted through "grammar schools," and the students in these said schools were giving the best classical learning. Most celebrated intellectuals like Bacon, Shakespeare, Marlow, and Spenser received a humanist education.

Overview of the English Renaissance

In England, the Renaissance took place in 1485, two centuries after it began in Italy, to the early 17th century. Many believe that the inauguration of the Tudor Dynasty signaled the beginning of this period. However, the ideas and style of the Renaissance movement were slow to saturate England; hence, the Elizabethan Age was regarded as the true Renaissance period of England. Other historians also call the English Renaissance as the *Early Modern Period*.

The English Renaissance is quite different from its Italian counterpart. The strongest art forms of the English Renaissance were music and literature; whereas, the dominant art form of the Italian Renaissance was the visual arts.

Literature and Theater

As mentioned, England had a strong tradition of literature written in their own language which eventually progressed with the popular use of the printing press in the mid-1500s. The literary culture produced the likes of poet geniuses like Edmund Spenser, the genius behind the verse epic, *The Faerie Queen*. Soon, playwright extraordinaire like Thomas Wyatt and William Shakespeare popularized dramatic poetry. During that time, the works of poets and playwrights circulate in manuscript form for some time before they were officially published.

Of all the Renaissance plays, the English theater contributed the most outstanding legacies. It started with the opening of "The Red Lion" theater in 1567. It was followed by several permanent theaters in London such as the Curtain Theatre in 1577 and the Globe Theatre in 1599. The English theater had the widest audience ranging from the court and nobility to the general public. They had the most crowded performances in the whole of Europe having a great host of playwrights including the big shots like Ben Jonson, Christopher Marlowe, and William Shakespeare.

Queen Elizabeth I herself was a product of the Renaissance movement, having trained under Roger Ascham. She wrote poems like *On Monsieur's Departure* during the most crucial moments of her life. The Italian literature had contributed greatly to the works of William Shakespeare. Even the publication of the *Book of Common*

Prayer in 1549 and the *King James Version* (or *Authorized Version of the Bible*) in 1611 created a huge impact on how even the common people of England should think.

Here are the literary notables during the English Renaissance:

- Ben Jonson
- Christopher Marlowe
- Edmund Spenser
- Francis Bacon
- Francis Beaumont
- George Chapman
- James Shirley
- John Donne
- John Fletcher
- John Ford
- John Webster
- Philip Massinger
- Philip Sidney
- Thomas Dekker
- Thomas Kyd
- Thomas Middleton
- Thomas More
- Thomas Nashe
- Thomas Wyatt
- William Rowley
- William Shakespeare
- William Tyndale

Navigation and Exploration

The Elizabethan Age witnessed the rise of the English navy when it defeated the Spanish Armada in 1588. The event also opened ways in order to improve the navigation system through the efforts of Francis

Drake when he circumnavigated the world. Other noteworthy explorers include Walter Raleigh (established Virginia Colony), Humphrey Gilbert (discovered Newfoundland), John Hawkins, Richard Grenville, and Martin Frobisher (discovered Labrador or Frobisher Bay).

While there are numerous motives which prompted the English exploration, the men were led to set discovery voyages inspired by the Renaissance spirit. The thought of spreading Christianity among the heathen also added to the thrill of exploration. Yet, perhaps the most powerful driving force to go beyond the horizons is *commerce* wherein the eastern spices play a vital role in setting the wheels in motion.

During the English Renaissance period, people lived on salt meat during winter and salt fish during the Lent—a great contrast during medieval times when spices like ginger, pepper, cinnamon, nutmeg, and cloves were more accessible. Spices were also used to create medicines and season the wine and ale. Aside from the spices, the English were also eager to acquire dyes, perfumes, gems, drugs, gums, and different kinds of woods that can only be found in the East.

Fashion, Clothing, and Textiles

Clothing and fashion were given importance particularly in the peers of nobility and the wealthy commoners during this period. Queen Elizabeth even created new Sumptuary Laws known as the "Statutes of Apparel" to specify who could wear a particular type of clothing. For instance, only duchesses, marquises, and countesses could use gold cloth, fur, and tissue in their gowns. People under the rank of knighthood were prohibited to wear silk trimming on hats and other sundries. These set of laws were strictly observed by all.

Linen and wool were ordinary fabrics during the Elizabethan era.

Linen, in particular, is favored since it's comfortable to wear and easy to wash. During that time, people rarely washed their clothes and linen eventually turned softer with use. Each fabric had its proper use:

- *Wool* keeps the body cool during the warm weather and warm during the cold season. It's an enduring fabric that does not absorb moisture and can take dyes well.
- *Felted wool* or *fulled wool* is durable and resilient. It doesn't need hemming as it doesn't unravel.
- *Cotton* was used to blend well with linen to make Fustian and to create other fabrics.

The luxurious fashion styles portrayed we see in Elizabethan artworks were observed by the elite, nobility, and royalty in that period. Upper classes used taffeta, silk, velvet, damask, and satin together with linen and wool for their clothing. They embellish their garments with lace, gems, pearls, embroidery, braiding, borders, and ribbon trims. Hats, belts, shoes, gloves, doublets and, breeches were made of leather.

As for the colors, natural dyes were the only available kind and were usually faded through time. Brown and gray were cheaper dyes which were often used by the lower classes. Blue dye was also inexpensive but was associated with apprentices and servants. Meanwhile, the black dye from Spain was rather expensive and was often used by the Queen herself. There were two dominant red shades—the crimson and russet. The former was an expensive shade used exclusively by the members of the royal family; whereas, the latter was used as a down-to-earth hue.

Layered clothing, particularly in women, was in fashion those days—the undergarments called smock and a kirtle, the bodice, several layers of petticoats, and a cloak. This style seemed to work well with the chilly and damp climate of England.

Government

The English government was constituted by three different bodies—the monarch, the Parliament, and the Privy Council. As the monarch, Queen Elizabeth I had the power to determine most of the laws in the kingdom, but she had to consult the approval of the Parliament in order to implement taxes. The Privy Council, on the other hand, was composed of the queen's closest advisors. The members had the power to give her sound advice and recommendations. When Queen Elizabeth came to the throne, there were 50 advisors in the Privy Council but eventually reduced to a party of 11 by 1597. Meanwhile, the Parliament had two groups—the House of the Lords and the House of Commons. The former was composed of the high ranking church officials and the nobles, and the latter was made up of the representatives of the commoners.

The Censure against the Concept of English Renaissance

The word "Renaissance" pertaining to this period of transition was popularized by the Swiss historian, Jacob Burckhardt, in the 19th century. The whole concept of the Renaissance has undergone much criticism by many seasoned cultural historians, and some of them strongly argued that the idea of "English Renaissance" should have never existed in the first place. For them, the English achievements could not even compare to those of the Italians with the accomplishments of Leonardo da Vinci, Donatello, and Michelangelo as a greater part of the Renaissance visual art.

However, these historians failed to regard the contributions of English in literary history. England had already established their foothold in the field of literature two centuries before the time of Shakespeare. Geoffrey Chaucer, dubbed as the Father of English Literature, initiated the style of using the English language as a medium of literary composition instead of the popular Latin. Chaucer also translated the works of Francesco Petrarca and Giovanni Boccaccio into Middle English. Even his contemporaries, John Gower and William Langland, also utilized the English language as their medium of the composition. In the mid-1400s, author of Le Morte D'Arthur, Thomas Malory became a significant figure in the literary field.

These aforementioned factors and figures made the historians and scholars contest the claim that the Elizabethan Era was England's true Renaissance period. The world-renown creator of the *Chronicles of Narnia*, C.S. Lewis, who was also a professor of Medieval and Renaissance literature at Cambridge and Oxford once remarked to a colleague that there was actually no English Renaissance, or that if it truly existed, it failed to create an effect.

Regardless of the contradictions, one cannot deny the fact that the revolutionary era in England truly transpired and its results are being relished by the current era, not only within the English soil but anywhere all over the world.

The Protestant Reformation in England

One of the major highlights during the English Renaissance period is the Protestant Reformation which triggered the religious, cultural, intellectual, and political revolution that divided Catholic Europe. It established principles and beliefs that have helped define the continent until the current modern era.

Historians often date the beginning of the Protestant Reformation to the 1517 publication of the *95 Theses* by Martin Luther and end in the 1555 Peace of Augsburg. The period features the coexistence of Lutheranism and Catholicism in Germany up to the Treaty of Westphalia in 1648 which concluded the Thirty Years War.

The major ideas of the Protestant Reformation included the

purification of the church and the belief in the Bible—not the dictates of the Catholic tradition—should be the sole provenance of spiritual authority. The reformers, particularly Martin Luther, were able to skillfully utilize the power of the printing press to spread their beliefs and ideas to a wide audience. Martin Luther published his prolific works between 1518 and 1525.

Despite the historians dating the Reformation with the publication of Luther's *95 Theses*, England had actually started to challenge the authority of the Catholic Church during King Henry VIII's quest for a male heir.

A New Development

England and Scotland were at odds for the most part of the 16th century. However, this conflict ceased to be when a Scottish king in 1603 ascended the English throne with the charm and presence that the English ruling elite approved of. This strange turn of events was greatly influenced by the peculiarities of the Tudor dynasty that had ruled England in the sixteenth century—the religious revolution initiated by King Henry VIII for his determination to marry often in order to acquire a male heir and the equal resolve his daughter, Queen Elizabeth I, not to marry at all.

Protestantism also played an important role in shaping England during that time. Even if the English aristocracy had a little respect for the throne after the death of Elizabeth I, the determination to retain England as a Protestant nation held them together.

Henry VIII

Initially, the Tudor king defended the Catholic faith, earning him the title "Defender of the Faith." He put Cambridge and Oxford, two of the most outstanding universities, to campaign against Martin Luther. He supported the finest theologians of these universities to abolish the growing thread of Lutheran "heresy." At this point, Luther's attacks created minor resonance in England.

However, the Reformation got opportune progress due to the king's personal affairs. King Henry's desperation to divorce Catherine of Aragon forced him to take extreme measures to go against his own theological conservatism.

King Henry declared that the absence of a male heir to the throne threatened the future of the dynasty and the kingdom itself. He then swiftly acted from 1532 to force the Parliament to pass the legislation that restricted the influence of the papacy in England and automatically made the monarch the new head of the English Church. Finally, in 1534, he had the absolute authority behind the English Church. He then proceeded to dissolve the monasteries throughout the kingdom and confiscated their wealth.

For the most part, the political nation was rather compliant than eager. Only a few people were prepared to defend the institutions of the old church and defy the king in the process — many received windfall profits from the sequestered church properties and monastic lands.

Edward VI

During the last years of King Henry VIII, a powerful evangelical party at Court had grown. Upon his death in 1547, the group rapidly established their foundations with the newly crowned king, Edward VI. In his short reign, the young monarch made efforts to establish Protestantism in England as modeled from the German and Swiss Reformed churches. He also established a powerful alliance with Archbishop Cranmer and the Duke of Somerset.

In the five year reign of Edward, the Reformation achieved a new English order of service, two evangelical Prayer Books, and the elimination of the Catholic paraphernalia from the churches.

Unfortunately, this short period failed to generate roots. On King Edward's death in 1553, these changes were quickly reversed by his elder sister, Queen Mary I.

Queen Mary I

In the month following her coronation, Mary immediately issued a proclamation that she would not force her subjects to follow her religion. However, she soon had the leading reformers including Thomas Cranmer, John, Bradford, Hugh Latimer, Hugh Latimer, and John Hooper arrested. She also had her first Parliament declare the marriage of her parents valid and abolished his brother's, Edward VI's, religious laws. The Catholic doctrine was restored according to the form it had taken in the 1539 Six Articles which also reasserted clerical celibacy of the priests. Due to this, married priests were then denied of their benefices.

Mary's husband, King Philip II persuaded the Parliament to repeal Henry VIII's religious laws in order for England to return to the Roman jurisdiction. It took months before the approval of Pope Julius III was granted even though the confiscated monastic lands were not handed back to the church. By the end of 1554, the Heresy Acts were revived leading to the execution of numerous 300 Protestants and the exile of about 800 wealthy and influential Protestants such as John Foxe. This goes down in history as the *Marian Persecutions*.

The first executions, death by burning at the stake, happened for more than five days in the early February 1555 including John Rogers (February 4), Laurence Sanders (February 8), and John Hooper and Rowland Taylor (February 9). The former Archbishop of Canterbury, Thomas Cranmer, was forced to witness the execution of his comrades, Bishops Nicholas Ridley and Hugh Latimer, on October 16, 1955. Queen Mary did not relent on this decision despite the condemnations from Alfonso de Castro, King Philip's own ecclesiastical staff and Simon Renard, an adviser. The persecutions continued until her death in 1558.

Elizabeth I

When Queen Elizabeth I had ascended to the throne in 1558, she immediately worked to reverse the works of her late sister which resulted in an insecure regime. Had the childless queen died in 1563 due to smallpox, the throne could have been handed to the Catholic Mary Queen of Scots and lead to religious civil war affecting even the neighboring lands in the continent. Even so, the remarkably confident queen together with her advisors addressed all complex domestic and foreign problems due to the restoration of Protestantism.

The issue with her legitimacy both in Catholic and Protestant perspectives was an important concern. Her illegitimacy under the English Church wasn't much of an issue compared to the Catholic claims that she was never legitimate at all. This matter alone put Elizabeth's favor in Protestantism over Catholicism.

Elizabeth and her advisors discerned the threat of a Catholic crusade against "heretical" England. To deal with this, the queen came up with a solution not to greatly offend the Catholics while staying on the favorable side of the English Protestants at the same time. However, she could never tolerate the action of the radical Puritans who were pushing for more extreme reforms.

To settle the religion, a Parliament was created in 1559 and reinstated the Protestant settlement of the late King Edward VI with the monarch as its head. However, Elizabeth impeded the full Calvinist Church recommended by some of the English exiles and foreign theologians who had returned to the kingdom upon Elizabeth's ascension. She retained Catholic elements such as the ecclesiastical vestments and the bishops. Queen Elizabeth I preferred pragmatism in addressing religious issues.

The House of Commons supported the queen's proposal, but they met opposition in the House of the Lords, specifically from the bishops. Fortunately, there were many vacant bishoprics during that time including the Archbishopric of Canterbury. Due to this circumstance, Elizabeth's supporters outvoted the conservative peers and the bishops. This also led to Elizabeth being forced to accept the lesser title as the *Supreme Governor of the Church of England* instead of the more controversial title of *Supreme Head*, which many people consider inappropriate for a woman to bear.

With the new Act of Supremacy in 1559, all public officials were made to swear an oath of loyalty to the monarch as the supreme governor; otherwise, they could face the risk of disqualification from their office. The laws pertaining to heresy during the time of Mary were repealed to avoid further persecution. Simultaneously, the new Act of Uniformity was passed, making church attendance and the use of an adapted version of the 1552 Book of Common Prayer mandatory although the penalties for failing to conform were not drastic.

Chapter 6: Religious and Civil Wars (17th Century)

The Reign of James I

When the son of Queen Mary of Scots, King James VI, was also hailed as the new King of England as King James I, he began a new lineage—the Stuarts.

The newly crowned king never had the same charm as his predecessor, Queen Elizabeth I, and never delighted in the same glory as hers. Nevertheless, he had his own set of achievements. First, he ended the long war with Spain in 1604; and secondly, he was accountable for the translation of the Bible which was later called the King James Version published in 1611.

The Gunpowder Plot

The Gunpowder plot was an assassination attempt for King James and the members of his Parliament. In the late sixteenth century in England, most people were Protestants, and the Catholics were the persecuted minority. Majority of the priests faced execution as they were treated as foreign agents while the common people face appalling fines for not attending the services of the Church of England.

When King James ascended the throne, the Catholics hoped that the king would treat them favorably since his Danish wife was a Catholic. At first, James stopped all fines for recusancy but the two failed Catholic plots to kill him in 1603 angered him. He reinstated the fines in the following year (1604). Still, many Catholics gave their loyalty to King James and did not partake in violent revolutions.

There were few Catholics, however, who resorted to radical measures like Thomas Percy, Robert Catesby, Thomas Winter, John Wright, and Guy Fawkes. These five men met in May 1604 and schemed what is historically known as the Gunpowder Plot.

The group executed their devious plan with Thomas Percy renting a house situated next to Parliament Houses then proceeded to "hire" Guy Fawkes as the custodian of the rented house. Part of his caretaking responsibility is the cellar underneath the House of Lords where they kept the barrels of gunpowder. They hid the barrels amongst the firewood. They also recruited other men to partake with the conspiracy.

Unfortunately for these revolutionaries, their plot was foiled. On October 26, 1605, William Parker, Lord Monteagle, received a letter from an anonymous individual warning him not to attend the parliament. Monteagle then consulted Robert Cecil, Earl of Salisbury and one of the king's ministers, regarding the message. With that, the government had uncovered the plot and began to search the Parliament buildings including the cellar beneath the House of Lords where they discovered huge amounts firewood. When they conducted a second search around midnight, they found Guy Fawkes.

The other conspirators were found and arrested. All of them were proven guilty of treason and were sentenced to death. The leader, Guy Fawkes, was hanged on January 31, 1606. Instead of helping the Catholics gain their voice, the assassination attempt led to even harsher treatments of the Catholic minority.

Every November 5, the English would celebrate with bonfires to complete with the burning of Guy Fawkes' effigy.

Conflict with the Parliament

King James had a disagreement with the Parliament regarding the rising cost of the government and of fighting wars compared to its income. The rents from royal lands could only be raised once the lease contract ended. Therefore, the Parliament was in the advantage. The Members of the Parliament intended to disagree to the increase of lease unless the king gave in to their demands. Because of this, King James had to resort to new ways in order to raise money.

The situation became even more complicated due to the conflicts over religion since many MPs were puritans. They wanted to completely eradicate the "flaws" of the Church of England by eliminating the remaining Catholic elements retained by Queen Elizabeth during her reign. Although a Protestant himself, the King did not concede to puritan views.

King James believed in the divine right of the Kings. For him, God has chosen kings to rule and with that, he became unwilling to work with the Parliament since he believed that the absolute authority was placed upon him alone.

When King James died in 1625, he was succeeded by his son, Charles I.

Charles I

Charles I, too, believed in the divine rights of the kings. He often quarreled with the Members of the Parliament. First, he married the Bourbon Roman Catholic princess, Henrietta Maria, which was a detested act in the Puritan point of view.

King Charles had also partaken in pointless wars. In 1625, he sent an unsuccessful expedition to Cadiz. Due to all of these, the Parliament strongly criticized his policies, even resorting to the rejection of raising extra taxes to support the Spanish war. This move deeply angered the king and he went as far as to dissolve the Parliament. Without the obstruction of the Parliament, he imposed forced taxes to finance his expeditions and wars. Those who refused to pay were immediately sent to the prison without trial.

By 1628, Charles was in dire need of money due to the cost of the wars. He was then forced to call the Parliament. The Parliament took this as their advantage, so they drew up the Petition of Rights, forbidding the king to levy taxes without their consent and order arbitrary imprisonment.

The King and the Parliament continued to clash regarding the issue of religion. By law, everybody under the sovereign of England should belong to the Church of England, but there were still some practicing Roman Catholics particularly in the Northwest.

In 1629, William Laud was the Bishop of London. His views strongly oppose the Puritans and Charles fully supported him. Meanwhile, the Parliament criticized the king and William Laud. King Charles called their reaction "impertinence" for he thought that the MPs held no right to oppose him. The Parliament responded by refusing to grant the king taxes for over a year. Because of this, the King sent a messenger to announce that he was dissolving the group once again. However, before the dissolution was proclaimed, the members physically restrained the speaker until they were able to pass three resolutions about the religion and Bishop William Laud. Only after then was the Parliament disbanded. This period without the Parliament was called The Eleven Years Tyranny.

William Laud was made Archbishop of Canterbury in 1633. Determined to suppress the Puritans, he checked almost all parishes by sending commissioners. He wanted to ensure that they still observe the traditions and rules of the Church of England. The bishop went as far as to stop the Puritan lecturers of their preaching.

The Bishops' Wars

In 1637, King Charles and William Laud infuriated the Scots by proposing religious reformation in Scotland as they introduced the new prayer book. The Scots went on riots in Edinburgh. In February

1638, the Scottish ministers and nobles signed the National Covenant, a document rejecting the attempts of Charles I and William Laud to conform to the Church of Scotland in accordance with the English church governance.

Meanwhile, Charles took the disturbance in Scotland as a rebellion against him. The event triggered the 1639 First Bishops' War. Charles did not consult the English Parliament to wage war and began to raise an army. They marched to Bewick-upon-Tweed, a town on the border of Scotland. The King avoided the Covenanters, the Scottish Presbyterian movement, for fear of defeat. In the Treaty of Berwick, Charles recovered the custody of his Scottish fortresses and dissolved the Covenanters' temporary government. Instead, the General Assembly of the Scottish Church and the Scottish Parliament were placed.

The failure at the First Bishops' War deepened the diplomatic and financial crisis that Charles was facing that time. His unpopularity went rock bottom when his efforts to raise funds from Spain and continuous support for his Palatine relatives resulted in the public humiliation of the Battle of Downs wherein the Dutch obliterated the whole Spanish fleet and rendered the English navy invalid.

In the early months of 1640, Charles summoned both the English and Irish parliaments in an attempt to raise funds for the new military campaign against the Scots (later called as the "Short Parliament). By March 1640, the Irish Parliament granted £180,000 along with the promise to raise an army of nine thousand. On the other hand, the earls of Strafford and Northumberland attempted for a compromise whereby the king would forfeit ship money for £650,000. Unfortunately, all of these were deemed insufficient to create unity and agreement in the House of Commons. Charles ignored further reforms proposed by the Commons as he was still backed up by the House of Lords. The protests of Northumberland fell on deaf ears, and the Short Parliament was dismissed in May 1640.

The Second Bishops' War happened in August 1640 when the Scots invaded England and seized Newcastle. Emboldened by what happened in the English Short Parliament, the Scottish Parliament declared that it could govern its own kingdom without the English King. The Covenanter army moved into Northumberland.

The English army cannot be compared to that of the Scottish which comprised of many Thirty Years' War veterans. There was no resistance at all until the Battle of Newburn. The Scots occupied the city, its neighboring county, the Durham.

It was inevitable for the king to call for the Magnum Concilium (or the Great Council), an assembly of the wealthy landowners and church leaders to discuss relevant issues concerning the kingdom. The council strongly advised for the restoration of the Parliament while Charles asked the council to help him obtain army funds against the Scots for the meantime.

England faced another humiliating blow in the Treaty of Ripon in October 1640, wherein the king signed for the cessation of arms. The treaty also stated that the Scots could have Durham and Northumberland and would be paid £850 per day until the English Parliament is restored.

Desperate for the money, Charles called the Long Parliament in November 1640. Out of the 493 members of the Commons who returned, 350 opposed the king. The Parliament soon passed the Triennial Act which stated that an assembly must be called every three years and the Dissolution Act which declared that the parliament could not be arbitrarily dissolved without its concession. Furthermore, it would be illegal to fine people who have not achieved knighthoods and landowners who had intruded on royal land, and the ship money was also abolished.

The Parliament also passed an act against the king's loathed adviser and First Earl of Strafford, Thomas Wentworth (notoriously known as "Black Tom Tyrant" during his rule as Lord Deputy of Ireland), declaring him guilty of high treason. Charles was forced to sign the act since he worried about his and his family's safety. Wentworth was executed on May 12, 1641, on Tower Hill.

Due to the drastic measures, the Parliament had been taken (mostly by the opposition led by John Pym); some MPs began to realize that they were going too far. Disharmony soon became apparent amongst the group.

The Grand Remonstrance, an anti-Catholic list of grievances setting 204 points of objection to the King's policies, a call to purge officials, the expulsion of bishops from the Parliament, and an end to the sale of land seized by the Irish rebels. Pym demanded that the king should let the Parliament control the militia. Many considered that this was an opening to something more dangerous than what Charles had been doing.

The country was beginning to be critically divided with some wanting to return the Church of England back to its state before William Laud. Others conceded to Pym's proposal of completely abolishing the bishops.

The king made the situation worse by forcing his way to the Commons and trying to arrest five Members of the Parliament (Sir Arthur Haselrig, John Hampden, Denzil Holles, William Strode, and John Pym) for high treason. However, the accused already slipped away by boat even before the king appeared. The botched arrest caused outrage as no English sovereign had ever dared to set foot on the Commons before and this was an explicit assault to the parliamentary privilege. All the efforts of his supporters to build his image as the country's defender against disorder all crumbled down. Charles was then forced to flee to Hampton Court Palace on January 10, 1642, then to the Windsor Castle two days later.

In March 1642, the Parliament then proclaimed that its ordinances were valid laws, requiring no royal agreement. Meanwhile, the king traveled northwards after sending his wife and eldest daughter abroad. In April, Charles tried to seize the military arsenal at Hull but the town's Parliamentary governor, Sir John Hotham, refused to grant him access. The king was forced to withdraw in York where he assembled the courts of justice, and his loyalists from both houses joined him.

The English Civil War

In the mid-1642, both Parliamentarians and Royalists began to arm. Charles raised his army using the medieval strategy, commission of array while the Parliament assembled volunteers for its militia. On August 22, the king raised his royal standard in Nottingham, signaling the start of war after the failed negotiations with the Parliament (also known as The Nineteen Propositions).

At the beginning of the First English Civil War, the king's forces subdued the Midlands, the West Country, Wales, and northern England. He organized his court at Oxford.

The Parliament had the edge over the Royalists since it was controlling London and therefore had the financial support for their army. Moreover, the navy assisted the Parliament, making it nearly impossible for the king to receive help from abroad. It also dominated the south-east and East Anglia.

Below are the most crucial events during the nine-year war between King Charles I and the Parliament:

The Siege of Portsmouth (September 7, 1642)

During the Civil War in 1642, Portsmouth's support was divided. The Mayor and most of the common folks aided the Parliament while the town's military governor, Colonel George Goring, supported the king and had command over the soldiers based in the town. The town itself was greatly fortified and equipped with 100 cannons and 1,400 barrels of gunpowder.

The Parliamentarian militia gathered at the north Portsea Island in order to prevent supplies getting into the town. There were many skirmishes between Goring's and the Parliament's forces. The last Royalist ship in Portsmouth harbor, the Henrietta Maria, was later captured by the group of Captain Browne Bushell.

Due to the pressure and lack of supplies, many of the Royalists surrendered. Sir William Waller's commissioners went to Portsmouth on August 28 for negotiation of peaceful surrender. However, Goring and his men refused the terms offered.

On September 2, the Parliamentarian forces at Gosport and Portsbridge bombarded the Royalist's hideout. The St. Thomas Church tower which served as a watchtower was heavily damaged. The next day, Colonel Richard Norton ambushed the strongpoint of Southsea Castle. Goring surrendered on September 7 and immediately left for the Netherlands.

Battle of Edgehill (October 23, 1642)

After King Charles fled from London, the country rapidly took sides—the conservative north aided the king while the south sympathized with the Parliament. The first battle of the Civil War had been a pitched battle. Had the royalists been more discipline, it could have also been the last.

The two opposing sides met at Edgehill in Warwickshire. The Parliamentarians were led by the Earl of Essex, Robert Devereux, while the Royalists were commanded by Prince Rupert, a veteran of the 30 Years War and the king's nephew.

Rupert initially turned the battle into their favor and made the Parliamentarian cavalry escape. However, instead of securing the victory, they chose to plunder the baggage train. In their absence, the opponent's remaining cavalry attacked their unit. The two sides were stalemates and gradually agreed to call it a draw. Charles retreated to Oxford, his winter base.

Roundaway Down 13th July 1643

Sir William Waller, a Parliamentary commander, managed to drive the Royalist army back to Devizes. Knowing that the Royalists were running off, with one company retreating into the direction of Salisbury, the commander let his troops relaxed before mounting a final attack on the Royalists. He failed to realize that the escaping troops turned north for reinforcements.

The Royalist reinforcements headed by Lord Henry Wilmot assisted the retreating forces. When Waller had seen that the Royalists were returning, he immediately assembled his army and assumed into battle position on Roundaway Down located at the north of Devizes. He positioned the cavalry at the sides and the infantry at the center.

The Royalists initiated the first attack which sent the Parliamentary cavalry fleeing. After that, Waller focused on Parliamentary infantry which firmly took their ground until another Royalist troop executed a sneak attack from behind. Caught sandwiched between two Royalist armies, many Parliamentarian soldiers escaped from the battlefield. The battle was won by the Royalist troops.

Battle of Newbury (September 20, 1643)

After the battle at Edgehill, the Royalists started to establish their control by seizing the majority of Yorkshire and winning battles in the West including the Adwalton Moor.

Robert Devereux, leading the only Parliamentarian army in the field, realized he was in trouble. He found that his supplies were dwindling, so he had to retreat back to London. However, the

Royalists blocked him at Newbury.

They engaged in a bitter battle on the first day. At midnight, when both sides decided to take a rest, both sides called their respective councils. The Parliamentarians were prepared to continue the battle despite their circumstances.

On the other hand, the Royalists decided to withdraw from the battle despite Prince Rupert's argument that they could win the battle. Unfortunately, he was outvoted. They missed their chance to annihilate the Parliamentarians and continued to suffer losses from then on.

The next morning, Robert felt relieved after discovering that the Royalists had left. The Parliamentarians returned to London where they were received with a hero's welcome.

Battle of Marston Moor (July 2, 1644)

The large-scale Civil War battle happened in Marston Moor and even marked a significant turning point. In 1944, the combined English Parliamentarian and Scottish forces sieged York. Charles immediately sent Prince Rupert's notorious cavalry to the rescue. Upon hearing that reinforcements were on the way, the Royalists abandoned the siege and gathered on Marston Moor.

However, the Parliamentarians brought in a new champion, an MP who had quickly risen through the ranks, Oliver Cromwell together with his Ironside cavalrymen. Cromwell built a reputation which rivaled Rupert's.

The numbers of men involved in Marston Moor were enough to call it the largest battle yet. It began at around seven o'clock p.m. and lasted for about two hours. In such a short period, approximately 4,000 Royalists were killed, and 1,500 were taken prisoners while the Parliamentarians and Scottish forces suffered 300 deaths.

The victory meant handing York and Northern England to the Parliamentarians. It also boosted the reputation of the Parliamentarians particularly the cavalry of Oliver Cromwell. It also shattered the myth of Rupert's invincibility and left the Royalist army in the north devastated.

Battle of Naseby (June 14, 1645)

Cromwell quickly established the New Model Army, a highly trained professional fighting force, after his victory in the Marston Moor. He, together with Thomas Fairfax, commanded this unit. This group practically won crucial battles specifically achieving a landmark battle at Naseby.

Prince Rupert's cavalry had achieved initial victory against the New Model Army but—again— lost when they had focused on looting the Parliamentarian baggage instead of securing their overall victory. This lack of discipline enabled the Parliamentarians to regroup and eventually defeat the Royalists. Upon Rupert's return, his cavalry already lost its will to fight. They lost the battle and with it, the war.

This loss marked the beginning of the end for King Charles himself. He lost his main army, and the Parliamentarians also apprehended correspondences showing that he was seeking Catholic help. Dressed as a servant, he fled from Oxford, on April 27, 1646, and surrendered to the Scottish forces at Newark.

The Fall of Charles I

The Royalists had a series of defeats from 1645 to 1646 through the alliance of both the Parliament and Scottish forces and the formation of Oliver Cromwell's New Model Army. Charles surrendered to the Scots who handed him over to the English Parliament. He got away and hid in the Isle of Wight in 1647. He tried to persuade dissatisfied Scots to invade.

The radical MPs including Cromwell were convinced that there would always be unrest as long as the king lived, so they put the king into a trial for high treason. King Charles was found guilty and was executed for treason on January 30, 1649, outside the Whitehall Banqueting House in London. His death concluded the English Civil War.

The Interregnum

Majority of the Parliament members wanted to convert the Church of England to Presbyterian. Moreover, they wanted that the attendance of church services should remain mandatory. However, the army disagreed because they wanted to have the freedom of worship.

In 1650, Charles II instigated another war having an arrangement with the Scots. Cromwell and his army headed to Scotland. At first, his campaign went rather badly as they were short of supplies and sickness spread in the ranks. In September 1650, he defeated the Scottish forces at Dunbar, killing 4,000 Scots and taking 10,000 prisoners before capturing the capital, Edinburgh. Cromwell then proceeded to the Firth of Forth, clearing the road to England along the way.

The Instrument of Government, a new constitution, was approved by the Council of Officers on December 15, 1653, and Oliver Cromwell was inaugurated as the Lord Protector the following day. At first, Cromwell ruled with a council, but in September 1654, he called for a new parliament. Unfortunately, the Protectorate Parliament rejected the Instrument of Government, so he dissolved it in January 1655.

In 1655, the country was divided into eleven districts wherein each was ruled by a Major-General. In 1656, another parliament assembly was called, but this time, some members were removed from the office. However, when the Parliament reconvened in January 1658, the excluded members in 1656 were reinstated. This time, the members criticized the new arrangements as they could not accept the newly nominated upper house. Their actions led Cromwell to dissolve the Parliament again in February 1658.

When Oliver Cromwell died on September 3, 1658, he was succeeded by his son, Richard, as Lord Protector. However, Richard had no power base from the Army and the Parliament. He resigned in May 1659.

The Long Parliament voted for its own dissolution in order to hold fresh elections for a new parliament which was later called the Convention Parliament. The new parliament then proclaimed that the government of England should be constituted by the King, Lords, and Commons.

The Parliament declared Charles II as the rightful English sovereign in 1660.

The Rule of Charles II: England in the Late 17th Century

During the reign of Charles II, the Parliament passed a series of four legal statutes (1661-1665) called the Clarendon Code. It aimed to re-establish the supremacy of the Anglican Church, persecuting the non-conformists or the Protestants who did not belong to the Church of England. The Corporation Act (1661) stated that all town officials should be a member of the Anglican Church.

In 1670, Charles created a secret treaty with King Louis XIV of France. It was known as the Treaty of Dover. By this, Louis promised to support Charles with money so he could no longer become dependent on the Parliament. In return, Charles had to join the French monarch in a war with Holland and that the English king had to announce that he was a Roman Catholic.

In 1672, Charles issued the Royal Declaration of Indulgence which suspends the law against the non-conformists. In 1673, the Parliament passed the Test Act which prohibited the Catholics as well as the non-conformists from holding a public office.

In 1679, the Parliament passed the Act of Habeas Corpus, making it illegal to imprison a person without a trial.

Charles had no legitimate children. When he died in 1685 at the age of 54, the throne was passed to his Catholic brother, James II.

The Glorious Revolution

In 1687, King James II presented a Declaration of Indulgence, preventing all laws against non-conformist Protestants and Catholics. The following year, he ordered the Church of England clergy to proclaim the declaration in the churches.

In June 1688, James had a son. The English could have been willing to tolerate James as long as he would not make his heir a Catholic. Despite this, he declared that his son would surely be brought up a Catholic. At his response, the Parliament declared the throne vacant.

Due to James religious tendencies and tyranny, he was removed from the throne through the Glorious Revolution in 1688. His daughter, Mary, and her husband, William of Orange, were then declared as the new monarchs.

Mary and William were "invited" by the Protestant aristocracy to lead an invasion from the Netherlands. They soon overcame James' troops at the Battle of the Boyne. They let the king flee away to France where he lived for the rest of his life under the shelter of King Louis XIV.

The new English monarchs were later called the "Grand Alliance." The Parliament then officially approved that all the future kings and queens of the country would have to be Protestant. Upon the death of

William in 1702 (Mary died earlier in 1694), James II's second daughter, Anne, was crowned queen.

In 1707, the Act of Union joined the English and Scottish Parliaments in order to create a unified Kingdom of Great Britain. It also declared London as the center of political power.

Queen Anne died in 1714, leaving no heir. Her distant German cousin, George of Hanover, was then summoned to rule the kingdom.

Chapter 7: Georgian Era (1660-1830)

The Georgian era spans from 1714 to 1830, being named after the four Georges of the Hanoverian house and is often extended to include William IV's reign which ended upon his death in 1837. The term "Georgian" is often used as reference to the architecture, social, and political history of that particular period.

The Georgian era witnessed the rise of Britain as a global power, establishing itself as the center of the growing empire. The change occurred in the 1770s under the rule of George III as the world's first industrialized country. The period was defined by its extreme luxury and poverty.

The inauguration of the Kingdom of Great Britain in 1707 signaled the new British identity celebrated by the Rule Britannia anthem (1740), the British Museum foundation (1753), and the Encyclopedia Britannica publication (1768). However, England was still able to keep its own unique character during the early Georgian era. Its refined style, etiquette, arts, architecture, and literature strongly contrasted with the uncouth Georgian mode like casual violence, extreme sports, poverty, and epidemic addition in gin. Handel's oratorios prospered at the same time as the infamous debauchery practices as told by his friend, William Hogarth.

George I

When Queen Anne died in 1714, she was succeeded by her German and Protestant relative, George I of Hanover. Since he couldn't even speak English, the new British monarch soon faced opposition from the Jacobites who supported the restoration of the Catholic Stuarts into the throne. However, the rebellions were mainly concentrated in Scotland and were suppressed by the end of the year.

The monarch turned to the help of the Whigs since the Tories were rather sympathetic to the Jacobites. The contention eventually involved his only son, the Prince of Wales, and worsened their already sour relationship.

George I actively campaigned in British foreign policies. His sharp diplomatic judgment helped him establish an anti-Spanish alliance with France in 1717-1718.

When the South Sea Company collapsed in 1720, despite the heavy royal, aristocratic, and government investments, the kingdom faced dire economic crisis. This event resulted in the installment of Robert Walpole as the first Lord of the Treasury in April 1721. His position can also be identified as the Prime Minister. Together with his ascension comes the decline of the popularity of the monarchy. With this, George became detached from his involvement in the government.

George I continued to be unfavorable in the eyes of his subjects for the remainder of his life partly because of his inability to speak in English and mainly because of ugly rumors concerning his treatment of his wife and the notoriety of his German mistresses.

When George died in Hanover on June 11, 1727, he was succeeded by his son.

George II

George II was also German-born just like the previous monarch. He held the titles Archtreasurer and Prince Elector of the Holy Roman Empire along with his title as the Sovereign of Great Britain and England. He was considered as a powerful ruler and practically the last British ruler to personally lead his troops in the battle at Dettingen in 1743. George Frideric Hander, a celebrated Baroque composer, was commissioned to create his coronation anthem, "Zadok the Priest," which has since been played in every British coronation.

George II considerably expanded the British Empire during his rule.

His achievements included the development of the Gregorian calendar and replacing the Julian calendar by 1752. Since then, the New Year was officially moved from March 25 to January 1.

King George's War (1740- 1748)

In 1740, the deaths of two European sovereigns embarked the continent into war. King Frederick William I was succeeded by his son when he died on May 31, 1740. Frederick, known as ruthlessly ambitious, also inherited the most progressive army in the whole of Europe and the most efficient bureaucratic government institutions his father developed. These elements helped Frederick (historically known as "Frederick the Great").

On October 19, 1740, Emperor Charles VI of Austria died leaving the throne to his daughter, Maria Theresa. Since Charles thought that his daughter would find a hard time defending the throne, he spent the last years of his life designing the *Pragmatic Sanction of Prague*, a convention that assured Maria Theresa's imperial dominions, coercing other European monarchs to sign it. Unfortunately, Frederick's miscalculation.

The Prussian heir broke its commitment and immediately seized Silesia, appropriating the rich Austrian province as part of his kingdom. He completely underestimated the Austrian monarch who instantly declared war on Prussia, invaded Silesia and turned the whole Continent against him. The war was only concluded in the 1764 Treaty of Paris, confirming Prussia's ownership of Silesia.

In the early phase of the war (1740-1748), Prussia and Austria fought in Silesia and Bohemia while the French invaded Bavaria. The French proceeded to threaten the Netherlands, prompting the Pragmatic Army (from the Pragmatic Sanction) to assemble in order to counter the French forces. The army consisted of the Austrian and German militia—including the Hanover, the jurisdiction of George II.

King George sent his English troops to join the Pragmatic Allies, ready to fight not just for the Austrian monarch but to defend his beloved Hanover. The English troops were dispatched to Flanders in mid-1742 and stationed there until 1748. They fought four battles: Dettingen (1743), Fontenoy (1745), Rocoux (1746), and Lauffeldt (1747).

On June 16, 1743, the Pragmatic Army headed south to Frankfurt, Germany. There, George II joined them and fought the Battle of Dettingen against the French forces of the Duc de Noailles.

In early 1745, the Duke of Cumberland, King George's favorite son, became the Pragmatic Army's commander-in-chief. He led the army to the City of Tournai which was then sieged by Marshal Saxe. This went down in history as the Battle of Fontenoy.

After a brief interlude in 1746, the British resumed their help in the battles of Roucoux and Lauffeldt, and the war ceased in 1746 although it was considered as the calm before the storm, the Seven Years' War in 1755.

The Jacobite Rising (1745)

The last Jacobite rebellion, also known as the *Forty-five Rebellion*, was the most formidable among the Jacobite dispute for the throne. The prospect in 1745 looked hopeless even if the rising this time comprised of fewer Scottish Highlanders compared to the 1715 revolution. However, the daring young prince, Charles Edward (historically known as the Young Pretender and Bonnie Prince Charlie) who motivated the rebels to get as far as Derby and the absence of the government militia led to a serious insurgency.

In a matter of a few weeks, Charles earned the sympathies of Scotland and even became the victor of Prestonpans (September 21). He won the Battle of Falkirk Muir on January 17, 1746, and retreated to the Highlands. However, the Duke of Cumberland, William

August, was able to suppress their forces on April 16 at the Battle of Culloden located near Inverness. At least 80 rebels were executed while the escapees were hunted down and arbitrarily killed or driven into exile. The government tried to track Charles down, but he was able to escape to the Continent on September 20, 1746.

The Seven Years' War (1753-1763)

Britain played a major role in the Seven Years' War and emerged as the top colonial power, having gained new territories through the Treaty of Paris (1763) and established itself as the world's leading naval power.

At first, the odds were against Great Britain which suffered many deaths due to the plague, scurvy and the French forces in North America (1754-1755). They even lost Menorca in 1756. Their major ally, Austria, switched sides with France, so they have to immediately establish ties with their former opponent, Prussia. However, things changed in 1759 which signaled the beginning of what the British call *Annus Mirabilis* (or the "Year of Miracles"). They won numerous battles beginning with their success over the French in Germany, North America (New France), and in India. In 1761, they had a conflict with Spain. The following year, the British forces were able to capture the western and eastern capitals of the Spanish Empire, Havana (Cuba) and Manila (Philippines). They were also able to stave off the Spanish forces from Portugal.

George III

George III, the first Hanoverian King to speak English as his first language, succeeded the British throne in 1760 at the age of 22. In addition to the crown, he also inherited the ongoing world war (Seven Years' War), changing social issues, and religious discord. Despite all of these, he defeated France during the Seven Years' War, Great Britain rose up as a dominant European power in India and

North America and led a successful resistance against the Napoleonic forces in 1815. He was also the longest living British monarch before Queen Victoria and Queen Elizabeth II.

Early Reign

In 1761, King George was married to the daughter of a German duke, Charlotte of Mecklenburg-Strelitz. Although it was a political union, George remained faithful to his wife and sired 15 children with her.

George III worked hard to accelerate the end of the Seven Years' War, forcing William Pitt the Elder, the British war minister who wanted to extend the conflict, to resign. The following year, the king appointed his former tutor, John Stuart, Earl of Bute, as his Prime Minister. The earl became the main influence in the early stages of the king's reign. However, he was forced to resign due to the alleged sex scandal with the Dowager Princess of Wales, the mother of George III.

In 1764, the new minister George Grenville initiated the Stamp Act, a means of raising revenue in British America. The decree was vehemently opposed in America, particularly by the pamphleteers whose paper was also included in the taxation. The Parliament repealed the act two years later, but the mistrust generated still persisted in the colonies.

The American Revolution

In 1770, Frederick North (popularly known as "Lord North") became the Prime minister. The event also marked the beginning of a twelve-year period of parliamentary stability. Three years after his inauguration, he introduced an act taxing tea in the British colonies. The Americans responded with a strong complaint of taxation without representation and soon organized what was famously known as the Boston Tea Party. However, the Prime Minister held on to his decision since he had the king's support.

On April 19, 1775, the American Revolution started with the Battles of Lexington and Concord. The following year, the Declaration of Independence depicted the British king as a tyrant who foolishly misused his rights to govern the colonies. Little did they know that the Parliament—and not the crow—was the actual decision-making body for colonial policies even though George had direct and indirect influence over them.

In 1781, Britain was defeated at Yorktown. The king drafted an abdication speech but decided to go with the Parliament's idea of peace negotiations. The Treaty of Paris in 1783 recognized the United States and relinquished Florida to Spain.

Later Rule and Mental Illness

In 1778, George experienced violent bouts of insanity which required him to be restrained with a straitjacket. He underwent various treatments for months. Because of this, Great Britain experienced a temporary political crisis. Fortunately, he recovered a year later and reigned for another 12 years. His popularity even rose after this ordeal, and he became a symbol of stability amidst the period of France's revolutionary chaos.

In 1804, the British monarch suffered insanity for the second time although he recuperated immediately. However, he succumbed to his fatal illness in 1810 so his son, George IV had to become the prince regent. George IV displayed characteristics of a promising monarch as he defeated Napoleon in the Battle of Waterloo in 1815.

George III died mad, blind, and deaf on January 29, 1820. The cause of his death was unknown although it might have been caused by porphyria or arsenic poisoning according to the 2005 analysis of hair samples.

George IV

George IV was the eldest son of George III and Charlotte Sophia of Mecklenburg-Strelitz. He became the sovereign de facto during his father's illness before he was finally crowned as the king of Great Britain and Ireland on January 29, 1820, at the age of 58.

George IV described himself as someone "rather too fond of women and wine." His lifestyle and friendship with Charles James fox together with other hedonistic politicians made his father regard him with contempt. In 1784, he met the only woman he ever loved, Maria Fitzherbert. They were secretly married on the 15th of December, 1785 but the contract was later declared invalid since the members of the royal family under 25 were prohibited to marry without the king's consent.

In order to persuade the Parliament to pay his debts, George IV was forced to commit into a loveless marriage on April 8, 1795, with Caroline, the daughter of the Duke of Brunswick. However, the couple immediately separated only a few weeks after their only child, Princess Charlotte, was born. Caroline returned from Italy in 1820, just a few months after George ascended to the throne in order to claim her rights as the queen consort. However, a bill from the House of the Lords deprived her of those rights on the grounds of adultery. Caroline died the following year due to cancer although some rumors say that she had been poisoned.

In 1810, when his father, George III, yielded to his sanity, George IV rose as the regent under the Regency Act. When the statute expired, he decided to continue employing his father's ministers instead of appointing new ministers from among his old Whig friends. This was considered as a great decision as it benefited the whole of Europe because the 2nd Earl Grey and other top Whigs had prepared to abandon their war with France and let Napoleon take over the continent. In 1815, the British defeated Napoleon and his forces.

George IV's character was partly enhanced by his linguistic prowess and other intellectual abilities particularly his shrewd judgment in arts. During his lifetime, he served as the benefactor of John Nash, the architect who developed the Regent Street and Regent's Park in London; and sponsored Sir Jeffry Wyatville's rehabilitation of the Windsor Castle. His most popular achievement was the Royal Pavilion at Brighton with its Chinese and Mughal Indian ornamentation designed by John Nash.

William IV

Known as *Silly Billy* and the *Sailor King*, William IV was king of Great Britain and Ireland from 1830. William was born at Buckingham Palace, London on August 21, 1765, as the third son of George III and Queen Charlotte. He joined the Royal Navy at a young age of 13. He enjoyed his voyages, performing his services in America and the West Indies. He became an admiral in 1811.

When the only daughter of King George IV had died in 1818, the king's brothers hastily married in order to produce heirs. That same year, William married Princess Adelaide of Saxe-Meiningen. With the death of his brother in 1830, William ascended the throne.

Initially, the newly crowned king was very popular. His humility to take a simple coronation heavily contrasted the extravagance during the reign of his elder brother. However, William's reign was dominated by the Reform crisis. It started soon after the Duke of Wellington's Tory government, which William backed up, was defeated during the general election in 1830.

Lord Grey who led the Whigs rose up into power and immediately worked on the electoral reform against powerful opposition in Peers and Commons. In the 1831 general election, many in the Commons had given their support to the Whigs while the Peers continued to reject the Reform Bill. In the winter of 1831 to 1832, Great Britain faced a political crisis, and there were riots in some parts of the country.

Eventually, the king conceded to create enough new Whig peers to get the bill through the House of Lords who finally passed it. The 1832 Reform Act repealed some of the worst oppressions of the electoral system and even incorporated the authorization to the middle classes.

When King William IV died on June 20, 1837, he had no surviving children so his niece, Victoria succeeded him. His death also marked the end of the Gregorian era.

Chapter 8: The British Empire and Victorian Era (1837-1901)

At 18, Victoria, niece of William IV, inherited the throne and crowned queen when his uncle died of liver disease in 1837.

Originally, Victoria should have succeeded the throne of the kingdom of Hanover, but because of the Salic Law which excludes females from succeeding Hanover's throne, she was disqualified as heiress to the kingdom.

Victoria as Queen

Queen Victoria (1819-1901), while still living, was the first English monarch to have the period of her reign named in her honor.

Owing to the facts that she never thought of being queen, unmarried and inexperienced of politics, she relied on Lord Melbourne (1779-1847), her prime minister as to whom the city of Australia was named after.

She eventually married her first cousin, Prince Albert of Saxe-Coburg- Goth (1819-1861). Both of them were King Leopold I of Saxe-Coburg-Gotha's (King of Belgium) niece and nephew.

Victorian Era

From medical, technological and scientific knowledge, advancement to location change and population growth, fast developmental progress and changes were prime characteristics of the Victorian Age. It was also an age that started in confidence and optimism that led to economic expansion and prosperity that transformed and deeply affected the country's disposition. Over time, it gave way to uncertainty and doubt to Britain's world standing.

As of today, the 19th century is associated with religious observation, family ethics, institutional faith, and Protestant work ethics.

In 1851, Prince Albert organized the first world fair or known as The Great Exhibition. The proceeds were used for building the South Kensington Museum in London. Later, its name was changed into the Victoria and Albert Museum.

Britain asserted its influence and domination almost everywhere around the world that resulted in numerous wars such as:

- Boer Wars with the Dutch-speaking settlers of South Africa (1880-1981 and 1899-1902)
- Opium Wars with Qing China (1839-1942 and 1856-1960)

Also, the United Kingdom was alongside the Ottoman Empire versus Russia in 1854 and was brought to the Crimean War (1854-1856). One of the most prominent figures of that war was Florence Nightingale (1820-1910) who pioneered modern nursing and fought for women's condition to improve.

At the age of 42, Prince Albert died an untimely death in 1861 that devastated Queen Victoria. The latter retired in a semi-permanent mourning state. But nevertheless, she was involved in a romantic relationship with John Brown (1826-1883), her Scottish servant. In fact, there were even rumors of a secret marriage happening between the two which became the object of the film: Mrs. Brown.

The latter years of the Victorian reign remained under the control of two prime ministers, namely:

Benjamin Disraeli (1808-1881) who was the Queen's favorite. In 1876, he crowned Queen Victoria as Empress of India. In return, he was made Earl of Beaconsfield.

William Ewart Gladstone (1809-1898) was the rival of Disraeli. He was liberal and often in dissonance with the Queen and Disraeli.

Between 1868-1894, he enjoyed the strong support of his party that enabled him to stay in power for 14 years. He advocated both universal education and universal suffrage for men. He also legalized trade unions.

Large and patriarchal, the majority of the 19th-century families encouraged respectability, social differences, hard work, and religious conformity. Even though this kind of lifestyle was often contested by its contemporaries, still, it was well- grounded and effective. Educational and employment opportunities for women that were usually portrayed as whores or Madonnas increased, and they were also given roles aside from their common roles in the family.

Because Victorians value politics much, they believed in exporting their evolved representative government throughout the British Empire as to which they also believed it to be perfect. This era birthed and spread political movements such as liberalism, organized feminism and socialism.

Geographical explorations by the opening up of Asia to the west and Africa gave excitement to British Victorians, but due to the continuous defiance of Ireland and the humiliation from failures of the Boer War, they were distracted. But still, British Supremacy remained unchallenged at sea throughout the century.

Work and play expanded dramatically at the peak of the Victorian Era. Travel and leisure opportunities for all were stimulated by the national railway network. Race meetings, football matches and visits to seaside resorts were enjoyed by the urban society. Literacy increased, popular journalism was embraced, and novel ascended and became the most powerful and popular icon. Significant changes in medicine, accompanied by specialization and developments in surgery, and hospital infrastructures were made possible due to scientific thought progress in the 19th century. Medical breakthroughs in anesthetics were distinguished and publicized by the Queen herself after she took chloroform for the birthing of her son in 1853; and in antiseptics as introduced by Joseph Lister (1827-1912).

The growth of hospitals, construction of asylums, and specialized workhouses for the most vulnerable members of the society was eagerly accepted by the public, and their faith to the said institutions was evident.

The longest and most glorious reign that any British monarch ever had was ascribed to Queen Victoria. She reigned 64 years, and she ruled 40% of the world and was a queen to a quarter of the world's entire population.

Chapter 9: The Word Wars and Aftermath (18th-20th Century)

World War I (1914-1918)

The First World War or World War I is a series of battles between the Allies (which consists of France, Belgium, Russia, Serbia, and Great Britain) and Central Powers (Germany and Austria-Hungary). In commoner's viewpoint, most think that there is no need for Britain to go to war. However, English historians, as well as other experts, simply didn't agree with that.

The main reason why Britain had to go to war is the fact that it had a 'Gentleman's Agreement' of some sort with France and Belgium, which is a neutral country during that time. For the Germans, the best and fastest route to Paris is none other than Belgium itself, bringing that country up as a strategic target for an invasion. They also have their eyes in Iran, which supplies the oil for the British Navy. And to make matters worse for Britain, the Ottoman Turks also joined the Central Powers during that time, forcing the British to make plans in defending the Suez Canal, which lead to the Persian Oil fields as well as India.

Having considerably lower numbers in soldiers compared to their allies during that time, the British shipped native Indian forces from their subcontinent as Chinese volunteers in order to provide sufficient men for the Western European troops. Later on, troops from New Zealand, Australia, and Egypt also joined the war, supporting Britain's war efforts.

Trench Warfare

One of the most notable events during the First World War is none other than trench warfare. Due to the fact that the Central Powers use the breech-loading rifle as well as the fast and deadly machine gun, fighting them, head-on is just a stupid move. Because of this, the Allied soldiers decided to dig trenches in order to protect themselves from the incoming gunfire. These trenches became more important after the invention of accurate field guns, hence making trench-digging a very important skill in the military even nowadays.

For the first three months, the Germans marched so fast that it became almost impossible for soldiers in Paris to finish digging up defensive trenches. What made them survive the ordeal, however, is the fact that there was still no motorized transportation such as jeepneys and motorcycles during that time, delaying the German's transport of ammunition as well as provisions for the entire war. And since the battle theatre is in the French capital, the soldiers used their trains when transporting their cargo as well as reinforcements, making it possible for them to drive the Germans away.

Pushed back towards their own border, the Germans also made use of trenches as defensive measures and improved it according to their own taste and style. This led to more intense trench warfare, increasing the number of casualties on both sides. Because of this, the British also made adjustments by conscripting coal miners in the second half of the war, whose aims is to dig right under Germans' defensive lines and blowing enemy soldiers away along with their trenches.

World War I Aftermath

The outcome of the First World War dramatically changed the face of entire Europe. Aside from the suffering economy as well as deaths on both sides, the losers literally lost everything, which was seen in the collapse of both the Austro-Hungarian and Turkish Ottoman Empire, which reigned for more than four centuries. Because of this, new countries were founded and rose in the Middle East, namely Iraq, Saudi Arabia, Jordan, Syria, and Israel. The Germans, on the other hand, also lost most of their territory, even forcing themselves to give most of East Prussia to Poland. France also forced them to pay for all the damages they caused.

Russia didn't survive the war, either. Despite it being a part of the Allied Forces, the country not only lost a significant number of men; it also lost most of its treasury, eventually making it hard to sustain its citizens. Because of this, many peasants and their families in St. Petersburg starved to death, forcing the citizens, bourgeoisie and the middle class to assassinate the Tsar and found the Union of Soviet Socialist Republics under the communist Vladimir Lenin.

World War II

Being forced to pay for the damages they caused during the First World War, the German economy suffered much, making them start another one, which was later known as the Second World War or World War II.

Known to be a strong country, Britain not only defended their homeland as well as their territories from the Germans. This time, the Germans under the dictatorship of Adolf Hitler also had two other troublesome allies in the form of Italy and Japan, forming the so-called Rome-Berlin-Tokyo Axis. The British, on the other hand, had its whole empire, Russia, China, and the USA as members of the Allies.

On the 3rd day of September 1939, the British along with France declared war against Hitler and Nazi Germany under Anglo-Polish Military Alliance because of their Blitzkrieg invasion of Poland and having annexed Czechoslovakia (Ceylon) Austria and Rhineland.

Setting his eyes from the Atlantic to Moscow, Adolf Hitler wants to conquer all of Europe. At the same time, the Japanese under Emperor Hirohito also wanted to gain control of Asia under the so-called 'Greater East Asia Co-Prosperity Sphere.' The British also have to secure their hold in Asia since the Japanese have their eyes on Burma and Malaysia, which happened to supply Britain with rubber as well as oil.

By September 9, the British landed in France, providing military support. What they don't know, however, is that the Germans had an agreement with the Russians to attack Poland simultaneously. Because of this, Poland has fallen in a span of one month.

According to historians, Hitler did not really intend to attack Britain at first, due to the fact that he simply respected the country and the reigning Queen of England was known to have German origins. What changed his mind, however, is that he simply cannot trust Winston Churchill, who recently became prime minister. In addition to that, he was afraid that Britain and the USA would possibly join forces and attack him in the process. This is the reason why the Germans started attacking London mostly via air raids on July 3, 1940, which lasted for three months. But despite all of these, the British successfully resisted the invasion, forcing Hitler and Nazi Germany to give up his plan on October 12, 1940.

World War II Aftermath

Because of the war, almost all of Europe except Ireland was in ruins, particularly Britain having exchanged blows with the Germans for five long years. Under the so-called Marshall Plan, the Americans acted as the bank, financing the countries that needed money the most for their reconstruction and re-stabilization of their economy. Despite their evil deeds, the Germans became the primary beneficiaries for this due to the fact that the country's economic collapse was the reason behind the Second World War.

Britain didn't escape the after-effects of the war, either. As a matter of fact, the country continued living off food rations for seven years after the war since the country simply cannot provide enough food for themselves. This is also evident when the country hosted the 1948 Olympics, which showed the contrast in appearance between the European competitors and the Americans.

Chapter 10: Modern England in the 21st Century

Geography

As a country that is now a part of the United Kingdom of Great Britain, England shared land borders with Scotland to the north-northwest and Wales to the west. Lying on the west of England is the Irish Sea and the Celtic Sea to the southwest. Separated from Continental Europe by the English Channel to the south and the North Sea to the east, England covers about five-eighths of the whole island of Great Britain sitting in the North Atlantic and includes more than a hundred of smaller islands.

The country's terrain mostly consisted of low hills and plains especially on its southern and central parts while there is mountainous terrain in the North such as the Lake District and Pennines and in the West, the Shropshire Hills and Dartmoor.

London is considered the capital of England with the largest metropolitan area in both the United Kingdom and the European Union.

The Kingdom of England including Wales ceased being a separate and distinct sovereign state on the 1st of May 1707 when the Acts of Union implemented the Treaty of the Union creating a political union with the Kingdom of Scotland - the United Kingdom of Great Britain and Ireland. In 1922, the Irish Free State formally withdraw from the United Kingdom which led to it being renamed the United Kingdom of Great Britain and Northern Ireland.

The Transition

In the early 21st century, England continuously progressed from an industrial society where most people were employed in the manufacturing and mining industries to work in service industries. By 2011, about 80 percent of the labor force work service-related jobs.

At the beginning of the century, unemployment was relatively low at 5.5%, but it sharply increased since the recession in 2008 until it reached 8% in 2011. It only decreased again at 4.3% in 2017 after the Great Recession.

England's population grew mainly because of immigration. In 2001, the population reached 52 million, by 2013 it increased to 63.7 million, and in 2018, it grew to approximately 66 million.

Meanwhile, the internet greatly influenced the lives of more than half of the households in England by 2006. In 2018, about 90 percent of the households had access to the internet. This revolution is expected to lead to another kind of movement. Emails and social networking have played a key role in communication and people's lifestyle. Business transactions like banking and shopping can be done online. Even gaming and entertainment can be done via the internet.

The English Economy

At present, the English economy strongly relies on services with the main industries include education, music, travel, fashion, food, and luxury cars. Here is the list of the top money-makers in each industry field:

- Education: Oxford University and Cambridge University (plus hundreds of English language schools)
- Music: EMI Records Ltd., HMV, Virgin Records, Warner Music

- Travel: Virgin Atlantic, British Airways, Costsaver, Trafalgar
- Clothes and Fashion: Burberry, Vivienne Westwood, Dunhill, Paul Smith, Hackett, New & Lingwood
- Food: Cadbury-Schweppes, Unilever, KitKat
- Luxury Cars: Aston Martin, Rolls Royce, Bentley, MG, McLaren, Lotus, Jaguar, Bentley
- Brexit: Leaving the European Union

In mid-2016, the British people voted to leave the European Union (EU) by a 52% to 48% margin. This led to huge consequences concerning Britain, the whole of Europe, and the global economy.

In 1973, Britain joined the European Economic Community and the EU in the 1990s. However, Britain never completely acknowledged the legitimacy of the union's control over the British institutions just like the other members did. For instance, Britain refused to adopt the common currency or join the Schengen Area which removes internal border controls.

Since the start of the Great Recession in 2008, Britain's background skepticism greatly intensified due to the poor performance of European economies. The continent took the recession hard and even had a hard time recovering.

Two of the leading common arguments in favor of Brexit concentrated on the EU's inconvenient economic regulations and the liberal rules for internal migration. Even advocates like Boris Johnson, the mayor of London during that time, criticized the continuously growing power of the unelected EU bureaucrats in Brussels. He pointed out that the increasing "works" of the EU negatively affect the nation's decision-making. He was talking about rules like prohibiting the recycling of a teabag, that children below eight years old shouldn't be allowed to blow balloons or there should be a limit on the power of vacuum cleaners. Such regulations were deemed importunate and extremely undemocratic.

Constitutional Framework

England itself does not have its own formal government and constitution for it operates on a nationwide British basis. We may give credit to the English for the evolution of Parliament which has been related to the Anglo-Saxon practice of regular gatherings in its medieval form. The English are likewise credited for the success of the Revolution of 1688 which affirmed the freedom of speech, parliamentary control of the army and taxation, the rule of law, and religious toleration. Unlike Wales, Scotland, and Northern Ireland which all have their own assembly of parliament, the regional government never exists in England.

Local Government

England has a distinct form of local government which has evolved through the centuries, Historic counties or shires that were developed during the Anglo-Saxon still continue as geographic, administrative, and local units. It was in 1888 that the Local Government Act regulated the administrative functions of these counties and redrawn some of the boundaries to create new administrative counties including the country of London which is formed from parts of the historic counties of Kent, Surrey, and Middlesex.

Culture

England's contribution to the world and the United Kingdom of Great Britain is countless and numerous with its culture too vast for anything. Historically, England is a country of homogenous origin and developed coherent traditions, but as the British Empire expanded and expanded people from all over the globe, the English culture has been blended with diverse contributions from Asians, Afro-Caribbean, Muslims, and other immigrant groups. Other areas of the United Kingdom had likewise experienced the same cultural and social diversification. With these similarities, England is not always distinguishable from Scotland, Wales, and Northern Ireland.

The former insularity of English life was replaced by a cosmopolitan familiarity with exotic things. Italian, Chinese, and Indian cuisines became a natural part of some meals being offered in restaurants just as guitar-based rocks naturally blends with Afro-Caribbean salsa and South Asian rap.

Although England has become ever more diverse culturally, it continues to exert a strong cultural influence on the rest of the world. English films, music, and literature garnered wide audiences all over the world as the English language has become a preferred international medium of cultural and economic change.

Social Customs and Daily Life

English daily life and customs in rural and urban areas show a significant difference. Much of the English literature explores the difference between life in a town and country as well as the comparison of being on a farm or factory.

Today, even though the English had traveled much to other parts of the world, yet their ties to the rural past remains strong and evident. Those who have been used to living in urban areas usually retire to villages and country cottages. Even in the smallest home in an urban, one is most likely to find a garden.

There are many holidays in England that is likewise celebrated throughout the world like Christmas. Christmas for the English is less a commercial event than an opportunity for festive gathering and singing.

Remembrance Day has held every November 11 in honor of British soldiers who died in World War I. There are also remembrances that are distinct to the English and inexplicable to outsiders including:

- St. George's Day (April 23) - honors England patron saint
- Guy Fawkes Night (November 5) –is held in commemoration of a Roman Catholic conspiracy to blow up the Houses of Parliament in 1605.

St. George's Day is hardly celebrated in England contrary to patron saint's celebrations in Ireland, Wales, and Scotland. This lack of official celebration for St. George's Day contributes to the ambiguity of being English as distinguished from being British.

A military parade called "Trooping the Colour" commemorates in the summer to celebrate the monarch's birthday. This has been a practice since the 18th century.

Food and Cuisine

English cuisines are mostly based on pork, chicken, fish, beef, and lamb traditionally served with potatoes and another vegetable with minimal embellishments. For fish-based cuisine which usually used cod or haddock, these are deep fried in batter and served with deep-fried potato chips.

When English is traveling home, the most popular carryout dishes are fish and chips usually wrapped in old newspapers to keep them warm.

It is also normal especially for middle-income families to have the Sunday joint as the main meal of the week. The Sunday joint is a substantial piece of pork, beef or lamb roasted in the oven in the morning and served at midday. However, this tradition changed around the 1950s and 1960s when immigrants from China and India arrived bringing with them their own distinctive cuisines. Chinese and Indian restaurants then became a familiar sight in almost all parts of England.

The American fast-food chains started dotting the landscape, and the rapid post-World War II growth of holiday travel to Europe particularly to Spain, Greece, France, and Italy helped exposed the English to new foods, variations, flavors, and ingredients. Many of these had found their way into a new generation of cookbooks filling up the typical English kitchen.

Literature

England has attained the most influential cultural expression in its literature. Each stage in the development of the English language has produced its masterworks for more than a millennium.

Before the arrival of the Anglo-Saxons, little is known of the English literature though echoes of the Celtic pasts are echoed in Arthurian legend. The Anglo-Saxon literature presented in the Old English language is a remarkable diverse work of art. Surviving pieces include corpus hymns, lyric poems, songs, riddles and spells dating back from the 9th to the 10th century.

Following the Norman conquest of 1066, the French help shaped the vocabulary and the literary preoccupations of Middle English. Geoffrey Chaucer displayed both the earth vernacular and the philosophical concerns of this period in Canterbury Tales and Troilus and Criseyde. On the other hand, Piers Plowman of William Langland was an early expression of political and religious dissent that later characterized English literature.

The Elizabethan era in the late 16th century fostered the flourishing Renaissance and the golden age of the English literature. William Shakespeare's popular plays apparently represent the culmination of the Elizabethan English but somehow were able to achieve a depth of characterization and richness of invention that had fixed them in the dramatic repertoire of almost every language.

The 1611 publication of the King James Version of the Bible has blended the literature of the period with a remarkably vigorous language and religious imagery while serving as an important tool in spreading literacy throughout England.

The 17th century long lists of conflicts in both religious and political aspects provided a backdrop for a treasure of poetry.

Music

Musical arts in England can be traced back to plainsong and were later blended with the help of monks and troubadours who were traveling throughout Europe which freely intermingled and spread out quickly in many regions.

England was able to produce notable producers including:

- John Dowland
- Thomas Tallis
- Thomas Morley
- William Byrd

Baroque composers George Frideric Handel and Henry Purcell established musical stature remain unquestioned.

Sports and Recreation

While England has a vigorous and lively cultural life, its commerce is increasingly concentrating on the exploitation of leisure from gambling, tourists holiday package tours, and transformation of the traditional English pub through trendy interior decorations.

Weekends are usually spent on countryside trips and for outdoor activities from hiking, fishing, and mountaineering. England manages to share to the world some sports including cricket, rugby, soccer, and football but now failed to outshine other nations in international competitions. Although England participates in sports like basketball, angling, snooker, and swimming, yet most preferred leisure activities are connected with home activities.

Elizabeth II: The Longest Reigning Monarch

On September 9, 2015, at exactly 5:30 p.m. (BST), Queen Elizabeth II became the longest-serving British monarch, surpassing her ancestor, Queen Victoria. According to BBC, the queen had served the country for 23,226 days and about 16.5 hours. Yet that day, the 89-year-old queen chose to simply enjoy the day doing her queenly duty by inaugurating the Scottish Borders Railway in Scotland.

The following year, on October 13, Elizabeth II became the world's longest reigning sovereign after the death of King Bhumibol Adulyadej of Thailand.

Conclusion

Referring to the history of England, it is difficult to separate it from the history of Britain. Since the arrival of the Anglo-Saxons into the Roman's Britannia in the early part of the 5th century A.D. up to the time of the Unions that bound England, Wales, Scotland, Ireland, and the Northern Ireland, the history of England is complicated and intricately interwoven with that of the British Isles.

The name of the country and the word "English" is 'taken from the Old English word for "Angles" while "British" and "Britain" are derived from a Roman term for the inhabitants' language of the British Isles called "Brythonic" or "p-Celtic."

For non-English, it would be very difficult to distinguish which are British and which is English. With the union of countries unified under the United Kingdom of Great Britain and Northern Ireland, these countries had lost their own national identities although the English language was more identified with the English than the British – although they are one.

Religion played a significant role in the formation of the history of England with Catholicism and Protestantism serving as major tools in the powerplay of significant figures. The long lists of successions side by side with unending struggles, violence, and life's dramas added to the configuration of political and religious settings.

Today, these two dominant factions managed to work separately ignoring what had happened in the past although we can't deny that each one still bears each own organizational power and influence.

Regardless of the past and internal struggles, England remained and will always be a strong and formidable force to reckon with. Its long lists of influences, powers, challenges, turmoil, and struggles embedded in its historical saga are not something that can easily be forgotten. No one can deny the fact that England was one of the world's formidable forces the world ever had.

Irish History

A Concise Overview of the History of Ireland From Start to End

Eric Brown

Legal & Disclaimer

The information contained in this book and its contents is not designed to replace or take the place of any form of medical or professional advice; and is not meant to replace the need for independent medical, financial, legal or other professional advice or services, as may be required. The content and information in this book has been provided for educational and entertainment purposes only.

The content and information contained in this book has been compiled from sources deemed reliable, and it is accurate to the best of the Author's knowledge, information, and belief. However, the Author cannot guarantee its accuracy and validity and cannot be held liable for any errors and/or omissions. Further, changes are periodically made to this book as and when needed. Where appropriate and/or necessary, you must consult a professional (including but not limited to your doctor, attorney, financial advisor or such other professional advisor) before using any of the suggested remedies, techniques, or information in this book.

Upon using the contents and information contained in this book, you agree to hold harmless the Author from and against any damages, costs, and expenses, including any legal fees potentially resulting from the application of any of the information provided by this book. This disclaimer applies to any loss, damages or injury caused by the use and application, whether directly or indirectly, of any advice or information presented, whether for breach of contract, tort, negligence, personal injury, criminal intent, or under any other cause of action.

You agree to accept all risks of using the information presented inside this book.

You agree that by continuing to read this book, where appropriate and/or necessary, you shall consult a professional (including but not limited to your doctor, attorney, or financial advisor or such other advisor as needed) before using any of the suggested remedies, techniques, or information in this book.

Table of Contents

Introduction

Just like any history, the history of Ireland seems an endless series of struggles and bloody battles as the local natives fight against invading foreign forces. Often perceived as a remote, distant, and isolated backwater, the Irish history denies any truth of it even when it is often discussed merely as an offshoot to that of the English.

Ireland has its own distinctive character as exemplified by its history. Ireland close connection with Britain somehow has had profound influences on the country in many ways although the influence in culture managed to flow in both ways and yet remained to be just one portion of the adverse and fascinating history.

The country's history is embedded not just in the cityscapes but scattered throughout the numerous landscape and throughout the country in the form of historical monuments and archaeological edifice. A closer look at the landscape itself reveals the historical imprints that account for what Ireland is today.

Those long years of hostility and tumultuous battles with the colonists had helped engraved in every Irish their own national identity which have been long trampled by foreign invaders and which today have to mold them to appreciate their freedom.

This book "The Irish History" is written to make everyone aware of how Ireland had gone through those periods of hostility and colonization despite the power struggle between religion and politics which lead to loss of lives and properties of the common people, still, they fought both for survival and for redemption of their lands which have been stolen in broad daylight.

The History of Ireland is a challenge to everyone, especially to those descendants of the people who have fought hard so that they can take back their lands for their children and future generations. Many generations have passed since the last Civil War, but the lesson of the

War is enough to make everyone aware through this book that power struggle can occur anytime and unless you unify and get ready to protect your lands, there will always be invaders to come and take it from you.

Nationality is not only seen in arms struggles but in the unification of your dreams and hopes for a better future of the lands that have been your home and that of your forefathers who have willingly sacrificed their lives for the freedom of the next generations.

Chapter 1: Ireland in the Early Time

The topography of Ireland as we can see today was actually made up of waves after waves of glaciers a long time ago and before the coming of settlers. But underneath those covering sheets of glaciers, Ireland was made up of very old rock.

During the mountain-building era – the Caledonian orogeny and Armorican phase, a large portion of north-western Europe were folded to form the mountains of Himalayas. The long period covering the Ice Ages reduced these mountains with the remnant of the once vast mountain chains discovered in Scotland, Scandinavia, and Ireland. About 75% of the land area of Ireland today is below 492 feet while the highest point is about 3,414 high which is the Carrantoohill, County Kerry.

The majority of the regions of Ireland were formed by glaciation in the last period of the Ice Age of 20,000-10,000 years ago which retained deposits of sheets of drift material in lowland areas. Such material later formed the unevenly laid fertile agricultural land consisting of gravel and clay. The shape of the material varies across the province. Its undulating form around Dublin makes the land great for farming while in central lowlands; the material was formed with an extremely irregular surface. Lakes were formed in the hollows which later turned into quagmires which are a distinguishing characteristic of the region today.

The ice melted last to the north of the central plain where it molded the landscape into countless numbers of tightly-packed elongated, teardrop-shaped hills of sand, gravel, and rock-forming other moving glacier ice. These drumlins, as they are called extend from Donegal Bay in the west to Strangford Lough in the east which are not conducive for agricultural farming and tend to produce a natural barrier to settlement throughout the history of Ireland.

Areas in the upland were stripped bare of soil by the ice which has become one of the sources of the drift material scattered across the lowlands. Ice that once covered the mountain-side valleys formed greatly curved basins referred to as "corries."

During the next 2000 years, the formation of the ice slowed down until only the Ulster remained under the sheet of ice. The rising sea level brought a flood to the lower lands, but a land bridge still manages to connect the southeastern tip of Ireland to the southwestern portion of England. The Irish Sea which was trapped between the ice sheet in the north and the land bridge formed a vast freshwater lake. At this point in time, the first plant appeared to reclaim the rocky wilderness that formed Ireland Britain. Grass began to cover the land, and Juniper trees started to grow. Using the land bridge, many wild animals including the Giant Deer wandered off into Ireland [1].

Low-land areas surrounding Ireland, Britain, and Europe were gradually flooded as the sea level rose to overwhelm the land bridge and filling up the freshwater lake with salt water. After the flood, the land bridge still showed up on many occasions. The vast Dogger Bank lying between Britain and Denmark was entirely submerged in water, and today it lies 50,165 feet below the North Sea when 10,000 years ago, it was covered by a great rain forest.

With the melting of the ice, rivers and lakes were formed in the landforms left behind by glaciers. The new river pattern in Ireland was entirely different from those previous ones making it difficult for us to imagine what Ireland looked like in the ice age and also because the previous landscape was completely destroyed.

Even with its destruction, the Ice Ages were able to leave behind a beautiful topography that played a significant role in the unfolding history of Ireland. The first humans are thought to have first set foot in Ireland 9000 years ago or during 7000 B.C. Although people have made some alterations on the landscape, still, it could not contest the great changes that the Ice Age had once brought.

Mesolithic Ireland

Recorded to be one of the last places in Europe to be discovered and settled by humans, the first humans who settled in Mesolithic Ireland [2] originally came from Scotland. It was said that they traveled here using boats and settled at the place known nowadays as Antrim County around 8000 B.C. It is believed that, during that time, momentary land bridges reappeared from the Irish Sea and Northern Scotland due to rising land and levels, allowing both human and animal migration in this place. Compared to other European countries, the human presence here is believed to be only about 10,000 years old.

The early humans in these parts are known to be fishermen, concentrating their search for food on seashores, lakes, rivers, and waterways. These early residents rarely venture inside the forest, leaving Ireland's forest ecosystem untouched and unaffected.

The earliest recorded Mesolithic activity in Ireland is found in Antrim, the country's only source of flint as well as in Sligo and Londonderry. Archaeologists also found charcoal and Mesolithic hut remains in Mount Sandel and have said to be dated between 7000 and 6500 B.C. In addition to that, they also found thousands of flint tools in The Curran, a place near Larne in Antrim and pieces of evidence of Mesolithic settlement in Lough Boora, thereby proving concrete evidence of Mesolithic activity in the country.

Around 4000 B.C., near the end of Mesolithic Era, the settlers started copying coiled pottery technology from more advanced Neolithic tribes from Eastern Europe. However, unlike in France, these 'Mesolithic Irishmen' did not leave any earthworks even though they have the knowledge to make pottery as well as in building huts and making tools. It is said that the earliest earthenwares discovered in Ireland are Neolithic.

In the last part of Mesolithic Era, Ireland's climate became wetter, turning lakes in the western part to bogs. Because of this, the land was unable to sustain or support the entire population, either resulting in settlers migrating to other nearby European countries or death due to starvation.

Mesolithic Ireland Life

Life in Mesolithic Ireland consists of flint, skin huts, a meat-rich diet with fruits and nuts on the side, and a nomadic way of living. Just like in any other starting lives in Europe, people of Mesolithic Ireland consist of hunters and gatherers. Using their flint harpoons, they primarily spear and eat fish during the early stages of settlement and lived near rivers and lakes inside skin huts. As the fish supply in water areas dwindled, they then moved inside the forested areas where they hunt birds and game as well as gathered fruits, berries and nuts. The skin covering used in their huts proved to be useful since they can just bring it wherever they go. It is recorded, however, that they just venture inside the forested areas but set up their camps near waterways, most probably to ensure a safe and stable water supply as well as fish.

Hunters mainly look for deer and wild boar inside forested areas for food as well as their skins, which were used either to make clothing, repair the skin canvass in their huts or to make new ones.

The discovery and practice of Farming are what first signaled the Neolithic Age. Not only did this practice provide the people with food, giving them another handy option besides hunting, gathering, and fishing; but it also gives rise to the concept of building bigger and permanent homes until eventually, communities. Needless to say, farming gave the people time to invent more useful things, improve the existing ones and innovate their technology. [4]

It's sad to know, however, that it is not the Mesolithic people in Ireland who suddenly 'discovered' and practiced farming during their time. Instead, this was practiced by the Neolithic settlers from Britain, who came to Ireland and drove the Mesolithic people away from their territory. Shreds of evidence found from Cashelkeelty in Kerry suggest that farming started in the country from 3900 to 3000 B.C.

In order to build their permanent farms, these Neolithic settlers started farming by clearing out upland forests either by using their stone axes or by burning it. Ireland doesn't have lots of native cereal crops, so these settlers brought wheat and barley to plant in their farms. And since wild pigs are the only animals here that can be potentially raised as livestock, the settlers also brought cows, goats, and sheep along with them.

The Neolithic settlers' plan worked at first. However, as time passed, erosion and overgrazing in the newly-cleared uplands resulted in acidification, eventually turning those into peat bogs that are unable to sustain plant life. In other words, most of Ireland's upland peat bogs are primarily caused by Neolithic settlers' farming practice and not just the climate.

In addition to farming, Neolithic settlers also utilized Porcellanite technology. Tougher than flint used by Mesolithic people, Porcellanite was used in their axes, knives and other tools. This rock enabled them to clear larger trees in the upland forests faster than using flint tools. And unlike flint, which is supplied only in Antrim, porcellanite was also mined here as well as in Cushendall and Rathlin. Archaeologists found porcellanite axes not only in Ulster but also in other parts of Ireland, extending up to Southern England. This evidence suggests that the Neolithic Irish settlers are trading with Neolithic Britons as well as exchanging knowledge and technologies with them.

Neolithic Ireland Life

Compared to Mesolithic Irish, archaeological evidence suggests that Neolithic Irish settlers lived in larger and permanent houses as well as having larger communities. Pieces of evidence found in Ceide Fields in Mayo county that Neolithic Irish communities may have farmed large tracts of upland. And since they practically stay in one place, Neolithic Irish settlers build their houses from materials such as tree trunks and mud-covered woven branches they obtained from clearing upland forests. In addition to that, they may have also made large multi-purpose buildings in the center of each community.

It can be safely assumed that a Neolithic settler lived in a wattle-and-daub house and was a part of a community consisting of at least thirty people living together. At first, they occupied the uplands since it is easier to clear away compared to lowlands, making it ready for both farming and habitation. The materials obtained from the trees have been used for many things, primarily for building houses and fuel. Field boundaries were later set up by building stone walls.

In addition to farming, Neolithic settlers [3] also raised sheep, cows, goats, which they brought along with them, and wild pigs, which are abundant in the area. Though being small at first, a Neolithic community gave rise to other communities until eventually; these communities formed a tribe, establishing trade relations to one another.

When it comes to cooking food, Neolithic Irish cooked their food and lit their fires indoors, as suggested by the small hole in the roof of their houses, allowing the smoke to escape.

The third remarkable invention that the Neolithic Irish used in this era is none other than Pottery itself. According to archaeological pieces of evidence found throughout Ireland, the settlers made their own pots by coiling long pieces of wet clay round and round and building a basic-shaped pot before smoothing it down. 'Customized pots' are decorated either by pressing twigs, stones or fingers when the clay is still wet before baking it in a hot fire.

Depending on its size, these pots are either used as oil lamps, in cooking as well as in storing food and water. Decorations in customized pots do not only improve a pot's individual look; it may also have served as identification of some sort to its owner.

It is still uncertain when it comes to the topic of how the Neolithic people bury their dead. Archaeological evidence found in one place suggests that cremation of the deceased is common. In another place, however, human bones are also found, suggesting that entombment of the deceased is also practiced. Given this situation, it can be assumed that religious beliefs and traditions in a particular tribe or community had influenced Neolithic people on how they bury their own dead.

As the population in the uplands increased, the farming practices of the Neolithic people, as well as overgrazing of their livestock, resulted to the entire land becoming peat bogs, making it acidic and unable to support vegetation. Because of this, exploration and settlement started in the lowlands.

Chapter 2: The Bronze Age to Iron Age

While the Bronze Age in Ireland is coming to an end, Celtic Influence spread almost throughout Europe. This influence (not an empire) started in the Alps in Central Europe before spreading to Iberian Peninsula (modern-day Spain and Portugal), Gaul (modern-day France), Teuton (modern-day Germany), Balkans and even Turkey. During that time, the well-known Roman Empire is just starting, practically ignoring the territories beside them. It was also during that time that Ireland and Britain were known to the Celts as Pretanic Islands.

The discovery and utilization of metals became the signal of a new age. A key event in human history, metals is nonetheless the first materials that can be mined, melted and molded into any desired shape. It can also be molded and crafted into useful things such as tools and utensils or decorations for both humans and their home. And last but not the least, it can also be made into stronger and tougher weapons that are way deadlier than those made with wood and stone. However, compared to other European countries, the Bronze Age started in Ireland two thousand years later.

Around 2000 B.C., settlers from France traveled to Ireland, most probably by boats, and shared the knowledge of bronze-working with the Neolithic Irish, which signaled the arrival of the country's Bronze Age. Having relatively large copper deposits, production of bronze, an alloy of copper and tin, became possible throughout Ireland. However, copper is found only in locations that are actually devoid of any human activity during the Mesolithic and Neolithic Age. Because of this, those who learned metalworking left their respective communities and started their new life in copper-rich locations such as Western Munster, Cork and Kerry counties. [5]

Mining Copper, one of the two key elements in making bronze, is somewhat dangerous if done carelessly. According to evidence found inside Mount Gabriel in Cork County, the copper ore was possibly extracted by lighting fires inside the mine and, as the walls become hot, it will then be doused with water so that their tools could easily remove the ore. Aside from the risk of the entire wall breaking down, dangerous gases can also be found inside the mines, gases that are mostly flammable and poisonous by nature.

On the other hand, there isn't much tin to mine inside Ireland, probably giving the possibility of the country importing their much-needed tin from the place that is now known as England.

During that time, what is copper made into?

Since tools are the main requirement even after the Neolithic Age, copper was usually crafted into tools such as axes, picks, and other farming implements. Cooking and eating etiquette is also evolving slowly during that time, giving rise to crafting of kitchen knives, cauldrons, bowls, and platters. And most of all, weapons specifically made to kill wild animals as well as human beings became popular, marking its increase in manufacture. Needless to say, these weapons also gave rise to various conflicts and wars against opposing communities and tribes during that time.

Aside from Bronze, the Bronze Age also signaled the discovery and first use of gold. Known for being useless when it comes to crafting tools and such, gold became a highly desirable material when it comes to making ornaments and other decorations because of its color and rarity. Since it is very valuable, its possession and usage may have given rise to the separation between rich and poor classes in the society, if not aristocracy. Because of this coincidence, that period in the Bronze Age somewhat became the 'First Golden Age' in Ireland.

Bronze Age Ireland Life

Even though that some pieces of evidence found from Carrigillihy in Cork county suggest the existence of stone houses during this time, most people in this age still lived in wattle-and-daub houses. The only noticeable improvement when it comes to housing is the usage of circular wooden fences that serve as a boundary of some sort as well as additional security.

Cooking methods also improved because of Fulacht Fian, the cooking place for Bronze Age people. A wood-lined trough dug from the ground, and the fulacht fian was filled with water before putting a heated stone in. When the eater inside it boils, large chunks of meat are added. A very common sight in southwest Ireland, fulacht fian is being used until 1600 A.D. According to Geoffrey Keating, these things are also used for boiling water.

The discovery of metal also improved Bronze Age agriculture. Compared to porcellanite of the Neolithic age, tools and other farming implements made from bronze are more reliable and don't easily wear out. In addition to that, bronze tools can be sharpened and melted again if broken.

It's also a sad thing to know that this age also signaled mankind's first use of weapons that were specifically designed to kill other humans. Because of the growing population, food supply became a problem, giving rise to disputes between various communities. Eventually, the disputes left unsettled by words alone resulted in armed conflict, leading to the demand for weapons made to defend oneself as well as kill enemies.

The Arrival of the Celts and Iron Age

While the Bronze Age in Ireland is coming to an end, Celtic Influence spread almost throughout Europe. This influence (not an empire) started in the Alps in Central Europe before spreading to Iberian Peninsula (modern-day Spain and Portugal), Gaul (modern-day France), Teuton (modern-day Germany), Balkans and even Turkey. During that time, the well-known Roman Empire is just starting, practically ignoring the territories beside them. It was also during that time that Ireland and Britain were known to the Celts as Pretanic Islands.

As the Celtic influence arrived in Ireland and Britain in year 500 B.C., the Celts also brought Iron and the knowledge of its use along with them. Compared to bronze, iron is stronger and more durable. However, it also requires more heat as well as effort and skill to work with, limiting its use to making tools as well as weaponry. It is the reason why bronze objects are still widely-used during that age.

It is still uncertain as to how Celtic Influence really arrived in Ireland. For some historians, Celts used their knowledge of Iron as well as numbers to spread their influence, effectively erasing any existing culture from Bronze Age. Others said that those Celts actually came from the Iberian Peninsula who escaped the Roman Empire, finally settling in Pretanic Islands. Still, others said that the Hallstatt group of Celts arrived before the end of the Bronze Age and started to spread their influence but failed to make it effective throughout the country. However, their influence was later supported by the La Tene cultural group, who arrived in Ireland after 300 B.C.

Though being regarded as pseudo-historical, the earliest records that we have about Celtic Ireland are from Greek, Carthaginian, and Roman writers who probably got their story from sailors who ventured in the British Isles. In 4th Century A.D., the Roman writer Avienus called Ireland in his writings Insula Sacra (Holy Island) and its people gens hiernorum, which were thought to be a Latinization, Ierne (Greek word for Ireland). The Greek writer Pytheas called the British Isles Pretanic Islands, which came from the Celtic word Priteni. And in year 52 B.C., Romans started calling Ireland Hibernia, which is probably extracted again from Ierne.

The most interesting record of Ireland's historical account is that of Greek writer Ptolemy. Published in his book Geographic, his map of Ireland was based on an account from year 100 A.D. but compiled in the second century A.D. It is sad, however, that there are no surviving originals in existence nowadays. The only copy remaining is dated from the year 1490 A.D. This map of Ptolemy enabled the historians to identify and name some of the Celtic tribes in Ireland during that time. Many of these tribe names have been badly corrupted by being passed via word-of-mouth, and most of them are unidentifiable with known tribes. The map also contains names of rivers as well as islands that can be identified nowadays.

Celtic Ireland Life

Even if the Celtic Culture managed to influence almost all Europe, part of Celtic Ireland's culture is still under Bronze Age influence. This cultural influence can be seen in their Heroic Tales such as the Ulster Cycle. Doubted by most historians at first, these tales describe the way of life of Celts during that time. Even if the description of events is somewhat exaggerated and may have undergone various revisions, the stories accurately describe the way of life in Celtic Ireland.

A culture mainly based around war, Celtic Ireland is believed to be divided into dozens, if not hundreds, of small and petty kingdoms. In each Kingdom, druids, poets, and blacksmiths are respected greatly; Druids for their soothsaying and prophecies, Blacksmiths for their skill in crafting tools and weapons of war and Poets for recording and putting the achievements and exploits of their warriors to verse, their heroism being sung in every important event.

It is also recorded that competition for the 'hero's portion' is done during the celebratory banquet after every victorious battle. The victor after the challenge will not just have the food prepared to fit the hero; he will also have the 'bragging rights' up until the next battle.

Political Structure

The aristocracy during this time is determined through individual strength and valor. In other words, a warrior who wants to become the next king should prove himself worthy in every battle while staying alive. Needless to say, it is expected that he should bring home the head of their enemy king or commander after the battle.

Unless the former king dies, the strongest and most valorous warrior will be given the privilege to take part in a 'Rite of Combat' against their own king. Depending on the conditions set beforehand, the loser will either be put to death or banished out of their kingdom.

At the time of the late Celtic Period, the country is believed to have been divided into two hundred small kingdoms or less (Tuath), each ruled by a king. Depending on their individual power, a king can be either classified to one of these three existing ruler grades during that time: Ri Tuaithe, Ruiri or Ri Ruirech. Ri Tuaithe rules over a single kingdom or territory. A Ruiri or Great King, on the other hand, is an overlord who either had an allegiance of or overseeing a number of other kings. A Ri Ruirech or King of Overkings (overlords) is the most influential, ruling an entire province. Because of the Ri Ruirech's sphere of influence, the whole country is divided into at least ten warring provinces during that time, until it eventually settled into four different provinces (Connaught, Ulster, Munster, and Leinster) as of today. The royal sites, however, remains intact in most of the displaced provinces.

As for the common folk, life means living inside wattle-and-daub houses and farms protected by a circular enclosure. Most of these farms have access to higher grounds where their animals graze. Almost every farmer plant grain crops and practice dairying. And since most farms are self-sustained, most of them don't need to trade just for food. The only problem for the common folk during this time is the passing-through warriors as well as invaders, who raid livestock as well as burn and pillage their farms. It is believed that there are at least a million people living in Ireland by year 400 A.D. However, their numbers decreased because they were affected by the recurring famine and plague, which had found its way to Europe during that time.

Chapter 3: The Advent of Christianity

The early Christian era occurs between 400 A.D. – 800 A.D. The first Christians to travel to Ireland probably came from Gaul (France) and Britain. There are no historical records showing how the Early Christian Era began in Ireland. However, historical records began to be recorded when the monastic settled in and started making manuscripts.

Pre-Christian Ireland Irish people are practicing druidism before Christianity was introduced in Ireland. They built many ritual sites like the Passage Tomb of Newgrange that was built in ancient Ireland during the Stone Age.

As a symbol of the importance of their beliefs and sun worship, the druids erected many monuments throughout Ireland.

Christian Missionaries in Ireland

Many people believed that Palladius was the first to introduce and establish Christianity in Ireland for he was the first canonical bishop to Ireland. This led to the belief that the first Christians to settle in the land of the Irish were the four "Palladian Bishops", namely:

- St. Ailbe of Emly
- St. Abban of Moyarny
- St. Ciaran of Saigir
- St. Declan of Ardmore

These four settled in Munster or southern part of Ireland.

Palladius' Arrival

When St. Palladius set sail for Ireland, he arrived at Hy-Garchon (today's Wicklow) on 431 A.D. unfortunately, he stayed there for a very short period of time. He was banished by the denizens of Hy-

Garchon off their lands. So, he left and sailed to the Orkney Islands in Scotland. He never set foot again in Ireland.

St. Patrick's Arrival

Though there is no exact date to tell of St. Patrick's arrival in Ireland, he was believed to have settled there around 432 A.D. St. Patrick was enslaved in Ireland. He escaped and returned to Britain, his home and then became a cleric. Later, he returned as a Christian Missionary in the northern and western part of Ireland.

St. Patrick came to a small island off the coast of Skerries coast (now known as Inish- Patrick) wherein near this location; he converted Benignus, a son of an Irish chieftain. Until the Vikings invaded the land, it is believed that the monastery that St. Patrick founded flourished on the island.

St. Patrick also converted a local pagan chieftain named Dichu mac Trichim in Saul (modern-day County Down) who then donated a barn in return. This barn was later converted to a church and served as a gift to St. Patrick.

In the next 30 years, St. Patrick continued his life as a Christian missionary in Ireland. He converted many pagans, local chieftains into Christianity and established worship places.

From Pagans to Christians

Though Palladius mission to Ireland seemed unsuccessful, on the other hand, St. Patrick's became fruitful. People may seem to perceive St. Patrick as a pirate or a warrior and grew weary of his appearances at first, but later they noticed his gentle approach. This act gave them little reluctance to be baptized and be converted to Christianity. To convert native Irish pagans to Christians, St. Patrick may have used different illustrations.

The shamrock is one of those famous illustrations that most people believed St. Patrick used to teach trinity to his followers. He also used some familiar things to the pagans for his illustrations. There were also some important figures that were popularized by Christianity in Ireland. They were St. Finnian of Clonnard, St. Brigid of Kildare, St. Brendan, St. Enda and Columcille.

Christianity in Ireland's History

Christianity played a major role in Irish history and society. As Christianity flourished, monasteries were built all over Ireland. Languages, literature, and art taught by the disciples gathered popularity throughout Europe. Because of this, not only scholars were attracted to Ireland but invited Viking raids as well.

After the Anglo-Normans Invasion, the English became involved in Irish affairs by the 12th century. New laws were instituted that oppressed the Irish Catholics. As ordered by The Crown of Ireland Act 1542, all monasteries in Ireland were forced to shut down.

In 1649, prior to Oliver Cromwell's invasion, many places of worship were removed. To remove Irish people from land ownership, the Cromwellian Act of Settlement 1652 was proclaimed, and in 1655, the Cromwellian Act of Settlement was altered by The Act of Explanation that enforces the return of one-third of the land by the Cromwellian settlers as compensation to the Catholics.

After 4 years, Oliver Plunkett was appointed by Rome as the Archbishop of Armagh. He then began a programme that reorganized structures and revived the Church which was almost destroyed in Ireland.

More Penal Laws were passed in 1673 together with the Test Act that commands the institution of the Holy Communion to be taken in the Anglican Church's manner by the clergy and laymen. This Act was refused by Oliver Plunkett that led to his arrest in 1679. He was charged with treason and executed in London on July 1, 1681. Since then, Oliver Plunkett was considered an Irish martyr and became a celebrated saint.

More anti-Catholic penal laws that outlawed the Catholic clergy were introduced after the Flight of the Wild Geese in 1691 and when William of Orange conquered Ireland. The state of affairs in Ireland became severe with poverty when it landed in the hands of non-Catholics in the 19th century. When Daniel O'Connell founded the Catholic Association in 1823, he succeeded in peacefully fighting for full emancipation. But in the latter part of the century, the land fight becomes violent resulting in land wars.

Christianity in Ireland Today

As of 2011 Census in Ireland, Christianity still remains as the predominant religion of the country. Majority or 84% of the Irish population is Catholic, and The Church of Ireland ranks next. Still, Christianity is taught and practiced in schools and many families remain as devoted followers of the church

Chapter 4: Ireland in the Middle Ages

Medieval Ireland

Early medieval Ireland (800 A.D.-1166) was a well-settled, prosperous, rural country that has a very tumultuous history. It was famous for its monasteries not only because these serve as centers for religion and education, but Irish monasteries were also places of great wealth and commerce. Ireland became an irresistible attraction for Vikings and raiders that left ineradicable marks in their history and country.

Ireland was divided into tuathas or small kingdoms. There were about 80-100 tuathas. Each kingdom has an Oenach (local assembly) composed of professionals, landowners, and craftsmen. The Oenach's function was the following:

- Create policies
- Declare war or peace on other groups or tuathas
- Elect or dispose of their king

The territory of Irish kings was owned by all freemen of their kingdoms. But still, the subjects owe their kings (the Uí Néill's were one of the few powerful kings that reigned over these groups) military services and taxes. For reasons that benefit everyone, the Tuatha becomes united. Though in-fighting existed among families at times when they have comes to select a new king, all in all, life was good in Ireland.

Tuatha kings, poets, and clergies were considered sacred in Ireland. They don't have to do manual work. Basically, Gaelic society was a case system that starts from landowners that were freemen down to those that don't have lands. Laws of the organization were specific and written between 600-900 A.D. in the Brehon Laws.

The Age of the Vikings

Vikings are a group of people who lived in Northern Europe, especially in areas known nowadays as Denmark and Norway. Also known as Norsemen, Ostmen, and Nords, Vikings are warriors known for their ferocity as well as valor in battle.

Because of political pressure in Scandinavia (the collective name for Denmark, Sweden, and Norway) during that time, nobles, as well as royals of various provinces, were forced to find territories of their own elsewhere. Most of these are younger sons who had failed to inherit any estate that their father owned. Along with their trusted band of fellow warriors, these men began to travel westward, raiding and pillaging nearby settlements. They sold their booty mostly for gold, food, and materials needed for forging and weapon crafting. These raids became possible because of their longboats, the primary mode of transport that became synonymous with Vikings as of today.

The first-ever recorded Viking raid in the British Isles occurred in year 793, wherein the monastery in Lindisfarne was raided and pillaged. Two years after that, the monastery in Rathlin Island was sacked as well. These raids happened not only because of the fact that Vikings are pagans (not Christian); monasteries are known to be the richest source of goods as well as slaves. [5]

How Viking Raids are Done

Believed to be done in a hit-and-run style, Viking raids are executed at a fast pace. Once they set their eyes on their target (mostly monasteries), the Vikings will land their longboats near their target. Longboats are preferred by Vikings because of their 'ramming' capabilities, so landing near sandbars or rocky areas doesn't pose many problems.

After the landing is done, the Vikings divide into smaller raiding teams, whose numbers vary depending on their target. Most of the time, the Viking leader attacks the target monastery along with the primary team while others pillage the nearby villages for potential slaves and goods. After that, they sack the entire location and carry their booty back to their longboats. These Viking raids mostly happen to a certain location at least once a year, unless it is really rich with booty.

Vikings are known far and wide for their brutality and harsh treatment towards their prisoners. That is the main reason why Viking raids are feared as well as hated by people during that time. However, not all Viking raids are successful. According to various historical records, some raids in Ireland were repelled such as in Ulaid in year 811 as well as in Munster and Connaught the next year.

It is probably because of this reason that the succeeding raids intensified, making it more ferocious and terrifying than it was before. At first, a raid only consists of three or four longboats and lasts for a week or two (or until their longboats run out of space for their booty) before returning to Scandinavia. This time, however, the Vikings brought fifty to a hundred (depending on their target location's size) longboats, landed on shores and set up their camps nearby. They attacked, pillaged and sacked Irish fortresses, monasteries, churches, and farms as well as the surrounding countrysides for months. According to records, these kinds of raids started in the year 836 and lasted for fifteen years. During this time, Irish kings were unable to repel such raids, resulting to most of the populace as well as monks getting enslaved and their goods looted in addition to their territories getting sacked.

After almost all of the intensified raids died down, the Irish initiated their counterattack and were successful in regaining some of their lost territories. In year 848 (three years before the last intensified Viking raid), the Irish regained Cork, which became a Viking town during that time. They also regained Vadrefjord (864), Youghal (866) and Dubhlinn (902), which was a great merchant town by then, driving the Vikings to the Isle of Man.

These Irish victories, however, were short-lived. In year 914, the Vikings initiated a second intensified raid in Vadrefjord, successfully retaking the location. Next, they attacked Leinster and Munster the following year through a series of offensive attacks while pillaging the monasteries in Lismore, Aghaboe, and Cork. In year 917, they successfully retook Dubhlinn. The second intensified raid stopped in the year 950, in which Vikings had stopped their raids in Ireland, settled in the towns they built for themselves and became traders.

Viking Appearances

The Vikings coming from Norway landed in Dublin. Without warning, they attacked and raided Ireland. So, instead of being ranked as sacred people, poets suddenly became equal with the laborers.

The first known Viking raid happened in 795 B.C. when the Vikings left Norway for Ireland -a more promising land. The earliest Viking raiders mostly came from the western Norway fjords. Their route was sailing down Scotland's Atlantic coast then over to Ireland. They also sailed to the Irish west coast, to the Skellig Islands off the coast of County Kerry during their early raids. These raids became the reason why the Christian Irish culture had their golden age interrupted and led to two hundred years of war. The Vikings also destroyed a number of towns and monasteries all over Ireland.

Viking Settlement

As winter months came, the Vikings settled along Irish coasts, and Ireland became their winter playground. They settled in Dublin, Cork, Arklow, Limerick, Wexford, and Waterford. In Kilmainham (in the west side of Dublin), archaeological evidence shows that there was a small Viking settlement in the mid- 840's A. D. in Ireland. There were also Irish journals that described the Vikings' inland movement often by the rivers' way (e. g. Shannon River) and back to their coastal settlements.

Among the Vikings, Thorgest was the first to put up an Irish kingdom. He sailed up the Shannon and the river Bann to Armagh in 839 A.D. where he carved out a kingdom containing Connacht, Meath, and Ulster. Thorgest's glory lasted for 6 years just when some of his subjects had enough. He was caught and drowned by the king of Mide, Màel Sechnaill mac Mail Ruanaid in Lough Owen.

After Thorgest's death, as high king, Màel Sechnail defeated a Norse army at Sciath Nechtain. He contacted the emperor of France, Charles the Bald asking to be allies as Christians against pagans. Unfortunately, it turned out to be unsuccessful and was a poor decision made. The Vikings erected a strong fortress in place of (the modern-day) the city of Dublin in 852 A. D. One of them declared himself as king, and they established a stronghold at Waterford the following year.

The Norse also built a fortified settlement near the Avoca River's mouth (modern-day Arklow in Wicklow County). According to the Annals of Ulster, Arklow was already occupied by 836 A.D. when the attack of the Vikings at Kildare was recorded.

Viking settlements in Ireland began earnestly in 914 A.D. When Waterford was taken; it became the first Irish city. It was the settlement of a Viking named Regnall. One can find the Tower of Reginald (Ireland's oldest civic building) here. Waterford was also the only Irish city that still has its Viking name retained.

Windy fjord or Ram fjord's name was originally Cuan na Gréine before it was called Harbour of the sun by the Irish. Wexton, Cork, Limerick, and Dublin were urbanized between 915-922 A.D. Modern excavations also proved of heavy Viking existence in Waterford and

Dublin. The Norse (means foreigner in Irish), a mixed Viking and Irish group began to influence Ireland after generations of plunder and courtship.

Even as of present, one can still trace Norse descents from among the residents of Irish coasts that have actual DNA evidence.

Viking Period's Everyday Life

The Viking raids made this a period of terror for Irish, especially to those who belonged to the Ecclesiastical communities. Being the primary target for booty, monasteries and churches became subject to periodic raids in which, some of these died and failed to resurrect even after this period. However, most of the monasteries and their structures remain intact, sparing themselves from the raider's wrath. This is probably due to the fact that Vikings knew that they will be filled with booty again, making it possible to initiate another raid sometime in the future.

Even the grad Fhene (commoners) weren't spared by the raids either. Even if their mud walls, as well as ditches, are enough to repel some Irish attacks, these defenses were practically useless against Vikings, who attack and raid in large numbers. Because of this, crannogs, as well as ringforts, became obsolete during the year 900s. Instead, these two were replaced by souterrains, which are heavily-defended underground chambers that are used mainly as places of refuge against Viking raiders. Because souterrains are practically hidden from enemy eyes, there are at least 3500 of those that managed to survive throughout Ireland.

If souterrains protected the common folk from raiders, monks and other members of the ecclesiastical community were protected by round towers during that time. Cylindrical in shape, round towers are defensive fortifications which had their entrances placed one floor high and are only accessible by ladder. In case of a Viking raid, the monks in the monastery will take as much food and valuables as they could, climb inside the tower, pull up its ladder before keeping it shut. Even if the raiders manage to enter the tower, the monks will just retreat upstairs, pulling the ladders up to restrict access. In the end, raiders either just gave up the pursuit or smoke the monks to their deaths.

End of Viking Rule

Due to the joint forces of the king of Meath and Brian Boru (941-1014 A. D.), the rule of Viking ended in Ireland. Brian Boru of mid-western Ireland gained influence through political conquests and maneuvers around the late 10th century. After he claimed the title of High King, he and his allies defeated the Vikings in 1014 at the Battle of Clontarf. When Boru was killed in battle, the Vikings lost their control over all Ireland and the Norse who remained became part of the Irish people. For 150 years, Ireland was free from invasion, but infighting weakened and drained the country from resources.

The Abbott of Clonmacnoise wrote a famous book in 1150. The book was entitled Chronicum Scotorum, and it was the story of Ireland from the Great Flood to the 12th century. The Normans (1167-1185) Ireland became a country with divided kingdoms by the 12th century. A few powerful regional dynasties fought against each other to gain control over all Ireland.

Ireland Lordship (1185-1254)

Seated at the southern banks of Shannon River, King John's castle was built in the 12th century.

Meanwhile, the Normans owned immense portions of Irish lands. They forefended the whole eastern coast from Waterford up to eastern Ulster, including Dublin as years passed. They also had gone as far west as Mayo and Galway. On the other hand, King John of England- Lord of Ireland warded the Norman regions and at the same time ensured that the Irish kings were under his power. Many Irish kings owed their armies and thrones to King John.

The Rise and Death of Brian Boru

Brian Boruma, or simply Brian Boru, came into power when his brother Mathgamain, Lord of the Dal Cais, was assassinated by the Christian Vikings of Limerick. At first, the Vikings were tolerated since they were more or less a peaceful lot even though their territory lies near the mouth of Shannon River. So after his brother's death, Brian Boru started his conquest of Ireland by killing the Vikings of Limerick, thereby avenging his brother.

Even though he's a Christian himself, he cared less about observing sacred traditions, leading his men right inside the monastery in Scattery Island, slaughtering King Imar and his sons who took refuge inside before desecrating the whole monastery. Because of what he did, Limerick became part of Munster. Four years after the death of his brother (in year 980), he also surpassed Eoganacht and declared himself as king of whole Munster. After that, he and his army eventually penetrated Laigin (Leinster) and Connacht through the help of Vikings of Vadrefjord.

Because of his exploits, the Ui Neill, which is the influential dynasty during that time, became alarmed of Brian Boru, eventually deciding to declare war with him. King Mael Sechnaill II, the leader of Ui Neill, fought Brian Boru by trying various tactics but eventually gave up after more than a decade of failed attempts. After their meeting at Clonfert, the two kings decided to divide Ireland, granting Brian Boru High Kingship over all of Munster as well as Dubhlinn (Dublin) and Laigin (Leinster). He, on the other hand, retained the allegiance of his own province and of Connaught for himself. However, the Viking King of Dublin and the lords of Laigin revolted under his rule two years after. Brian Boru retaliated by defeating Laigin at Glenn Mama and descended into Dublin the following winter, burning down its fortress. Because of this, King Silkenbeard of Dublin submitted himself and became Brian Boru's supporter. King Mael Sechnaill II also submitted himself to Brian Boru in the year 1002 because of their influential decline as well as the rising influence of Shannon River when it comes to Viking trade.

By the year 1005 and 1006, Brian Boru's power was almost complete. However, he was killed during the Battle of Clontarf in 1014 even though he managed to suppress Dublin and Laigin's second revolt. But regardless of what had happened, not only did his victory did secure Irish hold in both Laigin and Dublin for more than two centuries; he also managed to end the weakening Viking's power and influence in all of Ireland, eventually returning the whole country to the Irish for good during his time.

The Period of Dynastic Upheaval

Ireland had experienced dynastic upheaval right after the death of Brian Boru in the year 1014. Right after the Battle of Clontarf and upon confirming Brian Boru's death, King Mael Sechnaill II of the Ui Neill dynasty reasserted himself as High King of all Ireland. However, after his death eight years later, all of the existing dynasties fought against one another, eventually resulting in confusion and almost endless power struggle.

During the 11th century, Ireland's politics became similar to the rest of Europe. Rulers spend their time away from home and fought battles instead, leaving the kingdom to their stewards who, in turn, employ other essential staff in the name of royalty that will operate inside the palace. On the other hand, governors were appointed by kings to oversee their territories' everyday operations such as the collection of taxes as well as observing laws and edicts.

Warfare also improved during this time. In addition to existing Viking technologies that they acquired in the past, the Irish also learned mounted and naval warfare, which eventually led to the use of Admiralty as well as Cavalry. These posts were granted by the kings to their subservient lords, lords who were expected to be loyal to them at all times.

From the year 1086 to 1114, the High Kingship was under dispute. It was during this time wherein the kings of Munster and Ui Neill became mortal enemies just like their ancestors. However, the situation changed when Connacht's successor, Turlough O'Connor came to power. Using his large army and navy, he succeeded in destroying the power of Munster between the years 1115 and 1131 before spending the rest of his reign in trying to become Ireland's High King. The task of accomplishing this, however, was passed to his son Rory after his death in the year 1156.

After succeeding his father's throne, Rory O'Connor knew that he had to conquer Dublin (Dublin) to become High King in all of Ireland. This conquest became difficult due to the fact that King Muirchertach Mac Lochlainn of the Ui Neill and King Dairmait Mac Murchada of Leinster were allies and both have their eyes on the High Kingship as well. However, when the king of Ui Neill was assassinated by his own vassals in the year 1166, the citizens of Dublin had allied themselves with King Rory. With their help, King Rory had managed to capture Ui Neill as well as Leinster and drove the remaining enemy, King Dairmait Mac Murchada, out of Ireland.

Christian Church Reformation

The Christian church in Ireland had reached its peak of glory even before Vikings had entered the country. This is proved by the monasteries having amassed huge, if not exorbitant, amount of wealth. It may have been a good thing for them at first. However, this is the main reason why Vikings are targeting them most of the time.

During and after the time of Vikings, the Christian church does not only suffered material losses; most of them became corrupt and entertained secular thoughts. In addition to the fact that the church became decentralized, making every abbot in monasteries too powerful, some members of the ecclesiastical community do practice indecent and unchristian behavior: accepting bribes, acquiring concubines for themselves and, most of all, many of these abbots were not even churchmen, let alone Christian. If there were those who still observe sound doctrine during this time, they were just a minority and don't have any influence in church organization.

When the early period of medieval age came, the Christian church reformation in Ireland was initiated by some members of the ecclesiastical community along with the church in Europe, who was busy reforming the French church during that time. The revival in monasticism had influenced the whole continent, effectively bringing Ireland under their control. The Cistercian Order was the first medieval order to establish their base of operations in Ireland, founding abbeys while observing sound Christian doctrine at the same time. Other monastic orders came after them, who also found new abbeys as well as seizing control of the old ones run by corrupt abbots.

To establish English control over the country, the Archbishop of Canterbury in England planned to assert his control over the church there, having established a relationship with the church in Dubhlinn(Dublin). However, the reformed Irish church was organized under the Archbishop of St. Patrick's monastery during that time, which was supported by the synods of Cashel in 1101, Rath Breasail in 1111 and Kells-Mellifont in 1152, much to the Archbishop of Canterbury's dismay.

Because of the Christian reformation, the Irish Church was divided into dioceses, their leaders and members being required to observe sound doctrine at all times and, most of all, the monasteries were stripped of their rights to own much land. Even though this reformation had successfully removed most of the corruption in churches as well as monasteries, it also destroyed the basis of most Irish poetry and learning during that time.

Chapter 5: The Normans in Ireland

Following the defeat of the Vikings in the early part of the 11th century, the Irish immediately engaged in a series of battles to gain control of the territory as well as assert their authority. For 150 years, there was continuous unrest until in 1150, the majority of Ireland was controlled by four powerful clans:

- The O'Neills in Ulster
- The O'Briens in Munster (family of Brian Boru)
- The O'Connors in Connaught
- The McMurrough (Led by Dermot McMurrough who also held Leinster)

As soon as Rory O'Connor takeover the leadership of Connacht, he begins to seize Munster from the O'Breins, but McMurrough was able to dominate a nominal portion of Dublin which is an important trading center of Ireland at that time having the support of the O'Neills. However, things changed when the ruler of Ulster was assassinated in 1166 resulting in a power struggle in the North which left Dermot McMurrough without any strong support. Rory O'Connor grabs the opportunity and seizes Dublin first before also taking over Leinster. After his defeat, McMurrough left Ireland and O'Connor was soon recognized as High King of Ireland.

The Normans in Ireland

For a short period, Ireland gains peace but while in England, McMurrough was preparing for his return to Ireland. With promises of land and influence, he sought for the support of King Henry II of England along with other powerful English allies. He was able to gain the strong support of the powerful Earl of Pembroke, Richard de Clare, also known as Strongbow.

It was in 1170 when Strongbow first landed in Ireland with an army of skilled and well-armed men in addition to some loyal supporters of McMurrough. This troop will work for the reinstatement of McMurrough as King of Leinster.

Strongbow married Aoife, the daughter of McMurrough which sealed the alliance along with a promise that he would succeed to the throne and so he did in May of the year 1171. However, King Henry did not welcome the quick and increasing rise to power of his once loyal subject. He considered Strongbow as a threat and an affront to his authority. In August of the same year, King Henry set foot on Irish soil in a fleet of 400 ships and well-equipped army. This is the first time in history that an English monarch ever visited Ireland.

Being guided by his practical considerations, Strongbow met the King on the way to Dublin, where he pledged his renewed allegiance, and thus he was able to retain his lands. At this point, the other remaining kings including Rory O'Connor saw the King as an ally in curtailing the power of Strongbow.

The Treaty of Windsor

It was in 1175 when the Treaty of Windsor was made, giving Henry the authority to overlord all territories already inhabited by the Normans. Strongbow as a subject of the king held onto Leinster. Rory O'Connor had sworn loyalty to the crown and was paying an annual levy. To implement the treaty, the King assigned military commanders and awarded them lands to own. Not soon enough, they sought to expand the territory they owned. Being left by themselves, they have taken control of a significant portion of Munster and Connacht in 1178 with John de Courcy as their leader. They soon attempted to conquer the land of the Ulster in the North.

By the middle of the 13th century, the power of the once great clans diminished as the Normans were able to control the majority of Ireland.

Although the O'Neill managed to protect Ulster by not allowing the Normans to take a foothold of their territory although they were able to control the East Coast, with the ongoing battles, the O'Neill can lose their dominant position. The part of the province not occupied by the non-Normans is divided between 12 other families.

The Native Irish

Before the arrival of the Normans in Ireland, all the lands were considered communal. While there are chieftains controlling territorial areas and expect people living under them to contribute food and engage in fighting, yet the lands never belong to anyone. However, with the arrival of the Norman, the concept of land property was definitely changed. Aside from introducing the concept of land ownership, they likewise make the native people of Ireland believed that the lands belong to them.

Soon enough, Irish farmers who had been cultivating their lands for a long period of time became tenants and have to pay rents and taxes to the Norman rulers so they can continue working on the land. This situation continued with horrifying consequences.

To defend their properties and established themselves, the Norman began building enormous castles. Inevitably, intermarriage occurred and that a new ruling class emerged with a mixture of Norman and Irish heritage.

In England at this time, the Normans gradually adopt the Irish language, dress, and laws. However, these were largely despised as 12 parliaments sat in Kilkenny against these and worked for the stopping or reverse this cultural integration.

Under the Statutes of Kilkenny which the parliament was working were various measures curbing further assimilation including forbidding Normans to subject under the Irish law, to use the Irish language, to intermarry with the Irish or to give Irish names to their children. However, this did not work out as planned for even while Ireland is nominally under the King's rule, a large portion of Ireland was still operating independently of the English crown.

During the last part of the 15th century, only the area surrounding Dublin remained under the direct control of the English. This area was then recognized as "The Pale" which is translated in Latin as "palus" meaning border or fence. In fact, there was an attempt to separate this part from the rest of the Ireland areas.

Within the Pale, the English rule still prevailed but for the rest of the Irish Normans, they behave independently, thus the idiomatic expression, "beyond the pale" is used to describe unacceptable or uncontrollable behavior. Over the years, the English likewise show their intolerance to the situation which leads to their struggle to maintain their identity.

The Anglo-French Invasion

In 1176, Strongbow dies, and King Henry took over Leinster but granted all his rights as Lord of Ireland to Prince John, the youngest among his sons. Prince John was the Lord of England until he was crowned as King of England in 1199. [6]

There was extensive colonization in the lands where the Anglo-Saxon had settled. Agricultural lands were established, and goods are sold in local markets, nationally, and extended even to Europe. People from other parts of Europe such as French, Welsh, and Belgian, in addition to the English, came to settle in the lands owned by Anglo-French Lords. The remaining Irish were then assigned as serfs working on the estates. Changes in the life of the poor Irishmen were noticeable, but for the rich Irish, their lifestyle remains the same.

The colonization of the Anglo-French in Ireland continued until the end of the 1200s. The Irish Kings remain submissive to the power of the foreign invaders, but the people were hoping for the coming of someone who will come and liberate them from the hands of their oppressors – the Anglo-French.

In 1176, Strongbow dies, and King Henry took over Leinster but granted all his rights as Lord of Ireland to Prince John, the youngest among his sons. Prince John was the Lord of England until he was crowned as King of England in 1199.

The Anglo-French ruled over Meath and Leinster by 1177. There was extensive colonization in the lands where the Anglo-Saxon had settled. Agricultural lands were established, and goods are sold locally, nationally, and even to Europe. People from other parts of Europe such as French, Welsh, and Belgian, in addition to the English, came to settle in the lands owned by Anglo-French Lords. The remaining Irish were then assigned as serfs working on the estates. Changes in the life of the poor Irishmen were noticeable, but for the rich Irish, their lifestyle remains the same.

The Anglo-French were expanding their colony, and it took off when John de Courcy invaded and ruled over Ulaid which was later known as Ulster. The O'Brien kingdom in eastern Munster was granted to William de Burgh, and Philip of Worcester, and Theobold Walter in 1185 who later founded the Butler Dynasty that played a significant role in the Irish history. It took them eight long years to subdue the region – later known as Osmond.

The colonization of the Anglo-French in Ireland continued until the end of the 1200s. The Irish Kings remain submissive to the power of the foreign invaders, but the people were hoping for the coming of someone who will come and liberate them from the hands of their oppressors – the Anglo-French.

The longest war from the year 1226-1235 happened in Western

Ireland. Richard de Burgh invaded the Irish Kingdom of Connacht but did not expect that the Irish were able to develop their military facilities since the time of Strongbow that it took them long and hard winning the battle.

It was also during this period when the FirzGerals or Geraldines conquer north Kerry and Waterford and later owned more lands in Kerry, Connacht, and Fermanagh. The FitzGerald built a castle at Belleek, Fermanagh which the locals burned and getting back control over Fermanagh.

By the mid-13th century, Hugh de Lucy died, and so the Irish kings – Donegal and Tyrone stopped paying tribute to the English to which the King made little response. This motivates the Irish kings to form an alliance with the King of Connacht. In 1259, They entered Ulster by force and killed the colonists and burning downtowns. The revolution was extending to Mu8inster where the Irish residing in there revolted against the Anglo-French Lords. In 1261, the Irish were able to defeat the English army sent by the king to avenge the colonists. The revolt quickly fizzled out when key leaders were killed in battles.

After the revolution, Walter de Burgh, also Lord of Connacht was granted the title as Earl of Ulster. In 1296, Walter de Burgh became the ruler of all Connacht and the whole of Ulster. He was next in power to the King of England. In the south, emerging families were the Butlers of Osmond and the Geraldines of Desmond. Leinster at this time was divided into smaller Lordships as the families divided their lands among their heirs.

Meath, on the other hand, was divided into two – the Trim and Meaths while the Lordship of Leinster was divided into four parts – the liberties of Kilkenny, Wexford, Carlow, and Kildare.

Restraint of Norman Invasion

The Normans had undergone sequential events that resulted in the downshift and eventually stopped their settlement and power in Ireland. The English Lordships were attacked by Gaelic rebels that relied on raids and surprise attacks. Because of this, many Norman knights were killed, Norman resources were put to strain, and many Gaelic chieftains had their territories returned. At the same time, Norman colonists lost their English financial resource as King Henry III and Edward I, his successor, was occupied with warring factions in Wales, Scotland, and England. There was chaos within Norman ranks, and Norman lords fought each other.

On the other hand, residents and settlers were pulled closer to the heart and spirit of the Irish countryside by the new strength of Gaelic Ireland and West European politics. Ireland faced a transition during the late 12th to the early 13th century: from acquisition of lordship to colonialism. Norman Invasion produced numerous castles, borough towns, import tenants, churches and an increase in commerce and agriculture. Changes became permanent as the Normans altered Gaelic society with productive land usage.

Irish lifestyle elevated (in some ways) and most Irish people in Leinster and Munster even have Norman surnames. Not only Irish people were influenced by the Normans. Normans also acquired the DNA, language, and Irish customs.

Norman Declination, Gaelic Revival and the Black Death (1254-1536)

There were three significant events in the 14th century of Irish history.

Edward Bruce of Scotland Irish Invasion

Bruce rallied Irish lords against the presence of Englishmen in the country in 1315. He suffered defeat at the battle of Faughart, near Dundalk. Though his troops caused massive destruction especially in populous areas of Dublin, the local Irish lords won back their lands (in the midst of chaos) that were generations lost to their families.

Murder of William Donn de Burgh, 3rd Earl of Ulster (June 1333)

His land was divided among his family, and those in Connacht openly sided with the Irish and rebelled against the English crown. So, all of Ireland that is west of Shannon River turned to the Normans and was completely lost to the English rule. Then, the Burkes allied with the Dublin administration after more than 200 years.

Black Death During Medieval Times (1348)

Black Death landed on Irish shores and struck the English and Normans that resided in towns and villages the most. The Irish that lived in rural places were luckily unaffected. According to a celebrated account in chronicles of Kilkenny (Cill Chainnaigh), from a monastery, it described the plague as the beginning of human extinction and the end of the world.

Gaelic Irish language dominated after the plague ended. The English dominated area became constricted to the Pale- a fortified region around Dublin. Norman lords that lived outside the Pale adopted Irish customs and language so as to save their own skins. They became more Irish than the Irish (according to some people) and were known as the Old English. They sided with the native Irish against England in military and political conflicts during the next centuries, and they became Catholics after the Reformation.

Inside the Pale, authorities became alarmed that the whole of Ireland would become Irish. So, in 1367, they passed The Statutes of Kilkenny- special legislation that banned those of English descent to speak the Irish language, wear Irish clothing and inter-marriage with Irish people. This gained least attention and followers as their government in Dublin had almost zero authority.

The control of the government in Dublin continued to decrease during the 15th century. This time, England was engaged with their own affairs in the War of The Roses. Many English kings commissioned the powerful Fitzgerald, Earls of Kildare, authority over their territories. As time passed, the English monarchy became remote to Irish politics. As the Gaelic lords expanded their powers, they decreased English rule in Dublin.

Chapter 6: Ireland During 15th -16th Century

The Church Reformation

Throughout the medieval period and even until the 20th century, the church plays a significant role in Irish society as well as in their culture. At this point, the churches were fairly distributed across Ireland ruled by native Irish lords and also those lands ruled by Anglo-French lords that it was, therefore, difficult to rule over the land and assert control over churches. The King of England had, in fact, attempted to place Anglo-French Bishops over all dioceses in their lands. However, this was met with great condemnation by the Pope who expressed his outrage over such discrimination.

Dating back from the Normans invasion of Ireland, the title, "Lord of Ireland" was used by the Normans and English monarchs to refer to their Irish conquests. The Crown of Ireland Act in 1542 has renamed Ireland as the Kingdom of Ireland and granted King Henry the title as the King of Ireland. This was done through the command of King Henry himself as the Lordship of Ireland was granted by the Papacy. Worried that his title as the Lord of Ireland would be withdrawn by the Pope as he had been excommunicated twice - in 1533 and 1538, he mapped this out. [7][8]

The King further arranged that he would be declared to head the Church in Ireland with George Brown, the Archbishop of Dublin as the main instrument in the establishment of the state church in the Kingdom of Ireland who was appointed by the King upon the death of the incumbent bishop even without the Pope's approval. He arrived in Ireland in 1536.

With King Henry's death in 1547, reforms were continued by his successor – Edward VI of England. When the Church of Ireland likewise considers Apostolic succession for continuity in the hierarchy, the Roman Catholic Church disputed this claim asserting that only bishops approved by and in communion with the Holy See are considered legitimate. [9]

Edward the IV of England

Edward the VI of England, son of King Henry formally established Protestantism as the state religion. As his father reformation had been political, the son was as much religious but he reign only for six years and his principal reform act had much less impact in Ireland. [10][11]

Queen Mary of England

When Queen Mary I of England ascent to the throne in 1953 - being a faithful Roman Catholic - reversed Henry and Edward's efforts in the past. She imposed orthodox Roman Catholicism and then married Philip of Asturias who became the King of Spain in 1958. [12]

The Queen arranged for the Act of Supremacy which asserted England as being independent of Papal authority to be repealed resulting to forcing the dismissal of bishops in possession of diocese formerly appointed by her father without the Pope's approval. However, monasteries remain dissolved in the preservation of the loyalty of those who purchased monastic lands.

Soon enough, Queen Mary started planning for the mass confiscation of Irish lands for settlers from Great Britain. In 1955, Mary and Philip were granted the papal bull to reconfirm their position as the Catholic King and Queen of Ireland.

Queen Elizabeth

In 1959, when Queen Elizabeth, half-sister of Queen Mary I succeeded the throne, she managed to pass another act of Supremacy in 1959 declaring the English crown as the supreme head of the Church in England in place of the pope and that any act of allegiance to the pope will be considered a treason because the papacy is claiming both political and spiritual powers over those who are following him.

The English Regained Control over Ireland

Two of the most influential families in Ireland were the Fitzgeralds who resided in south-west Ireland and the Butlers who lived in Tipperary. Despite being descended from Norman settlers, both of these families had long lived in Ireland, and they already considered themselves Irish by heart. Unfortunately, these two families have a totally different perspective when it comes to the Englishmen. More than any other families in Ireland, the Fitzgeralds cultivated pure hostility to the English. The Butlers, on the other hand, supported the English king. In 1463, one of the FitzGerald earls showed support to the English. For this, he was captured by his own relatives and was murdered in 1468.

Because of this failed attempt to expand England's jurisdiction in other parts of Ireland, the English began to collaborate with Kildare's Earl Garrett Mór (also known as Gerald FitzGerald) who governed the western border of the Pale. This alliance between the English King and the earl brought great advantages to both parties—with Garrett Mór gaining more power and influence in Ireland as its Lord Deputy, and the king gaining control over the earl's territory.

In 1485, King Henry VII ascended the throne in England through the support of the Butlers despite the opposition from many of the Irish lords including Earl Garrett Mór of Kildare who supported the previous king. King Henry VII didn't like how Garrett Mór gained so much influence and power in Ireland that he was becoming a huge threat to the English authority in Pale. The newly crowned king then decided that it was high time to re-establish their control over Ireland like how the Normans had once relished it 250 years prior to his reign.

The relationship between the King and the earl of Kildare even got worse in 1487 when the latter supported Henry's rival to the throne, Edward, and even acknowledged him as the rightful heir to the English throne. Henry went livid with rage and had Garrett Mór abducted and imprisoned in the Tower of London for treason. After that, he immediately passed a law putting an end to the independence of the Irish Parliament in the Pale. Instead, London itself will have direct authority over Ireland.

Unfortunately, the monarch soon realized that he couldn't control the other lords in Ireland without the help of Earl Garrett Mór of Kildare. He then begrudgingly reinstated Garrett Mór as the Lord Deputy in 1496 knowing that if he could control the earl, he would have a better chance of spreading the English authority all over Ireland.

In 1513, Garrett Mór was succeeded by his son, Garrett Og. The son continued his father's rule as the Lord Deputy of Ireland in the reign of King Henry VIII, the son of Henry VII. Unfortunately for Garrett Og, his influence over Ireland began to decline with the king's marriage to the daughter of the FitzGerald's rival family, the Butlers.

Garrett Og was summoned to London in 1533, and because of this, a false rumor circulated that the Lord Deputy was executed. At the same time, Garrett Og's son also declared that he would no longer inherit the title as the succeeding Lord Deputy of Ireland. To top that, the Kildares were murdered and their castle destroyed. The territory owned by the Earl of Kildare was added to the Pale (currently known as the Kildare County). From then on, only

Englishmen ruled the Pale and ending all the chances of Irish Lords to claim the title.

Since there are almost no loyal supporters left from the Irish Lords, King Henry VIII was forced to compromise and resort to a more peaceful policy. He signed peace treaties with many Irish Lords, and in return, they swore their loyalty to the English throne. This diplomatic tactic managed Henry to gain control of most parts of Ireland immediately.

Ireland in the Tudor Dynasty

During the sixteenth century, Ireland was controlled by different governments. Some parts were ruled by various Gaelic chiefs together with their families known as clans. These people follow their own customs, laws, and language. On the other hand, many groups from Leinster, Munster, and Pale swore their loyalty to the English monarch; thus, they follow the English customs and law.

In 1541, King Henry VIII of England from the family of Tudors went against the Pope and gave himself the title King of Ireland with the support from prestigious families like the O'Neill. This led to an increase of English immigration and settlement in the country. Furthermore, the Irish and Gaelic chiefs who supported the English king gained titles in exchange for their loyalty and observance of the English laws. King Henry gave his word that their direct family line would stay in power. By the time of his death in 1547, the forty Gaelic lords who pledged their loyalty had been given English titles. Two of these famous clans, the O'Donnell and O'Neill, were given the title of earls.

The arrangement worked quite well for some time, but the Gaelic lords revolted against the king because of the overwhelming demands of the Tudor monarchs. As the king's retaliation and also in compliance with the English law, their lands were confiscated.

The Tudors met strong resistance from the Gaelic lords. Some of them even attacked English loyalists and supporters particularly those who live in the Pale including parts of Louth, Meath, and Kildare.

The English Immigrants to Ireland and the Tudor Plantations

During their respective reigns, Queen Mary I (1553-1558) and Queen Elizabeth I (1558-1603) decided that the English must gain more power in Ireland. For this feat, they resorted to sending more loyal subjects to Ireland by granting them confiscated lands which were later identified as plantations. The loyal immigrants, on the other hand, were called settlers or planters.

From 1556 to 1557, Queen Mary 1 (also known as Mary Tudor) confiscated the lands of the Gaelic clans O'Connors and O'Mores and granted these lands to the English settlers. The new settlers got about two-thirds of the land while the native Irish were driven to the areas near Shannon which are known to be of poor quality. This, in turn, wreaked havoc between the new settlers and the Irish clans who fought back to regain their lands which continued for about 50 years.

The English settlers were forced to build stone houses and have their own weapon because of the attacks. They were also ordered not to marry into Irish families and even make them their servants. Additionally, they were forbidden to let Irish families rent in their land. Queen Mary 1 established that only loyal English subjects could live in plantation areas.

Queen Mary also ordered that the confiscated lands of O'Connors and O'Mores be divided into two counties; and that the Irish who lived west of the planted lands had to comply with the English laws. The Laois was renamed as Queen's County and its main town, Maryborough (currently Portlaoise). Even Offaly became King's County in honor of King Philip II who is the queen's husband. Its main town was also called Philipstown (currently Daingean).

When Queen Elizabeth I became the queen of England in 1558, she decided that Ireland is a strategic place to colonize. Aside from being in the same climate as her native England, Ireland is also targeted by the queen's archenemy, the Spanish Catholic monarch, King Philip. She feared that the latter would send forces to Ireland and use them to attack England.

Queen Elizabeth I decided to make Ireland more English by sending more immigrants, giving them lands at a cheap price. This way, the monarch can easily control the neighboring Gaelic lords and their clans. However, this step was met with resistance from the Irish natives. The revolt by the O'Neills of Tyrone (ended in 1561) and two attacks by the Fitzgeralds of Cork and Kerry (ended in 1575 and 1580 respectively). With the defeat of the Fitzgeralds in Cork, Elizabeth took this as an advantage and began to establish a plantation in Munster. The plantation that was once Fitzgerald's was quickly developed into towns and farming lands by 1587. Sadly, the settlement was devastated by a coordinated Irish attack in 1598, and it never recovered. Even so, many English settlers stayed behind in isolated areas.

The 1580 Rebellion

Prelude: The First Desmond Rebellion

Munster was ruled by the influential family of Desmond (branch family of Fitzgeralds in Munster), with its head being on friendly terms with Queen Elizabeth. However, the earl, together with some reputable families like the Fitzmaurices, found unrest with the English intrusion into the Desmond territories. They were also against the creation of the office of the governor (or Lord President) in the province of Munster as well as the favorable policies for the Butlers of Ormonde who are the Fitzgeralds' adversary; but what the

Desmonds could not accept was the government's unjust arrest of Earl Gerald, the head of the family, and his brother John in 1568 for being a part in a private war against the Butlers in 1565.

The First Desmond Rebellion began in 1569 led by the captain-general of the Fitzgerald army, James FitzMaurice FitzGerald, in the absence of Earl Desmond. However, he was defeated by the English forces with the support of the Butlers (led by the Third Earl of Ormonde, Thomas Butler).

Despite the rebellion, the English monarch pardoned the Desmonds and Fitzmaurice but has confiscated majority of the lands and properties of the family. In the aftermath of the First Desmond Rebellion, Fitzmaurice found himself impoverished and Earl Desmond was forbidden to demand military service. On top of these resentments, Fitzmaurice was a devout Catholic who had deep antagonism towards Protestantism, which had been introduced by the English. In 1575, James Fitzmaurice went to France to seek help from Catholic powers to restart another rebellion. He found support from the ruler of Spain, Philip II, and Pope Gregory XIII.

The Beginning

The start of 1580 rebellion (also known as the Second Desmond Rebellion) was marked with the assassination of two English officials namely, Arthur Carter and Henry Davells in a tavern in Tralee. John of Desmond and Fitzmaurice commanded about 3,000 men which include native Irishmen and a small number of European soldiers. However, their plans for encouraging more reinforcements were impeded by the efforts of Sir William Winter who seized the ships of foreign forces and interrupted their sea-routes.

Unfortunately, Fitzmaurice was killed at an encounter with Burkes of Clan William after his men stole some of the horses of Theobald Burke who was a cousin of Fitzmaurice. This incident left John of

Desmond as head commander of the rebellion. The rebels were able to take hold of the southern Munster as the English forces did not have enough troops to retake it. [13]

The Involvement of Earl Desmond

Nicholas Malby, the Lord President of Connaught, marched through the territory of the Desmonds and brought devastation in the countryside. He even demanded that Earl Desmond surrender his Askeaton castle, but the Irish lord refused his demand. With that, the earl was proclaimed as a traitor by the Lord Justice of Ireland, William Pelham. This meant that Earl Desmond should be captured and executed accordingly. Being a hunted man, the earl, along with the remaining Fitzgeralds, was forced to join the rebellion.

Earl Desmond claimed the leadership of the rebellion in quite a spectacular manner. He and his followers raided the town of Youghal, annihilating the English garrison there and hanging the officials for everyone to behold. They even went further by looting and abusing the civilians. The earl's force besieged the city of Cork before driving back into the mountains of Kerry. Meanwhile, the lord of MacCarthys, MacCarthy Mor, announced his joining by plundering Kinsale.

The English, in retaliation, sent Sir William Pelham, Sir George Carew, and Thomas Butler (the Third Earl of Ormonde) to subdue the rebels and devastate the Desmond territory in Cork, Limerick, and Kerry counties. They even killed civilians who lived in those areas in order to faze the followers of the Desmonds.

In the spring of 1580, the English forces took hold of the principal Desmond stronghold at Carrigafoyle Castle located by the Shannon river mouth. This move cut off the FitzGerald forces from the north of the country and blocked the landing of the foreign aid into the main Munster port of Limerick. When the news of the fall of

Carrigafoyle castle spread, the other Desmond forts were also easily destroyed. Many of the Irish lords including Mac Carthy Mor, Barry and Roche surrendered knowing that the English had the upper hand. By the summer of 1580, it might have looked like the rebellion had been completely obliterated; but it was again revived by the onset of the new rebellion in Leinster.

The Leinster Rebellion

In July 1580, Fiach McHugh O'Byrne from the Wicklow Mountains started the rebellion in the eastern part of Ireland. He collaborated with the local lords and clan leaders including the O'Tooles, O'Moores, and Kavanaghs. Many of them were already veterans in fighting the English garrisons. Furthermore, the rebels gave the epithet "King of Leinster" to Creon MacMurrough Kavanagh whose ancestors held this title even before the English invasion, as a sign of their rejection to the English crown. O'Byrne was later joined by Viscount Baltinglass, James Eustace, a marcher lord of the Pale who was motivated by his devotion in Catholicism.

In August, John Desmond and Nicholas Sanders met the Viscount Baltinglass in Laois in order to coordinate their troops. Unfortunately, both parties were unable to establish a common strategy, and there was limited assistance from the Barrow valley region. Nonetheless, the dawn of rebellion near the center of the English jurisdiction in Dublin was taken as an important concern to the English forces.

The former Lord Deputy of Ireland, Sir Henry Sidney, swayed the response from his membership of the Privy Council and a new Lord Deputy was dispatched from England together with 6,000 troops. The immediate order for the new deputy, Arthur Grey, 14th Baron Grey de Wilton, was to suppress the rebellion in Leinster.

On the 25th of August the same year, the English troops under the command of Baron Grey de Wilton were defeated by the combined forces of Viscount Baltinglass and Fiach McHugh O'Byrne. While they were trying to attack O'Byrne's fortress at Glenmalure in the midst of Wicklow Mountains, they were ambushed losing more than 800 soldiers in the process. William Stanley was then sent by the Baron Grey de Wilton to protect the Pale area of Leinster. O'Byrne and his allies were able to attack English settlements in the east and southeast but failed to advance their victory at Glenmalure.

During the rebellion and its aftermath, a number of people from Wexford and Pale were hanged as traitors. Amongst the persecuted were Margaret Ball (wife of the Lord Mayor of Dublin) and Dermot O'Hurley (the Catholic Archbishop of Cashel). These executions left a bitter taste in the Irish natives and resulted in the prolonged isolation of the Old English from the English state in Ireland.

Spanish and Papal Backing

On September 10, 1580, a squadron of Spanish ships headed by Don Juan Martinez de Recalde arrived with a Papal force of Spanish and Italian soldiers. The 600 Italian soldiers were under the command of Sebastiano di San Giuseppe (also known as Sebastiano da Modena) at Smerwick located on the Dingle Peninsula. The troops were sent by King Philip II to secretly assist the rebellion since it was financed by Pope Gregory. Earl Desmond, his brother John, and Baltinglass tried to collaborate with the expeditionary force but were intercepted by the forces under Grey and Ormonde. On the other side, Richard Bingham blocked off the ships sent by the Pope into the bay at Smerwick. As a result, San Giuseppe was left with no choice but to strengthen his men in the fort at Dún an Óir.

In October 1580, Baron Grey de Wilton with 4,000 of his troops landed at Smerwick and seized the garrison. The Papal forces were trapped at the tip of the narrow Dingle Peninsula, blocked by Mount Brandon on one side and the English force on the other. This means that the Spanish and Italian troops had no means of escape. Moreover, the English were geared up with heavy artillery by the sea which quickly destroyed the improvised fortress of Dún an Óir. After a three-day siege, the Italian commander surrendered on October 10, 1580. Baron Grey de Wilton ordered the execution of the Papal forces, sparing only the commanders. All the Spanish and Italian troops together with the Irish men and women were all beheaded and their bodies discarded into the bottom of the sea. English writer and explorer, Sir Walter Raleigh, was one of the English soldiers present during the siege and execution at Smerwick.

The Dusk of the Rebellion

The war extended for two more years with the civilian population as the sacrifice for all the bitter fighting. Their homes, crops, and livestock were all destroyed. Baron Grey de Wilton was described to be a heartless English commander. His black hat tactics include burning the civilian's corn, driving their cattle, and destroying their harvest. This resulted in famine, malnutrition, and plague.

Due to Grey's excessive brutality, Queen Elizabeth I removed him from the office as the Lord Deputy of Ireland. By mid-1582, it was reported that around 30,000 people died of famine in Munster and hundreds were dying in Cork city due to disease and starvation.

The rebellion slowly broke up. In April 1581, Elizabeth offered amnesty to the rebels except for their leaders. Many of the Desmonds' old-time supporters took this chance and surrendered. Meanwhile, Baltinglass escaped to France in August 1581. Fiach MacHugh O'Byrne made a false surrender in April 1581 but resorted into raiding after a short time. He surrendered for good in September 1582, finally ending the battle in Leinster. John Desmond was killed in a skirmish north of Cork in early 1582.

The Earl of Desmond himself was tracked down and killed in

Glenaginty in the Slieve Mish Mountains on November 11, 1583, by the Moriarty clan of Castledrum. The earl and his troops raided the property of the Moriarty, stole their livestock and even abused the sister of the clan chief. They were then chased after and killed in Glenaginty near Tralee in County Kerry. The rebellion was finally concluded in 1583 when the Earl of Ormonde took over the command of English forces. The earl used diplomatic approach to the campaign. He restrained the rebels to Kerry and West Cork, persuading many of the Desmonds to surrender.

Famine Memorial - Dublin

The Aftermath

Munster suffered from bubonic plague and famine for years after the Desmond rebellion. The population was greatly diminished, and the lands were left empty. About a third of the province's population died in the war.

Most areas in the Muster—about 300,000 acres of land— were confiscated by Queen Elizabeth. In 1585, the plantation in Muster was established, and new English settlers arrived to cultivate the land. Even huge estates were granted to some like Walter Raleigh. Many of these new settlers had a hard time finding the location of Muster and were also harassed by the local Irish, so they decided to return back home to England.

Ulster History Park

The Plantation of Ulster

At the dawn of 15th Century, Ireland became a place of mixed culture as well as races except for Ulster, which remained pure Celtic. Even though the rest of the country was a mixture of English, Viking, Celtic and Norman cultures, Ulster remained purely Celtic. It is due to the fact that this was the farthest place, making it safe against the Norman Invasion, as well as the reason that it was being defended by strong clans such as the O'Neills living in Tir Eoghain. And most of all, invaders were thinking that Ulster was not worth conquering.

It was during the year 1598 when Hugh O'Neill, the Earl of Tir Eoghain and his army decided to do a pre-emptive strike against the English, catching them off-guard. Because of this, he successfully drove the English out of Ulster. The English, however, decided to build forts around the southern part of the province, forcing the Irish to attack the forts instead. On December 24, 1601, O'Neill's army was defeated at the Battle of Kinsale, forcing him to retreat to his stronghold in Tir Eoghain (Tyrone nowadays). He did not surrender, however, so the English decided to strengthen their fortifications and destroyed Ulster's crops hoping to make him either attack again or surrender for good. In the year 1602, O'Neill and his army attacked again but were defeated at Omye (Omagh) by Lord Mountjoy and his men. A year later, O'Neill and the English signed a treaty in Mellifont, agreeing to the terms that his lands will remain under his possession, but he will revoke his Irish title as well as adopt English Laws in Ulster.

Despite the conditions in the Treaty of Mellifont, the English thought that it is not enough to make Ulster submissive towards their rule. They also knew that the Catholic Spain, who is allied with O'Neill, can supply Ulster with enough weapons in case they decided to revolt again. Because of this, the English resorted to a somewhat familiar solution: Plant Ulster with Protestant settlers. This time, however, the shortcomings of the previous plantations were all determined and applied with the right solution. The Laois/Offaly as well as Munster Plantations were greatly affected by Irish attacks, so they decided to build fortifications called Plantation Towns. By 1609, the English mapped the entire four million acres of land and gave it out a year later. It was then that the counties such as Antrim, Monaghan, and Down were planted privately. At the same time, English settlers were planted in Derry and Armagh while Tir Eoghain and Donegal were planted with Scots. Cavan and Fermanagh, on the other hand, were planted with both English and Scots.

Since most of the planted settlers were Scottish, these people brought Calvinism or Presbyterian teachings along with them. This is classified as Protestant, and their teachings are different from those of Catholic and Church of England (Anglican). Aside from Calvinism, the Scots also introduced a Puritan way of life as well as new farming methods, making Northeast Ireland very different from the rest. This made the native Ulstermen angry, resulting in the settlers getting attacked and their crops destroyed. But despite all of that, many Irishmen stayed and worked under the settlers, making the Ulster Plantation the most successful one as of date. [14]

Chapter 7: Cromwell and the Restoration

Oliver Cromwell led what is referred to in Irish history as the Cromwellian war in Ireland in 1649-1653 during the Wars of Three Kingdoms. Others called it the Cromwellian Conquest. Cromwellian.

Majority of the areas in Ireland were under the control of the Irish Catholic Confederation after the Irish Rebellion in 1641. In 1649, the English Royalists who were defeated by the Parliamentarians in the English Civil War created an ally with the Confederates until 1652 when Cromwell invaded Ireland on behalf of England Parliamentarians. This brought an end to the eleven-year war Irish Confederate Wars. However, the guerrilla warfare did not end with it and continued for about a year after this. The vast of the population at that time were Roman Catholics. Cromwell passed a series of Penal Laws that lead to the confiscation of the people's lands.

The reconquest of Ireland was too brutal that Cromwell was well-hated by the people. The impact of war on the people was too severe although there were no documented reports on the number of lives that were actually lost. After the war came a famine and the outbreak of bubonic plague. All these resulted in an extreme decline in the Irish population. The decline in population as a result of the Parliamentarian campaign was estimated to be within 15-83 percent range. Around 50,000 people were also transported out of the country as indentured laborers.

Cromwell was then too harsh on the Irish Catholics as a form of revenge for the <u>rebellion of 1641</u> where Protestant settlers in Ulster were massacred. He likewise needed to raise a large amount of money to repay the London merchants who provided subsidies for the war under the <u>Adventurers Act</u>. Those implicated in the 1641 rebellion were executed while those who joined Confederate Ireland had their properties confiscated. Many were sent to West Indies as laborers. Confiscated lands owned by Catholic landowners who did not participate in the wars were allowed to claim their lands in Connacht.[15][16][17][18][19]

Catholics were not allowed to live in the towns, and the religious practice of Catholicism was completely banned and priests were executed. Irish soldiers who fought for the Confederates and Royalist armies which were estimated to be around 54,000 based on William Petty's estimate find services in the armies of Spain and France.

Prior to these wars, Catholics in Ireland owned about 60% of the lands but during the English restoration, only 20% of these lands remained in their ownership, and this percentage further declined to 8% during the Commonwealth period. After the 1660 restoration, Catholics were not allowed to serve in any public office with the exception of the Irish Parliament.

The Parliamentarian Campaign in Ireland was considered to be the most ruthless of the Civil War period particularly the presence of Cromwell at Wexford and Drogheda. However, there are arguments that his actions, if based on the standards at that time can't be considered as excessive cruelty. Those who are defending Cromwell even argued that his actions applied only to men in arms and that accounts of civilian massacres are still being disputed.

Regardless of the point of views, the campaign remains notorious in Irish history being responsible for the greatest death toll among Irish people. The cited reason was the counter-guerrilla tactics employed by Edmund Ludlow, Henry Ireton, and John Hewson against the Catholic population where they burn crops in large quantity and kill civilians forcing them to join movements.

Long-term Results

The Cromwellian conquest completed the <u>British colonization</u> of Ireland, which was merged into the <u>Commonwealth of England, Scotland and Ireland</u> in 1653–59. It causes the destruction of the native Irish Catholic who owned lands and replaced them with colonists with a British identity. The sufferings and hatred caused by the Cromwellian settlement was a powerful source of <u>Irish nationalism</u> from the 17th century onwards.

After the <u>Restoration of the English monarchy</u> during the Stuart period, Charles of England restored about one-third of confiscated lands to their former landlords through the <u>Act of Settlement 1662</u> but lacked support from English parliamentarians, thus not all were restored.

Chapter 8: Ireland in the 18th -19th Century

In the 18th Century

Through Penal Laws, the colonists were able to accomplish their expected results. Within a few generations, the Irish were reduced to poverty as many were illiterate and unskilled. By the year 1750, 93% of the land that belongs to the Irish was transferred to non-Irish landowners. By the year 1770, they already owned almost 100 percent of the Irish lands. The Irish then was reduced to being a country of tenants.

Some eyewitness accounts of the life of an average Irish tenant farmer proved that the Irish peasant farmer is poor than the lowest serfs in German and Poland. Their life is one of deprivation and desperation. About half of those who lived in rural areas lived in small mud cabins with no windows. It was normal to see farm animals living in a cabin with the people. Only the abundance of peat helps these people to survive in the winter.

Lands that were once owned by the Irish were now being rented by them. In order to increase rental income derived from the land, greedy landlords are dividing and subdividing their lands, so families have less and fewer areas to live and paying more for the rental each time. The price of the rent is actually double the price one would pay if renting in England.

The farmers lived by growing potatoes, and many of them never tasted meat or bread. Their meals were always potatoes and sometimes include buttermilk.

All these inhuman treatments were not placidly accepted by the Irish and with the execution of the Penal Laws; their response was a sort of guerilla warfare carried out secretly.

In the 1760s, there were gangs of men wearing white shirts over their clothes; hence they were called "White boys" who roam the countryside at night burning barns, tearing down fences, and crippling cattle. They were also after tithes collectors, informers, and men of landlords torturing them to death. Landlord's houses and properties were being destroyed. There are also some reports of shooting through windows of manor houses. With these, landlords' houses were often barricaded and secured by stationed military men or soldiers.

By the end of the 19th century, the Irish started planning for the insurrection of 1798. The plan is for simultaneous revolts all over entire Ireland at the same time that a large army of French soldiers is about to land in Ireland. However, the ship carrying these soldiers ran into a strong storm as they are in sight of the land that most of these ships sank and were not able to reach the

The 1778 Rebellion

seashore. However, the Irish, armed with pikes and clubs push through with the revolt and did remarkably well against muskets and canons of their enemies. The battle occurred in Vinegar Hill in County Wexford. The Irish stood their ground, but then, the enemy had blown them up with cannon balls. Although the Irish lost the battle, it became an inspiration to the most popular Irish war song entitled, "The Boys of Wexford." In other parts of the country, many of the Irish were butchered while on their knees begging for mercy during the mopping-up operation of the colonists. In that war, more than 50,000 were killed, and the majority died in cold blood than in the battle.

Chapter 9: Modern Ireland

Ireland hasn't had Parliament on its own since 1801, only a handful of Irish Members of Parliament (MP) who sat in the Westminster parliament in London. Westminster decided not to give any compromises to the Catholics despite their exhibited persistence. In 1823, there was a radical move from the *Catholic Association* headed by Daniel O'Connell, a Catholic barrister, in order to urge the full liberty of the Catholics. It quickly turned into a political mass movement, forcing the London parliament to grant Catholic Emancipation by 1829 and practically freeing the Catholics from all their disadvantages.

O'Connell's success made him the most influential figure in Ireland, giving him more confidence to seek the revocation of the Act of Union of 1800 and the re-establishment of the Irish parliament. He designed the *Repeal Association* and based his campaign on that for emancipation. The agitation was identified as mass meetings with the attendance of hundreds to thousands of people. In 1843, the London Government gave its resistance by banning a Dublin rally of which O'Connell conceded his defeat. This memorialized the successful end of the repeal campaign.

In the 1840s, the group of Thomas Davis created the *Young Ireland* movement. Like the *United Irishmen*, the group aims to educate everyone who lived in Ireland to embrace their nationality regardless of their culture, faith, and roots. When the group staged an insurrection in 1848, everything came crumbling down. However, their expressed ideas strongly inspired and motivated the next generations about their concept of liberty.

The end of the European war in 1815 brought a drastic impact on the Irish economy. Due to the army needs for food supplies, tillage farming experienced relative growth during the warring times. Potatoes, in particular, became a staple. Unfortunately, the end of the war also marked the transition of tillage farming to pasture-based farming, causing agrarian unemployment in the process. There was also a population explosion of 8 million by 1841; two-thirds of this depended on agriculture alone. While Ireland was facing the uncertainty in the agrarian economy, the country yet had to face another blow to the economy—blight in potato cropping in 1845. This was followed by another failure in the following year to 1848 and coupled with severe weather, Ireland faced famine. By 1851, the population was reduced by about two million due to mixed factors like disease, starvation, and emigration of people to Britain and North America. [20]

Ireland in the second half of the nineteenth century was characterized by various campaigns for land reform and national independence. In 1858, the secret society of *Irish Republican Brotherhood (IRB)*, also known as the *Fenians*, was founded. Two of their most controversial leaders were John O'Leary and James Stephens. In 1867, the group organized an armed revolt. The members don't believe that diplomatic and constitutional attempts would bring them the goal they wanted to achieve. Nevertheless, the uprising was easily and quickly suppressed although the secret society still existed thereafter.

By the end of the nineteenth century, Ireland pursued the concept of cultural nationalism. In 1884, the *Gaelic Athletic Association* was founded, aiming to promote the national games. The *Gaelic League* (1893) founded by Eoin MacNeill and Douglass Hyde, attempted to restore the Irish language and culture nationwide. Simultaneously, Arthur Griffith established a new political party called *Sin Féin* ("We Ourselves") from 1905 to 1908. Its strategy centers on the conviction that Irish Members of Parliament should withdraw from the Westminster and build an independent parliament. The party had close ties with the IRB. In 1913, a socialist and separatist group called the *Irish Citizen Army* was created based on the Dublin labor dispute.

The Sin Féin representatives, headed by Éamon de Valera, then declared themselves as the first dependent Parliament (or *Dáil*) in Dublin. When the English tried to obliterate Sin Féin, it led to the War of Independence from 1919 to 1921. The Irish forces were commanded by Michael Collins. After more than two years of battle, a truce was agreed upon. The Anglo-Irish Treaty which was signed December 1921 stated that the 26 counties gained independence as the *Irish Free State*.

However, after the Free State had been established, a civil war between the newly found government and those who opposed the Treaty happened. Éamon de Valera led the opposition. Although the civil war ended in May 1923, it had claimed the lives of those who had led the campaign for independence including Cathal Brugha and Michael Collins.

Chapter 10: Ireland Today

Ireland or Irish Eire is a country located in Western Europe which occupies about five-sixths of the British Isles westernmost island.

While geographically isolated, the magnificent scenery of Ireland's coastlines faces the wide expanse of the Atlantic Ocean and has helped a lot in developing its rich heritage of culture and tradition initially linked to the Gaelic language.

The vast green-hued landscape of Ireland is responsible for the popular so-called "Emerald Isle."

Ireland is also famous for its treasured collections of folklore ranging from tiny leprechauns with hidden pots of gold to that of Saint Patrick who according to legend rid the island of snakes. Although many may have considered the country as an enchanted land, yet it is beset with many perennial concerns including political, immigration, and cultural issues along with the relations with Northern Island.

At the start of the 21st century, due to its diverse export-driven economy, long-term economic issues that best the country were abating. However, the occurrence of a calamity in 2008 brought Ireland's economic crisis.

Largely depending on agriculture, Ireland was long among the poorest regions in Europe with a principal cause of mass migration especially during the 19th-century cycle of famine. More than 40 million Americans were able to trace their ancestry back to Ireland as a result of this exodus. There are millions other people throughout the world who shared the same situation.

Ireland's capital is Dublin, an affluent city which is home to more than 25% of the country's population. Where there were old dockside neighborhoods before, now, new residential and commercial developments take over.

Ireland is divided into four provinces that are further divided into 32 counties. The provinces are:

- Munster
- Leinster
- Ulster
- Connaught

Counties of Munster

- Clare
- Cork
- Kerry
- Limerick
- Tipperary
- Waterford

Counties of Leinster

- Carlow
- Dublin
- Kildare
- Kilkenny
- Laois
- Longford
- Louth
- Meath
- Offaly
- Westmeath
- Wexford
- Wicklow

Counties of Ulster

- Armagh
- Antrim
- Down
- Derry
- Fermanagh
- Tyrone
- Donegal
- Cavan
- Monagham

Counties of Connaught

- Galway
- Leitrim
- Mayo
- Roscommon
- Sligo

The Currency

Throughout the 26 counties of the South, Ireland uses the Euro currency while 6 counties in Ulster use British Pound or Sterling including:

- Down
- Derry
- Antrim
- Armagh
- Tyrone
- Fermanagh

Ireland discontinued the use of Irish Pound, known as "punt" in Gaelic when the country joined the Eurozone.

Climate

The weather in Ireland is largely influenced by the Atlantic Ocean - wet, mild, and changeable. Normal weather condition is not too hot or too cold. It seldom occurs that the summer temperature would go beyond 30 degrees Celsius or 86 degrees Fahrenheit. This can happen once or twice in a decade.

Rainfall can occur anytime in Ireland but a prolonged period of rain is not common, and severe frost and snow are confined to months of December to February.

The Language

Ireland's recognized first official language is Irish Gaelic. However, more than one out of 10 Irish speak a language other than Irish or English. Fingal in Dublin has the highest numbers of non-native languages speakers in the country including Polish, French, and Lithuanian which the most commonly used language in the state.

According to the 2011 census, a total of 182 different languages were recorded to have been spoken across the State.

French is the most common first language used by about 56,430 people nationwide followed by those whose mother tongue is Lithuanian.

Other languages used are the following:

- German
- Russian
- Chinese
- Spanish
- Romanian,
- Latvian

- Arabic
- Portuguese

Lesser-known languages include:

- Shona - the principal language of Zimbabwe (a Niger-Congo language)
- Akan - principally used in Ghana and Ivory Coast

The use of foreign languages is seen as a threat to some people, and if the government will not do something to encourage the use of foreign language, there is a great possibility that these languages will disappear in the coming generations.

Culture and Tradition

The Irish tradition and culture are well known across the globe, and though many are celebrating and enjoying these traditions, still, many don't like their origins.

Here are some of the famous traditions that have helped shaped Irish cultural identity.

Saint Patrick's Day

Patricius was born in a Roman-occupied part of Britain and when she was still 16 years old; she was kidnapped by Irish bandits and sold into slavery as a shepherd. Every day, Patrick prayed to God and each day he believes that God will hear his prayers. After 6 years, he heard God call him to a port which was a hundred miles away from where he was that time. He decided to leave Ireland.

After some time, Patrick saw a vision of lost Irish children, and this convinced him to bring Christianity to Ireland, so he went back. He was famous for comparing the Holy Trinity to Shamrock which then became a famous icon forever linked to Ireland.

After living a long life preaching the Word of Christ, he died on March 17 451 A.D. When the Irish migrated to America in the 19th century; they celebrated St. Patrick's Day and from there, this even became famous and celebrated worldwide.

Pub Culture

In Ireland, the pub culture was integral to the people's daily lives as friends and families are commonly seen in pub houses where they meet and catch up on each other's lives. One of the famous icons that are featured in most pubs is the Guinness. Guinness is a popular alcoholic drink in Ireland and well-known in the world bringing in more than two million euro annually.

Brigid's Cross

Catholicism has been an important element in the history of Ireland, and one image that is being connected to it is the St. Brigid's cross. The image of the cross is made from wild reeds which were said to be created by St. Brigid while trying to convert a dying chieftain into Christianity to convey the story of Jesus Christ crucifixion.

Saint Brigid's day is celebrated every 1st of February which is also the first day of spring in ancient Ireland. Along with the image and the celebration of the event is the belief that the cross would protect your home from fire. This belief continues till the modern time in Ireland.

Halloween

Halloween is a day for trick or treats, and it provides thrills and scares across the world especially to children. However, only a few know that the event originates from the pre-Christian festival "Samhain," where the boundaries between the mortal and the other world would collapse and allow the dead to return to Ireland.

Some people would dress up in a scary costume to ward off bad spirits and would visit homes collecting food for offering to gods. Today, children have innovated this to trick or treat. Offerings are then placed in front of the Tlachta bonfire, and the tradition of great lighting bonfires still continues up to this time.

As part of the celebration, the Gaels carve faces into turnips and made into lanterns to protect themselves from the living dead. Now, these turnips have become pumpkins and are called Jack-O-lanterns.

This tradition originated from the tale about Stingy Jack, a blacksmith who was able to trap the devil using a cross, keeping him as a prisoner. To get out of there, the devil swore to Jack that he wouldn't take Jack's soul after his death. But when Jack died, he was not allowed to enter Heaven, and since the devil keeps up to his promise that he won't take Jack's soul, he was left wandering on earth with only a flame taken from the pit of Hell to light him through the darkness. Jack then place this flame that is never extinguished into a turnip, and that's how it came to be known as the Jack of the Lantern or Jack-O-Lantern. [20]

Irish Music

Pubs hosting live music throughout Ireland prove that music plays an integral part in the Irish culture. Traditional music makes use of world-known music instruments including acoustic guitar, fiddle, and piano combined with local instruments of the Irish natives such as Uilleann pipes, the Celtic harp, and Irish bouzoukis.

There are other Irish traditional instruments apart from the harp that was recently developed like the accordions, the bodhran, concertinas, and the Uilleann pipes emerging only in the 19th century. The guitar and the bouzouki are just off-shoots of the revival of the Irish traditional music in the middle of the 20th century. [21]

Music has taken a large part of Irish existence since prehistoric times.

Even though in the early medieval times, the church contributed greatly to the musical evolution in Ireland. The monastic settlements in Ireland, as well as the rest of Europe, produced what is now known as the *Gregorian chant*. In the secular establishments, musical genres in early Gaelic Ireland can be referred to as a triad of laughing music or *geantraige*, weeping music or *goltraige*, and sleeping music or *suantraige*. Vocal and instrumental music were passed orally back then. The Irish harp holds so much significance that it was declared as Ireland's national symbol.

As for the classical Irish music, it had followed European models as well and was first developed in urban areas and premises where the Anglo-Irish dominated (i.e., Christ Church, Dublin Castle, St. Patrick's Cathedral, and the residences of those with Anglo-Irish roots). Handel's Messiah (1742) became one of the most popular music of the baroque era. In the 19th century, public concerts include classical music to cater to all social classes. Unfortunately, Ireland wasn't generous enough to provide a living to Irish musicians, so the names of the more popular Irish composers of this period belong mostly to emigrants.

The Irish traditional music and dance became globally known in the 1960s. In the mid-twentieth century, Ireland began with its modernization and music was part of this new revolution. Traditional music fell out of favor, particularly in urban areas. However, during the 1960s, the revival of traditional Irish music was led by popular groups like the Clancy Brothers, The Dubliners, The Wolfe Tones, The Chieftains, and Sweeney's Men. Individuals like Christy Moore and Seán Ó Riada also contributed to this revival. Meanwhile, other groups and musicians like Thin Lizzy, Horslips, and Van Morrison combined the elements of Irish traditional music into the contemporary rock during the 1970s and 1980s. This style has become the mainstream nowadays as seen in the works of contemporary artists like The Corrs, Enya, The Cranberries, and many others.

Irish dance, on the other hand, has become famous worldwide in the 1990s with the introduction of Riverdance. Irish dance takes various forms including step dancing, jigs, ceili dances, and reels. It also requires unique fashion sense, with the costumes fashioned based on the designs drawn in the Book of Kells. Although the famed hard shoes that produce clicking sounds during the dance movements were crafted in the nineteenth century. Nowadays, these shoes are commonly made with fiberglass. [22]

Irish Notable Figures

Irish people are famous for their eloquence. Ireland has birthed to a large number of world-class artists, writers, musicians, and politicians.

Michael Collins (1890-1922)

Michael Collins was an Irish revolutionary, soldier, and politician who became a major figure in the early twentieth century during the Irish struggle for independence. He was the *Chairman of the Provisional Government of the Irish Free State* from January 1922 until his death in August 1922.

Collins was initially a member of London GAA and became associated with the *Irish Republican Brotherhood (IRB)* and the *Gaelic League*. He fought in the Easter Rising and was consequently imprisoned in the Frongoch internment camp as one of the prisoners of war. He was released in December 1916 and rose through the ranks in *Sinn Féin* and *Irish Volunteers*.

During the War of Independence, he became the *Director of Organization* and *Adjutant General* for the Irish Volunteers and *Director of Intelligence* of the Irish Republican Army. He also earned the fame as a guerilla warfare strategist due to his skills in planning and commanding many successful attacks on the opponents like the assassination of key British intelligence agents in November 1920.

In 1922 he formed a provisional government and became its chairman but was soon interrupted by the Irish Civil War in which Collins was commander-in-chief of the National Army. Sadly, he was shot and killed during an ambush of anti-Treaty forces on August 22, 1922.

Charles Stewart Parnell (1846-1891)

An Irish nationalist politician, he served as a Member of Parliament (MP) in the *House of Commons of the United Kingdom of Great Britain and Ireland* from 1875 to 1880. He was born into an influential Anglo-Irish Protestant family, became a land reform activist, and the founder of the *Irish National Land League* in 1879. He was famous for his skills in executing parliamentary procedures and in stabilizing radical, economic, and constitutional issues. Parnell is greatly admired as the best political party organizer of his time and also one of the most intimidating figures in parliamentary history.

Bono (1960- Present)

Paul David Hewson or Bono is an Irish singer, musician, songwriter, businessman, and philanthropist. He is best known as the lead vocalist and main lyricist of the rock band U2. His lyrics bring social, political and spiritual awareness. As a U2 member, Bono has bagged 22 Grammy Awards and have been inducted into the Rock and Roll Hall of Fame.

Outside his profession as a musician, Bono is famous for his activism for social justice causes, being active in his campaigns for Africa, and for which he co-founded the ONE Campaign, DATA, and EDUN. Due to his humanitarian contributions, he was given an honorary knighthood by Queen Elizabeth II. Bono was also named as one of the Time Persons of the Year in 2005.

Aside from the icons mentioned above, these famous individuals greatly contributed to the name of their country and respective fields:

- Samuel Beckett (playwright, Nobel Prize awardee)
- George Bernard Shaw (playwright, Nobel Prize awardee)
- William Butler Yeats (poet, Nobel Prize awardee)
- Robert Boyle (chemist, physicist)
- John Philip Holland (inventor)
- William Edward Wilson (astronomer)
- John Tyndall (physicist)
- Oscar Wilde (poet and dramatist)
- Brendan Behan (satirist, poet, and playwright)
- Jonathan Swift (satirist and essayist)
- James Joyce (novelist)
- Sean O'Casey (playwright)
- Edmund Burke (political theorist)
- Pierce Brosnan (actor)
- Collin Farrell (actor)
- Ronan Keating (singer)
- Westlife (band)

Potatoes

Potato isn't just a food staple in Ireland but also a popular symbol. The potato obtained its importance as a crop in Ireland right before the famine. It was not a native Irish crop but had been found by Spanish in South America in the 1500s and was shipped to Europe, reaching Ireland at around 1590.

The farmers realized eventually that potatoes could double the food and everyone would have enough to eat. They could also still have land to grow oats and get involved in dairying at the same time. The plant allowed the farmers to make extra money. Eventually, potatoes were also planted in Connaught and Leinster, even becoming the staple food for the farm laborers. The lands in the east were converted into tillage farms while the Ulster was used to grow flax for the Irish linen industry. That time, Dublin was progressing as an urban center. These factors helped the potato economy surge, and soon farmers were selling their excess crops to the regions where food are scarce. Also, new potato varieties like Apple Potato (1760), Cup Potato (1800), and Lumper Potato (after 1810) were introduced. Potatoes became a primary source of nutrition for the poorest people of Leinster and Connaught.

In the early 1800s, the population was boosted to over 8 million that many of the farmers and their laborers became almost reliant on potatoes. By 1830s, about thirty to thirty-five percent of the Irish had potatoes as their staple food. Fortunately, potatoes are excellent in nutrition. If milk is added, it can provide enough protein, minerals, carbohydrates, and energy needed for a balanced diet.

In 1700, a Connaught farmer could have eaten one meal with potatoes per day; in 1800, the number doubled. As the potato spread, farmers had little ability to acquire oats and milk. By 1840, a Connaught farmer was eating three potato meals per day, containing a total of five to six kilograms of potatoes.

On the eve of the Great Famine, a third of the Irish population in Connaught and Munster relied on potatoes as their main food source. Since potatoes could not be stored for a long time or transported well, a new crop needed to be grown per year. [22]

Irish Legends and Folklores

When it comes to literary treasures, Ireland proves to be one of the richest in Western Europe. Even the individual characters like the Banshee, leprechaun, and changeling have become world-renowned.

The Banshee, one of the most popular in the lot, is derived from the Irish *bean-sidhe* which means a woman of the fairy. It's an ancestral spirit that warms families of approaching tragedies like personal losses and death. According to legends, she can only warn the five prestigious families: the O'Conners, O'Neils, O'Gradys, O'Byrons, and Kavanaghs. Thus, she's also a spirit symbolizing prestige and affluence. Appearing before the family members (or hearing her wails) portends death. She is also known to accompany the dead to the afterlife.

Her appearance can be that of a young woman, a middle-aged lady, or an old hag. In some stories, the banshee is said to take other forms like the stoat, weasel, crow, and other animals familiar to witches. King James I of Scotland was rumored to have been confronted by a banshee shortly before his demise.

Some Irish myths can also be seen in the history of other places like the Tales of the Irish hunter-warrior, Fionn Mac Cumhaill and his conflict with a Scottish giant named Benandonner. In order to avoid getting his feet wet, he created the Giant's Causeway. To scare the opposition, he threw a mass of land into the direction of Scotland but missed. The mass landed in the Irish Sea and came to be what is known now as the Isle of Man; the pebble of the projectile forming Rockall; the hole from where he scooped the land was filled with water and became Lough Neagh. Related tales of this legend were also told in the Scottish and Manx folktales.

Perhaps the most popular character among the Irish legends and folklore is the gold-obsessed leprechaun, a fairy of the Tuath Dé Danann known to be a supernatural tribe of gods from the Otherworld and who also ruled as deities of Ireland. The pint-sized fairies are portrayed as mischievous cobblers who own great wealth and grant three wishes to any human who captures them. Originally, leprechauns were known to dress in red jackets instead of green. [23]

Irish Literature and Theater

189

Irish literature has great influence all over the world, and a big part of its soul is from the Irish cultural identity. Their rich collection of mythology was preserved by the monks during medieval times. They were written both in Latin and the Old Irish language. The Normans introduced the English writing in Ireland during the thirteenth century. By the nineteenth century, the Irish literature was mainly written in English.

Ireland has produced great writers including Jonathan Swift, author of Gulliver's Travels, and the first world-renowned Irish writer. Oscar Wilde, the humorous and controversial playwright and author of The Picture of Dorian Gray. Dracula was written by the very much Irish Bram Stoker and the children's favorite, The Chronicles of Narnia, was written by C.S. Lewis.

Aside from Oscar Wilde, Ireland also gave birth to successful playwrights like Samuel Beckett and George Bernard Shaw. Geniuses like Seamus Heaney, W.B. Yeats, and Patrick Kavanagh greatly contributed to the field of poetry. There are also those whose writing skills have been conveyed in both Gaelic and English languages like Flann O'Brien and Brendan Behan.

In the 1920s, the Irish literature was internationally prominent with the modernist authors like James Joyce accomplishing popularity with *A Portrait of the Artist as a Young Man* and *Dubliners*, and notoriety with his novels, *Finnegans Wake* and *Ulysses*. In the 21st century, Colum McCann and Roddy Doyle along with the female writers such as Emma Donoghue, Jennifer Johnston, and Ann Enright contributed to the steady popularity of the Irish writing. Irish literature is continuously experiencing revival, always claiming its place in the global literary world. [24]

Conclusion

What seemed to be an unending struggle of political and religious power in Ireland had long been over, but the memory that it left behind will remain a lesson especially to the common people who bore all the consequences.

The English have long pulled out their armies and commanders, but the thousands of lives that were sacrificed will never be regained back.

But what lesson have we learned from the past?

Until recently, Irish history tells how the Irish resisted and finally overcame the oppressive dominance of the English rule and its collaborators. However, lately, this was questioned by a new generation of Irish historians leading to a deeper understanding of the past and drawing a different conclusion and lesson from it.

Let us consider the famous Irish Potato Famine in 1840. In 1845, there was an infestation of a fungal parasite – Phytophthora infestans resulting in a partial failure of the harvest of Irish potato that year. Also because of wet weather, there was again another harvest failure in 1847 and 1848 which resulted in the death of more than one and a half million people who died from hunger and famine-related sickness. To avoid the calamity, an equal number of Irish migrated to other countries including the United States of America. Due to this and to subsequent mass migration, Ireland has failed to recover demographically. In 1841 the population of Ireland is 8 million and today, there are only 6 million.

Although the British had their fair share of the blame for the great disaster, notice that the unending conflicts between religious sectors played a dominant role in what happened to the Irish. When at first there was this power play between the King and the Pope, later it became Catholicism vs. Protestantism. The irony here is the fact that both parties employ violence and politics to get what they want. Instead of leading the people in the right way, their misdeed led to the death of many.

When Penal Laws were passed and used as instruments for curtailing the rights of the Catholics, including foreboding them to go overseas for education, and for teaching or operating schools, nonetheless, what created a great impact was the Act to Prevent the Further Growth of Popery which prevented Catholics from buying lands or inheriting it from Protestants and from leasing lands beyond the period of 31 years.

When at this time, potatoes were considered a major crop, the existing legislature and penal laws were enough to discourage the farmers from planting crops and improving their agricultural practice. With the set-up advantageous only to the landlords who were Protestants, the Catholic farmers were never motivated to develop their lands for farming.

While Irish agriculture remained to be labor-intensive and the land repeatedly subdivided, a family survived in a small area because of the high yield of potato. However, these restraints on the majority also meant that the commerce and national gross production of Ireland are not developing resulting in low economic status. Added to this was the migration of many Irish to other places which had a great impact on its demographics.

Therefore, it is easy to see that that the root of the problem was actually the nature of the land system. With a policy that allows landowners to keep a large area of lands and yet prevents agricultural improvements is bound to keep the national economy is a disastrous state.

Furthermore, there was this Corn Law preventing large-scale importation of grains into Ireland which further aggravates the food shortage until it was repealed in 1846.

From the history of Ireland, we can learn that not all governments are effective in relieving disasters. In fact, some even aggravate the situation because of the political power plays which in this case is even magnified with the violent participation of religious sectors.

Another thing is laws that affect economic choices can have long-term and frequently perverse results. In the case of Ireland, actions and laws that led to wrong economic incentives produce effects that are difficult to reverse.

Finally, if you found this book useful in any way, a review is always appreciated!

BIBLIOGRAPHY

[16] Adventurers' Act. (2007, April 19). Retrieved from
   https://en.wikipedia.org/wiki/Adventurers_Act

[3] A Brief History of Ireland. (n.d.). Retrieved from
   http://www.localhistories.org/irehist.html

[4] Celtic Ireland in the Iron Age: the Celts. (n.d.). Retrieved from
   http://www.wesleyjohnston.com/users/ireland/past/pre_norma
   n_history/iron_age.html

[17] Confederate Ireland. (n.d.). Retrieved from
   https://en.wikipedia.org/wiki/Confederate_Ireland

[19] Connacht. (2002, August 21). Retrieved from
   https://en.wikipedia.org/wiki/Connacht

[10] Edward VI of England. (2001, December 11). Retrieved from
   https://en.wikipedia.org/wiki/Edward_VI_of_England

[20] History - Modern Ireland. (n.d.). Retrieved from
   http://www.ireland-information.com/reference/modirel.html

[14] History of Ireland 1598 - 1629: Defeat of Ulster and the Ulster
   Plantation. (n.d.). Retrieved from
   http://www.wesleyjohnston.com/users/ireland/past/history/15
   981629.html

[9] Holy See. (2001, May 4). Retrieved from
   https://en.wikipedia.org/wiki/Holy_See

Ireland in the Age of the Tudors. (n.d.). Retrieved from
   http://www.askaboutireland.ie/learning-zone/primary-
   students/subjects/history/history-the-full-story/ireland-in-the-
   age-of-the/

[1] Ireland in the last Ice Age. (n.d.). Retrieved from
   http://www.wesleyjohnston.com/users/ireland/past/pre_norma
   n_history/iceage.html

[Ireland. (n.d.). Retrieved from
   https://en.wikipedia.org/wiki/Ireland#Arts

[13] Irish Rebellion of 1641. (2005, February 2). Retrieved from

https://en.wikipedia.org/wiki/Irish_Rebellion_of_1641

[5] John's first expedition to Ireland. (2004, November 4). Retrieved from
https://en.wikipedia.org/wiki/John%27s_first_expedition_to_Ireland

[12] Mary I of England. (n.d.). Retrieved from
https://en.wikipedia.org/wiki/Mary_I_of_England

[2] Neolithic Stone Age in Prehistoric Ireland. (n.d.). Retrieved from
http://www.wesleyjohnston.com/users/ireland/past/pre_norman_history/neolithic_age.html

[22] Prelude to the Irish Famine: The Potato. (n.d.). Retrieved from
https://www.wesleyjohnston.com/users/ireland/past/famine/potato.html

[13] Second Desmond Rebellion. (2006, July 21). Retrieved from
https://en.wikipedia.org/wiki/Second_Desmond_Rebellion#Second_rebellion

[22]Ten Irish Cultural Traditions and Their Origins. (2018, September 14). Retrieved from
https://www.irelandbeforeyoudie.com/ten-origins-irish-cultural-traditions/

[23] Top 10 Irish Mythological Creatures | Irish Folklore. (2017, September 11). Retrieved from http://blog.carrolls.ie/top-10-irish-mythological-creatures/

[2] Vikings in Ireland. (n.d.). Retrieved March 19, 2019, from
http://www.wesleyjohnston.com/users/ireland/past/pre_norman_history/vikings.html

[16] West Indies. (2002, January 27). Retrieved from
https://en.wikipedia.org/wiki/West_Indies

Welsh History

A Concise Overview of the History of Wales from Start to End

Table of Contents

Introduction

Britain in the primary Middle Ages was very compared the country it is nowadays. Rather than England, Scotland and Wales, the island contained of many kingdoms, the recognition and affluence of which varied, as some kings increased lordship over others, some smaller kingdoms were believed by their superior neighbors and others fell to foreign invaders – comprising Vikings, in the ninth and tenth centuries.

Today, many of the populations of Britain identify mainly as Scottish, English or Welsh. But this was not continuously the circumstance. In Wales, for instance, there is no solitary defining moment when one can say the people became "Welsh."

In the early Middle Ages, Wales separated into different three kingdoms – Gwynedd, Dyfed, and Ceredigion, for example – whose relations with each other designed a vital plank of native politics.

Chapter 1: The Emergence of Wales as A Country

Wales, constituent unit of the United Kingdom that forms a westward extension of the island of Great Britain. The capital and primary commercial and financial focus are Cardiff.

Celebrated for its strikingly robust landscape, the small country of Wales—which involves six distinctive regions —was one of Celtic Europe's most important political and social focuses, as it holds aspects of culture that are uniquely different from those of its English neighbors.

Chapter 2: The Defining of Wales

Between AD 650 and 750, Britain's lowland zone turned out to be immovably English. Indeed, even in southern Scotland, a large portion of the Brythonic and Welsh kingdoms went under English or Anglian control. However, before that occurred, those kingdoms delivered the first surviving body of literature in the Welsh language, specifically the Gododdin of Aneirin.

The English development squeezed especially hard on Powys. Powys is a principal area and county, and one of the preserved counties of Wales. It is named after the Kingdom of Powys which was a Welsh successor state, petty kingdom and principality that emerged during the Middle Ages following the end of Roman rule in Britain. The Heledd poem is an excellent lament on that kingdom's adversities.

On achieving the Welsh mountains, English development turned into a spent power, a reality which Offa, King of Mercia, perceived. There is proof that, in around 780, he ordered the building of a dike from ocean to ocean. The result was Offa's Dyke, the most critical landmark built in Britain in the second 50% of the first Christian millennium, went far in characterizing the region of Wales.

Ancient Wales

During the last ice age, individuals chased reindeer and mammoth in what is currently Wales. When the ice age finished around 10,000 BC, new animals such as the red deer and wild bear showed up in Wales. Stone Age seekers chased them both as well as gathered plants for food.

In around 4,000 BC, cultivating was brought into Wales, even though the general population still used stone tools. Around

2,000 BC, individuals figured out how to use bronze. At that point, around 600 Celts moved to Wales, carrying iron tools and arms with them. The Celts were warlike persons, and they constructed many slope poles crosswise over Wales. They were also talented; they were skilled craftsmen with iron, bronze, and gold.

In 43 AD the Romans attacked Southeast England. They moved to attack Wales around 50 AD, but the conquest took a very long while. In 78 AD the Romans caught Anglesey, the central command of the Druids, the Celtic ministers. They installed a system of forts crosswise over the land to control any resistant Celtic clans. This effectively squashed opposition. Sometimes towns grew up outside the forts as the soldiers provided a market for the citizens goods. The essential Roman town in Wales was Caerwent. By modern standards, such a town appears modest with only a couple of thousand occupants, but towns were small then.

Christianity landed in Wales in the third century, though it was initially repressed. The Roman Empire did not adopt Christianity as its official religion until the fourth century. Perhaps it is unsurprising then that there are records of two men named Julius and Aaron martyred at Caerleon in 304 AD. Mistreatment of Christians declined from then on and ceased nearly altogether in 313.

Anyway, in the fourth century, the Roman Empire went into decay. The last Roman troopers left Britain in 407 AD and the Roman lifestyle slowly evaporated. Wales split into independent kingdoms.

Wales in The Middle Ages

In the interim, the Saxons attacked eastern England. They walked westwards, and by the seventh century AD, they had conquered the outskirts of Wales. Hundreds of years of battling between the Welsh and Saxons pursued.

This warring continued until the ninth century, when the Vikings began their assault of Wales. Anyway, a man named Rhodri ap Merfyn or Rhodri Mawr (Rhodri the Great) progressed toward becoming ruler of Gwynedd in the northeast. In 855 he also proceeded toward becoming lord of Powys in eastern Wales. In 856 he prevailed upon an extraordinary triumph the Danes. Anyway, the Vikings kept on assaulting Wales, at interims, until the finish of the tenth century.

When William the Conqueror became king of England in 1066 he did not attempt to conquer Wales. Anyway, he granted land along the English-Welsh fringe to Norman masters that impressed him or earned his respect. A few of these masters would later infringe on Welsh land, though not at William's behest.

During the rule of William II (1087-1100), the Normans proceeded with their assaults on Wales. The Welsh opposed sharply, and a large portion of Wales stayed free. In the parts they succeeded in conquering, they created towns, the most imperative of which was Cardiff. The English rulers also established numerous monasteries in Wales.

In the mid-thirteenth century, a man called Llewellyn figured out how to make himself the leader of a large portion of Wales. In 1255 Llewellyn moved toward becoming ruler of Gwynedd. According to the treaty Llewellyn was made Prince of Wales. However he agreed to become the English king's vassal.

In 1272 Edward I progressed toward becoming lord of England. He was resolved to lead all of Great Britain. Since Llewellyn was his vassal, Edward summoned him to do homage. Each time he was summoned Llewellyn made some excuse. In 1276 Edward proclaimed him an agitator and raised a military, which walked into Wales. The next year, Llewellyn was compelled to submit and surrender some of his kingdom to the English. Resentment grew among the Welsh for half a decade until in 1282, they revolted.

Llewellyn was executed battling the English in December 1282, but his sibling Dafyd carried on the fight. Dafyd was caught in June 1283, and he was killed in October 1283. The rebellion was crushed.

Edward became leader of Wales. English law was forced upon the Welsh. Edward constructed a system of castles and installed trusted men to control the general population. Around these castles, villas developed, and out of them, the king made new towns. Nevertheless, the Welsh rose in resistance again in 1294, only the be squashed again in 1295. Yet in 1301 to try and gain the loyalty of the Welsh Edward made his son, who was also called Edward, Prince of Wales.

At that point in 1400, Owain Glyn Dwr drove another resistance. Between 1401 and 1403 the radicals relentlessly progressed, capturing Welsh towns and crushing the English in the fight. In 1404 Owain, took the castles at Aberystwyth and Harlech. The tides began to turn against the Welsh in 1405 and 1406, however, as the English dedicated more resources to the fight and began to recapture lost ground. The English recovered Aberystwyth castle in 1408 and Harlech castle in 1409. Eventually, Owain and his devotees fled to the mountains, but records indicate they continued to battle until 1413. Only then did Owain Glyn Dwr disappear from history—no further mentions are made of him in any written record.

In the late fifteenth century, towns and trade in Wales flourished. Much of the countryside also grew more prosperous. At that point in 1485, Henry Tudor landed with a military at Milford Haven. He walked through Wales into England, after the battle of Bosworth he became king.

The Battle of Bosworth Field was the last significant battle of the Wars of the Roses, the civil war between the Houses of Lancaster and York that protracted across England in the latter half of the 15th century. Fought on 22 August 1485, the battle was won by the Lancastrians.

In The 16ᵗʰ Century And 17ᵗʰ Century of Wales

In 1536 a law divided all of Wales into counties. Wales was to send MPs to the English parliament. A law known as the Act of Union divided Wales into [however many] regions. The sixteenth century also conveyed religious changes to Wales. In 1517 Martin Luther, a German, began the Reformation. He demanded changes in Christian belief and practices.

The Reformation was a movement in Western Christianity in 16th-century Europe. Although the Reformation is usually considered to have started with the publication of the Ninety-five Theses by Martin Luther in 1517, there was no schism until the 1521 Edict of Worms.

In 1536 Henry broke down the smaller monasteries in Wales. The rest were broken down in 1539. In the meantime, Protestant ideas were spreading through Wales. Nonetheless, even though Henry made himself the leader of the congregation, he was not willing to allow numerous changes. In 1542 a Protestant called Thomas Capper was scorched to death in Cardiff.

In 1553 Henry's Daughter Mary moved toward becoming ruler. She endeavored to reestablish the old Catholic faith. During her reign, three Protestants were scorched to death in Wales. When Mary passed just five years later, her sister Elizabeth took the throne and changed the religious landscape once more. Elizabeth I represented Protestantism. In 1588 the Bible was converted into Welsh.

During the sixteenth century, Wales was gradually became more extravagant. A great many people made their living from cultivating, and cow grouping was vital. Exchange and industry kept on developing. Wales exported more and more wool and woolen cloth. Meanwhile coal mining flourished. The Welsh iron industry also grew.

In 1642 came civil war between king and parliament. Wales was firmly in the royalist camp (except for the town of Pembroke which supported parliament all the way through the war) and many Welsh soldiers fought in the king's army. However by 1644 the king was losing the war. In September the royalists were badly defeated at the battle of Montgomery. In 1645 the parliamentary army captured south Wales.

North Wales had been faithful to the lord, but in 1646, parliamentary forces marched on their territory. In 1648 Parliament decided to disband its army. Many fighters had not paid for quite a while, and they realized they would not be paid the money they were owed if they disbanded. The commander of troopers in Pembroke was called Poyer, and he revolted. Meanwhile the king did a deal with the Scots, who guaranteed to reestablish him to his royal position. Poyer put his support behind the ruler, but troopers faithful to parliament Marched to Wales and squashed the resistance.

Wales in the 18th Century

In the mid-eighteenth-century, Wales continued its streak of prosperity, and a number of splendid mansions were built. The SPCK (Society for Promoting Christian Knowledge) established numerous philanthropy schools in Wales. They were given a massive lift by a man named Griffith Jones (1683-1761). He made coursing schools and these were portable schools. Educators would set up a school in one spot for a period between a half year and three years before moving to another location.

Also in the eighteenth century, Wales experienced a religious recovery. In 1735 the Welsh Methodists were founded by Howel Harris (1714-1773) and Daniel Rowland (1713-1790). At first the Methodists remained members of the Church of England but they also held their own meetings. Eventually in 1811, Methodists split and established their own church and clergymen, primarily due to antagonism from ministers of the Church of England.

In the mid-eighteenth century, Wales was still largely a provincial society. Welsh towns were small, even by the standards of the time and vast share of individuals lived in the farmland and lived by cultivating the land. However, toward the end of the eighteenth century, that had begun to change due to the Industrial Revolution, which had people flocking to work in the towns.

Wales in the 19ᵗʰ Century

In the nineteenth-century, coal mining and iron working in Wales boomed. Other metal businesses in Wales, for example, copper, zinc and tin, plating thrived. There was also a vital woolen industry in Wales.

The number of inhabitants in Wales developed quickly notwithstanding displacement. In 1801 the number of inhabitants in Wales was under 600,000. By 1851 it was about 1.2 million. By 1911 it was more than 2 million. Town living became a happy prospect for many Welsh citizens, but by the mid-nineteenth century, they had become overcrowded and grimy. As a result, there were flare-ups of cholera in Wales in 1832, 1848, 1854 and 1866.

There was also turmoil in the Welsh field. There were revolts in the years 1842-1844 known as the Rebecca Riots. The object of their fury were tollgates. (Turnpike Trusts claimed numerous streets in Wales, and you needed to pay a toll to use them).

Later in the nineteenth-century things improved. Wages rose and hours of work were cut. Towns turned increasingly healthy when sewers were burrowed. Moreover during the 1840s railroads were installed crosswise over Wales, which made it a lot easier for guests to visit Wales. The travel industry turned into an essential Welsh industry.

Wales in the 20ᵗʰ Century

The 1920s and 1930s were years of hardship for Wales. There was mass unemployment at that time. Unemployment had already reached 23% of the Welsh workforce in 1927. In the 1930s it grew worse and in parts of Wales half the workforce was unemployed.

Full business came back with the Second World War, but joblessness stayed low through the 1950s and 1960s. Traditional Welsh industries such as coal, iron, and steel-working continued to decline, primarily due to number of collieries were shut.

Luckily new enterprises came to Wales. In 1976 the Welsh Development Agency was shaped to urge industry to move to Wales. The Welsh tourist industry also developed increasingly vital. Other administration businesses also developed insignificance. The number of inhabitants in Wales climbed slowly in the twentieth century significantly more slowly than it did during the nineteenth. Today the number of inhabitants in Wales is 3 million.

In 1999 the Welsh Assembly opened. In 2011 the general population of Wales cast a ballot that the Welsh Assembly ought to be allowed to pass laws without consent from Westminster.

Symbol. The image of Wales, proudly displayed on the flag, is a red dragon. Supposedly brought to the colony of Britain by the Romans, the dragon was a famous image in the ancient world and used by the Romans, the Saxons, and the Parthians. During the War of the Roses, Henry VII flew the red dragon as his fight flag over the fields during the Battle of Bosworth. After his victory and coronation, he proclaimed that it be adopted as the official flag of Wales.

The leek and the daffodil are also critical Welsh images. Some attribute the symbol origin to Saint David, who according to legend defeated the agnostic Saxons over a field of leeks. Almost certainly, leeks were embraced as a national image because of their significance to the Welsh diet, especially during Lent when meat was not allowed.

The Urge to Unity

The presence of Offa's Dyke maybe developed the mindfulness of the Welsh individuals. Inside the age of its development, most of the nation's occupants had turned into the subjects of a solitary ruler.

Rhodri, lord of Gwynedd, had by his passing in 877 added Powys and Seisyllwg (mostly the provinces of Cardigan and Carmarthen) to his kingdom. The union between the North and Seisyllwg ceased with Rhodri's death. It resuscitated by his grandson, Hywel (died 950), who also presided over Dyfed and Brycheiniog.

Dyfed, Seisyllwg, and Brycheiniog were from this point on known as Deheubarth. The process of unity came to a climax under Hywel's great-great-grandson, Gruffudd ap Llywelyn, who by 1057 had united the whole of Wales under his authority.

The Viking Challenge

Rhodri won the designation Mawr (meaning the Great) to a great extent because of his triumph over the Vikings in 856. The Vikings started assaulting the coasts of Britain and Ireland during the 780s. Their assaults on rich and unprotected monasteries helped to decrease the essentialness of the 'Celtic' Church.

In Wales, there is little proof of Viking settlements. However, some towns such as Anglesey, Swansea, and Fishguard were given Scandinavian names. For quite a long time to come, living under the Law of Hywel would be central to what it meant to be a Welsh individual.

The Law of Wales

Welsh law is the main and secondary legislation created by the National Assembly for Wales, using devolved authority granted in the Government of Wales Act 2006 and in effect since May 2007. Each piece of Welsh legislation is known as an Act of the Assembly. The first Assembly legislation to be anticipated was the NHS Redress (Wales) Measure 2008. This was the first time in almost 500 years that Wales has had its own laws, since Cyfraith Hywel, a version of Celtic law, was stopped and replaced by English law through the Laws in Wales Acts, enacted between 1535 and 1542 during the reign of King Henry VIII.

Relations with England

The Viking invasions smashed the state arrangement of the English. Wessex endured and, in the rule of King Alfred, a crusade started to bring the entire of England under the standard of the Wessex dynasty.

Rhodri Mawr died fighting against the English.

Gruffudd ap Llywelyn, on the other hand, was progressively forceful. As a significant aspect of his battle to unite Wales, he seized extensive territories, long lost by the Welsh, to the east of Offa's Dyke. Harold, Earl of Wessex, attacked Wales in 1063 and Gruffudd was chased down and executed. Three years later William, Duke of Normandy, seized the throne of England.

National Identity.

The different ethnic gatherings and clans that settled in ancient Wales gradually consolidated, politically and culturally, to safeguard their region from first, the Romans, and later the Anglo-Saxon and Norman trespassers. The sense of national identity was formed over centuries as the people of Wales struggled against being absorbed into neighboring cultures. The heritage of a common Celtic origin was a key factor in shaping Welsh identity and uniting the warring kingdoms. Cut off from other Celtic organizations toward the north in Britain and Ireland the Welsh clans joined against their non-Celtic adversaries.

The development and continued use of the Welsh language also played important roles in maintaining and strengthening the national identity. The convention of handing down verse and stories orally and the significance of music in everyday

life was critical to the way of life's survival. With the entry of book distributing and an increase in reading proficiency, the Welsh language and culture could keep on flourishing through the nineteenth century and into the twentieth century, in spite of emotional mechanical and social changes, in Great Britain.

Ethnic Relations. With the Act of Union, Wales increased peaceful relations with the English while retaining their racial personality. Until the late eighteenth century Wales was overwhelmingly rural with the vast majority of the populace living in or around small towns; contact with other ethnic groups was negligible. The Welsh nobility mixed socially and politically with the English and Scottish upper class, creating a very Anglicized top level. The business that grew up around coal mining and steel fabricating pulled in settlers, firstly from Ireland and England to Wales beginning in the late eighteenth century. Poor living and working conditions joined with the entry of vast quantities of immigrants caused social turmoil and often prompted clashes—regularly savage—among different ethnic gatherings. The decay of strong industry in the late nineteenth century caused an outward relocation of Welsh and the nation ceased to pull in foreigners. The modest restoration of industry and the increased standard of living that came with it at the end of the twentieth century brought foreigners back again, though without the violence. Many individuals came to stay, but others came for an excursion; Wales provided an end of the week retreat for people of nearby urban areas in England. Even today, this pattern causes tension in Welsh-speaking, rural areas among occupants who feel that their lifestyle is being undermined.

Urbanism, Architecture, and the Use of Space

The advancement of Welsh urban communities and towns did not start until industrialization in the late 1700s. Rustic areas are portrayed by a dispersement of disconnected ranches, typically comprised of the more seasoned, conventional whitewashed stone structures, usually with slate rooftops. Towns developed from the early settlements of the Celtic clans who picked specific areas for their farming. effective arrangements developed into the political and monetary focuses, first of the kingdoms, and later the individual districts in Wales. The Anglo-Norman manorial custom of structures grouped on a landowner's property, like rural towns in England, was acquainted with Wales after the conquest of 1282. The village as a center of rural society, however, became significant only in southern and eastern Wales; other rural areas maintained scattered and more isolated building patterns. Timber-framed houses, developed initially around an extraordinary hall, rose in the Middle Ages in the north and east, and later all through Wales. In the late sixteenth century, houses started to vary in size and refinement, mirroring the development of a working class and increasing differences in riches. In Glamorgan and Monmouth Shire, landowners constructed block houses that reflected the vernacular style popular in England at the time as well as their social status. This impersonation of English engineering set landowners apart from whatever remained of Welsh society. After the Norman conquest, urban advancement started around castles and military camps. The Bastide, or castle town, even though not expansive, is as yet significant to political and regulatory life. Industrialization in the eighteenth and nineteenth centuries caused an explosion of urban development in the southeast and Cardiff. Lodging deficiencies were average and a few families shared residences. Financial riches and a populace increase created a demand for new development in the late twentieth century. Slightly over 70 percent of homes in Wales are owner-occupied.

In time, however, Wales was in fact subdued and, by the Act of Union of 1536, formally joined to the kingdom of England. Welsh specialists, etymologists, artists, essayists, and fighters proceeded to make significant contributions to the improvement of the more prominent British Empire even as vast numbers of their comrades worked at home to safeguard social customs and even the Welsh language itself, which delighted in a recovery in the late twentieth century. In 1997 the British government, with the help of the Welsh electorate, gave Wales a measure of self-sufficiency through the making of the Welsh Assembly, which is essential leadership specialist for most nearby issues.

Even though Wales was shaken by the decrease of coal mining, before the end of the twentieth century, the nation had built up a diversified economy, especially in the urban communities of Cardiff and Swansea. More rural areas, as mentioned above, drew tourists and retirees from England, turning the travel industry into a financial staple. Guests—including numerous relatives of Welsh—were attracted to Wales' stately stops and castles as well as to social occasions featuring the nation's commended melodic and scholarly conventions. Despite the consistent change, Wales keeps on looking for both more noteworthy autonomy and a particular spot in a coordinated Europe.

Chapter 3: The Rise of national consciousness

Was Welsh nationality perceived in the mid-nineteenth century?

In 1850 there were not many Welsh national organizations. the Calvinistic Methodists had virtually no presence outside of Wales. Meanwhile, the established Church of England comprised of four westerly wards of the Archdiocese of Canterbury, with the Congregationalists and Baptists having virtually no focal association.

The Welsh court system - the Courts of Great Session - was abolished in 1830, making the legal and administrative structure of Wales identical to that of England.

Aside from the Cymmrodorion Society, restored in 1820, and the Cambrian Archeological Society, established in 1847, there were no social or instructive associations at a national dimension, nor did the nation have any financial or expert associations which conveyed its solidarity.

It was commonly accepted that the United Kingdom comprised of three kingdoms: England, Scotland, and Ireland. England was considered to contain the territory of Wales, and the Welsh were considered English. This was a conviction epitomized in the associated flag and the illustrious standard. Generally speaking, any assertions that the United Kingdom consisted of four countries was not well received or supported.

Over the next century, Welsh loyalists succeeded on this point: the idea of four countries gradually supplanted that of three kingdoms.

The Truth of Welsh Nationality in The Mid-Nineteenth Century

While acknowledgment was slight, the substance was specific. The essential marker of the nineteenth century Welsh was language. There existed no registration listing the quantity of Welsh speakers until 1891. However, no less than seventy-five percent of the nation's occupants spoke Welsh in 1850, and a substantial part of that is suspected to have known no other language.

The imperativeness of the Welsh language demonstrated by the number of periodicals distributed in it: in 1866 it was the average used by five quarterlies, 25 monthlies, and eight weeklies, with an entire course of 120,000. Famous books of verse, especially those of Ceiriog, could sell 30,000 copies.

There were also different measurements of Welshness. Welsh religious conventions had unmistakable attributes; provincial settlement designs and tenurial practices were different from those of England; radical developments had very notable highlights; Wales' mechanical networks, a large portion of them situated in the upland nation, were unlike some other. Explorers in Wales, George Borrow pre-famous among them, had presumed that they were in a country of an exceptionally singular character.

Chapter 4: The Transformations Its People Experienced and Survived Throughout the Centuries

A consequence of globalization, new technologies and other factors, the changes in Wales have had profound social and cultural consequences – some of which resemble changes in other areas where there has been a rapid decline of heavy industry, whilst others are distinct to Wales.

To outsiders, it is generally assumed that work in Wales is basically in the overwhelming industries of coal and steel, which has been a fair representation of Wales for quite a long time. Indeed, the workforce crested at 271,000 in 1920. But following the 1984-85 diggers' strike, fuel all but shut down; there are presently no deep pits in Wales, and fuel only utilizes a minor 0.2 percent of the workforce. Steel shut at Shotton in 1980 and Ebbw Vale in 2002, and the steelworks that remain are as profitable as in the past, but with a much-decreased workforce.

At the high-value end of the range are the assembly of the European Airbus wings at Broughton, and vehicle motors at Bridgend, but the broadness of assembling encompasses materials, electronics, car parts, and customer products. Quite a bit of this work includes assembly lines, which is low expertise as opposed to highly valued work. As with elsewhere in the UK, though, work in assembly is in decline, with development occurring in the administration part. Whilst much of this work, in health, call centres, administration and offices is white collar, it has many of the characteristics of blue collar work; and for many it is part-time and even casual.

In the countryside, too, there has been a massive decline in traditional agricultural employment. Milk quotas, BSE then foot and mouth all took their toll on a farming system that is characterized by relatively small units that neither achieve the necessary economies of scale nor benefit greatly from the EU's Common Agricultural Policy. With food makers crushed by the ground-breaking general stores, strategies today incorporate the consolation of diversification and stewardship of the wide open.

In attempting to reinforce the economy, the Welsh Government faces a tough task. In Wales, profitability is low in terms of the Gross Domestic Product (GDP), the estimation of the merchandise and ventures that created per a head. It is because the GDP is quite low – under 75 percent of the EU standard – that a lot of Wales qualifies for EDF Convergence financing.

Another issue is that a significant extent of the populace is economically dormant – higher than in other countries of the UK. Wages are low, and the hole with the UK average pay has not been improving in recent years.

Cardiff is a somewhat different story. Albeit different areas of Wales (counting Monmouth shire and the Vale of Glamorgan) are relatively affluent, there has been an enormous development of work in Cardiff – in government, the media and other associated businesses – especially since the landing of devolution in 1999. In Cardiff today, joblessness is 4.8 percent, contrasted and 14 percent in Merthyr Tydfil and a Welsh average of 9 percent. These figures mask massive amounts of unemployment among youthful individuals from the workforce.

These changes have significant social outcomes. Frequently today, two grown-ups in a family need to work, and the feminization of the workforce has affected traditional gender roles. The reduction in skilled jobs in heavy industries and manufacturing is connected with declining levels of trade union membership as well as lower wages. The convergence of work on the A55 and M4 corridors gives these areas altogether different attributes from west Wales or the South Wales Valleys. The decrease of rural business has had significant ramifications for the maintainability of provincial networks, which have been so vital for the Welsh language and the country lifestyle.

All of these changes in the organization of work and the structure of the economy can be identified in the everyday life of households, with transforming relations of gender and generation shaped in part by the world of work. They relate closely to the distribution of income and wealth and patterns of inequality. They shape the health of the nation, and are the main driver of policies on education. Studying the world of work—in Wales and elsewhere – can lead us to a better understanding of numerous key areas of social life.

Chapter 5: The Dramatic Conversions Wrought By The Industrial Revolution

The Welsh economy in the mid-eighteenth century

In 1750, Wales was still an overwhelmingly rural nation. Its populace of around 500,000 had an expanding modern base.

In the mid-eighteenth century, there were substantial increases in iron making in Pontypool and Bersham, lead, and silver mining in Flintshire and Cardiganshire, copper purifying in Neath and Swansea and coal mining in West Glamorgan and Flintshire.

By the by, they stayed negligible in correlation with the rural economy. That economy was also developing, with the adoption of crop rotation, the use of lime, the enclosure of waste land and the development of proto-industrial production, especially in the woollen industry.

By 1851, Wales was the world's second driving modern country, behind England.

The modern take-off

The take-off into self-supported development happened in the second half of the eighteenth century. However, advancement ought not to originated before. The provinces of Wales separated into hundreds; there were 88 in all and, as late as 1811, 79 of them had a more significant part of occupants still dependent upon the dirt for their employment.

By 1851, 66% of the groups of Wales were upheld by exercises other than farming, which implies that, after the English, the Welsh were the world's second mechanical country.

It was north-east Wales which built up the best scope of ventures. By the late eighteenth century, there were 19 metal works as well as a number of cotton factories at Holywell, and there were 14 potteries at Buckley. Of course, lead and coal mines still proliferated. Bersham, where the Wilkinson family were pioneers in the use of coke as opposed to charcoal in the purifying of iron, was one of Europe's driving ironworks.

By 1830 Monmouth Shire and East Glamorgan were delivering a large portion of the iron sent out by Britain.

In the long haul, the improvements in the southeast were progressively critical. The hearth of Merthyr Tydfil - Cyfarthfa and Dowlais specifically - offered to ascend to Wales' first modern town. By 1830 Monmouth Shire and East Glamorgan were delivering a large portion of the iron traded by Britain.

Monetary advancement was also significant in the Llanelli-Swansea-Neath territory, in Amlwch with its vast copper mine, in Snowdonia where slate quarrying overtook copper mining, and in parts of focal Wales where plant strategies were supplanting household creation in the woolen business.

The ascent of vote hyphenated system

The political representation of Wales before the Reform Act

The Act of Union allowed Wales 27 Members of Parliament, a number that stayed unaltered until the Reform Act of 1832.

In the county constituencies, the vote was vested in freeholders owning land worth £2 a year; in the boroughs it was the burgesses who were generally the voters. Both the county and borough systems were open to manipulation by landed families.

There were few genuine freeholders and most county voters were enfranchised through leases granted to them by their landlords. Almost all boroughs were controlled by estate owners and it is they who decided who became burgesses.

By the late eighteenth century, a tight gathering of somewhere in the range of 20 families controlled the parliamentary portrayal of Wales.

The framework in Wales was less immoral than it was in England. There were no completely rotten boroughs, fewer towns with no representation at all, and the inequality between the counties was not as blatant.

Nevertheless, with voting a public act, less than 5% of adult males enfranchised, bribery rampant and estate owners virtually the only moneyed class, landlord dominance of the electoral process was inevitable.

It was generally chosen not by the casting of votes, but by private courses of action which guaranteed the rise of a solitary unopposed candidate. In the general race of 1830, for instance, not one of the Welsh supporters was challenged.

Chapter 6: Fascinating Things About Wales

Though many have heard about Welsh mines and the immense cathedrals planted over its rolling green hills, there are lesser known points that are just as captivating things from Welsh history that haven't instructed in schools.

They each tell a story about Wales at a particular time (and those times range from the prehistoric to the 20th century).

The vast majority of information comes from eminent Welsh historian John Davies' epic work, A History of Wales.

The banks of the Taff once had fortifications to prepare for assaults by the Irish

The Irish were a threat to Roman Britain. Fortresses were built along the River Taff and heavily guarded in order to prevent their crimes. Settlements of Irish existed in Wales long after the Romans. Names, for example, Llyn and Dinllaen are of Irish birthplace, as was the kingdom of Dyfed, where there are 20 stones engraved with letters in ogham from Ireland.

Vikings sold the general population of Wales as slaves

The Vikings more than once assaulted Wales in the tenth century. They attacked villages and town all along the coast from their fortresses on the Isle of Man and in Dublin. It's most likely in this time Scandinavian names, later embraced in English, were given to places like Swansea, Bardsey, Anglesey, and Fishguard. They built up small exchanging stations in Cardiff.

A saint was burned at stake for heresy in Cardiff

Thomas Capper's life "ended" Cardiff in 1542 when he was burned alive. He was a Protestant and the chief religious saint in Wales since Roman Times, a casualty of Henry VIII's oppression of the individuals who precluded from Catholic mass.

These were at one time the 'four capitals' of Wales

According to John Davies, Carmarthen, Caernarfon, Denbigh, and Brecon were once the four capitals of the four corners of Wales. Carmarthen was the most populas town in Wales in the sixteenth century with around 2,000 individuals. The other three had about each 1,000. By 1700, Wrexham was the biggest town in Wales, but Carmarthen had restored its lead by 1770.

The first word of wales

Although Welsh may have been recorded in writing as early as 600 [AD?], the first surviving words are found on a stone in a congregation in Tywyn, and they date from around the year 700. Early Welsh was the mechanism of Taliesin and Aneirin, writers of the time. It is especially significant as Latin was the primary written language throughout Europe and there was virtually no composed French, Spanish or Italian until after 1000. The adoption of the word 'Cymru' may have been around the same time, with the word 'Kymry' used in a poem from 633. Around then, the word alluded to the Old North as well as to Wales.

There were no less than 5,000 Mormons in Wales around 1850

A Wales native named Daniel Jones migrated to America in 1840, where he converted to the Church of Latter-Day Saints.

When he returned to Wales in 1845, he set up a church in Merthyr and there converted over 5,000 individuals. The religious registration of 1851 records 28 Mormon assemblages in Wales. In 1849, 326 Welsh Mormons migrated to Salt Lake City, presently the world capital of Mormonism. in 1949 there were 25,000 Mormons of Welsh descent in America.

When 'the first Welshman' lived

Human teeth have been found in Wales dating to 225,000 years back. Even though these have been portrayed as having a home with 'the first Welshman,' their proprietor was unlikely to be a progenitor of the Welsh. Instead, he or she was likely apart of a Neanderthal..." There were a considerable number of years since during which Wales was utterly uninhabited, including an ice age. Ridges was free of ice by 8,300BC. When that occurred, Wales "become" a piece of an island and an ocean, not a strait, isolated from Ireland.

Every bank in Pembroke shire flopped in 1825

In 1825, a financial emergency was declared due to [reason]. This lead to the shutdown of many—if not most—Welsh banks that had been established in market towns before 1770. These incorporate all the banks in Pembroke shire. numerous ranchers "lost" their investment funds. The circumstances at the time inspired revolts in the field, including at Carmarthen, Abermule, and Maenclochog.

There were harsh dissents against the Irish crosswise over Wales

In 1851, around 20,000 individuals in Wales had been born in Ireland. They were in anxious conditions and therefore arranged to work for wages lower than the Welsh. Thus there were "severe challenges" against them. These occurred in Swansea in 1828, in the Rhymney Valley in 1825 and sporadically elsewhere. Irish lived in ghettos, and John Davies wrote that "the conviction emerged that uncleanliness and boisterousness were a natural piece of their character."

A home in England is to thank for The national song of devotion

When Wlad Fy Nhadau was written in 1856 by Evan and James of Pontypridd, but it only because of the National Eisteddfod in Chester in 1866 that it turned into the national song of praise. It was sung with such passion that it promptly was embraced as an athem. A guest to that expressed: "When I see the enthusiasm which these Eisteddfods stir in your entire individuals I am loaded up with profound respect."

In Blackwood in 1842, there was one bar for Every five individuals

After the Beer Act of 1830, there was a tremendous increase in the quantity of spots individuals could go for a drink. there were 200 bars around the Dowlais Ironworks alone. alone. It was not long for laws to be passed to curb the excessive drinking. The first teetotal society in Wales established in

Llanfechell, Anglesey in 1835. A survey in Mountain Ash professed to have set up that 90% of individuals supported shutting bars on Sundays.

In 1603 there were around 18 schools in Wales

Grammar schools for the less wealthy were established in Welsh market towns (though you could find Welsh pupils at Eton and Westminster). They were established to teach the basics of Latin. Welsh was not tolerated in the schools - it was deemed irrelevant to ambitions in the gentry and a career.

The termination of the Welsh language predicted in 1682

William Richards prophesized the inevitable demise of the Welsh language. Bardic schools were failing, parents no longer gave their children Welsh names and many customs were being looked at as meaningless. In the meantime, Thomas Jones went further, anticipating that Welsh individuals would be "expunged from history." The Anglicization of the Welsh upper class was among the underlying drivers. However, this proved to be incorrect thanks to Griffith Jones, a [profession] who set up schools all across Wales in order to ensure the continuation of the Welsh language. In the next 100 years, Welsh could spread quickly. The eighteenth century, Wales was one of only a handful couple of nations with a predominantly educated populace.

Individuals in Haverfordwest were the last individuals to experience the ill effects of the plague

Even though outbreaks of the plague had been substantially reduced in the 16th century, Wales continued to have sporadic outbreaks, like the rest of the UK. There was an occurrence recorded in 1652, but the last was around 1700. Although better treatment was available by that point, the death rate during this particular outbreak was substantial—multiple times more than usual—primarily because of a starving population.

The Law of Wales was relatively revolutionary

It dates to the tenth century, but the Law of Wales took ladies and children into the record in manners that were not found in English law up to this point. The original copy is in Latin, but there are a few duplicates, including those written in Welsh. One example of its fairness is its recognition that the union of a man and woman was a contract and that it could come to an end. Accordingly, it itemized how property and duty regarding children ought to shared if that occurred. It was later condemned as the work of the devil by Canon Law.

Sex outside marriage was a noteworthy issue before the courts

Between 1633 and 1637, a third of the punishments meted out by the Council of Wales related to these offences, which were considered as serious as violence and subversion. Around 10% of childrens brought into the world with only one parent present.

Better food was served in jails than in workhouses for poor people

The years 1834-45 were "among the most agitated ever," wrote John Davies. There was widespread distress and extraordinary destitution and so every one of Wales' 48 "associations" (areas assembled into associations) were obliged to manufacture a workhouse A Poor Law said no one could be helped at home - so they had to move to a workhouse to get help. Married couples were not allowed to go there together - so families were part up. Workhouses were horrendous, and it guaranteed in Carmarthenshire that "individuals wanted to kick the bucket rather than enter it."

The word 'Sais' was first given to a Welshman who learned how to communicate in English

'Sais' is used today in Welsh to portray somebody English, here and there in a deprecatory manner. In any case, it was first used in the fifteenth century to depict a Welshman who knew how to communicate in English. Welsh individuals had little reason to know the language in medieval times, and the use of the word recommends the information was uncommon and viewed with scorn.

A house of prayer was assembled every eight days

Between 1801 and 1851, it is estimated that a chapel was completed every eight days. There were enough chapels in the 19th century to seat half the country's population. A leading Christian historian has claimed religion "had been more successful in retaining the informed allegiance of the mass of the population in Wales than in any other country in Europe".

The Romans thought that it was difficult to curb the general population of Wales

There were at least 13 campaigns between AD48 and 79 and the Romans weren't used to the guerrilla fighters of the Welsh mountains. But they did manage to form a network of forts, with corners at Carmarthen, Caernarfon, Caerleon and Chester.

In 1966 you could head out from Holyhead to Chepstow without leaving a Labor supporters

The Labour party dominated Welsh politics in the 1960s. In 1966, it won 32 of the 36 constituencies, taking Monmouth from the Conservatives and Cardiganshire from the Liberals, who had held it since 1880. You could travel from Holyhead to Chepstow without leaving a Labour constituency, using the ferry from Ynyslas to Aberdyfi.

Jewish shops assaulted in Tredegar in 1911

In 1911, a riot broke out in Tredegar primarily due to anti-Jewish sentiments. Jewish businesses and properties were attacked and damaged, but there were no casualties also spread to places including Bargoed and Brynmawr. It was in the same time as against Semitism in Russia, but there are questions as to whether the attacks in Wales specifically coordinated at Jews. This incident occurred at the same time that antisemitism was on the rise in Russia, but it is questioned whether the attacks in Wales were specifically coordinated against the Jewish.

In 1932, nearly half of Welsh men was jobless

The sorrow that started during the 1920s was "the focal occurrence in the historical backdrop of twentieth-century Wales," Wrote John Davies. Individuals left the nation in huge numbers, and there were fewer individuals remaining in 1931 than in 1921. In 1932, 42.8% of men were out of work.

Although the depression affected every developed country "the experience of Wales was exceptional in severity and length". In many nations, it was over by the mid-1930s, but in 1939 there were still 100,000 men out of a job in Wales. In 1926, Coal diggers of South Wales lost a joined £15 million in wages - that is more than £1 billion in today's money.

Chapter 7: Welsh Economy

There is a long-standing joke in Wales that the economy is something of a dinosaur in comparison to whatever remains of the UK's.But even though customary industries like coal mining have decline in Wales, the economy was not disparaged, largely thanks to the success of the tourism industry.

In the 21st Century, where – owing to the recent recession – more and more people are curious about how the UK economy functions, we should investigate a couple of things you might now know about the Welsh economy.

Startup Comes to Wales

A successful Welsh businessman named Tim Morgan pioneered a startup called DeskBeers. The company's objective is to bring specialty lagers to workplaces on Friday afternoons, with the goal being to improve staffers' weeks. Until now, DeskBeers has primarily operated in London, but is currently in development in Wales. It is projected to have a high demand as soon as it begins. More ideas like Tim's, please!

Tourism Is Booming in Wales

If the travel industry in Wales has ever needed a lift, it got a noteworthy one in 2014, when £150 million was siphoned into the Welsh economy to promote popular travel destinations.

This resulted in over 1,000,000 more travelers visiting the nation in 2014 than in 2013, with the travel industry presently immovably observed as a substantial zone of the venture.

One of the First Laser Projection will call Wales home

Truth is stranger than fiction - Premiere Cinemas will assume control over Cardiff's rundown Odeon Film, breathing new life into the city with a groundbreaking film that will be one of the first in the UK to embrace laser projection.

A minimum of 4 screens will be laser, whilst at least one will be 4K quality, emulating Premiere's successful business model throughout the UK.

House Prices Are Low in Wales

Mirroring a UK pattern, of house costs in Wales have been falling gradually for over a year.

This means that more and more mid-market sectors are now being challenged to lower their prices too.

Disinflation in Wales

The prices of goods and services in Wales has fallen to an all-time low, with the Consumer Price Index coming in at 0.5%.

The Euro-zone doesn't want mass-scale flattening, but commentators have acknowledged that the deflation in Wales is much welcomed. Fuel costs have fallen as well, freeing up cash for Welsh citizens to spend on different types of merchandise and luxury goods. Hurrah!

Welsh Economy of North Wales

The success of the North Wales economy is critical to the achievement of Wales, with Welsh Secretary Stephen Crabb watching: "When the North Wales economy is progressing admirably, Wales is progressing admirably."

The point is for an assortment of dynamic and inventive firms in North Wales to be allowed to flourish, with internal speculation depicted as of late as being "extremely useful for Wales."

Lloyds Bank Has the Gay Vote

Stonewall, a group of campaigners and lobbyists for equality and justice for gays, lesbians and bisexuals, placed Lloyds Bank, which has a massive workforce presence in Wales, in the top 10 of their 'best places to work if you are gay' list.

It shows that the correct sort of groundbreaking balance culture is being sharpened at the financial mammoth, prompting efficiency and collaboration. And it's nice to see this is perceived.

Chapter 8: The History of Welsh Devolution

Early Days

The foundations of political devolution in Wales can be traced to the end of the nineteenth century. In 1886, Cymru Fydd ('Young Wales') was set up to advance the destinations of the Liberal Party in Wales and to crusade for Welsh 'home rule.' Even though Cymru Fudd's prosperity was fleeting, its exercises corresponded with other political improvements, including the passing of specifically Welsh Acts without precedent for the UK Parliament. It also compared with the start of administrative devolution in Wales through the Creation of the Welsh Board for Education in 1907.

Post-War Wales

After the Second World War, a Series of improvements began from Westminster to Wales.

Petitions to make a Secretary of State for Wales were turned down by the Labor Government of 1945-50. As a concession, it established a Council for Wales and Monmouth shire in 1948. It was a selected body that advised the legislature on Welsh undertakings.

In 1951, another minor government post of Minister of State for Welsh Affairs was created by the conservative UK government. Initially it was held by a minor clergyman in the Home Office, but from 1957 on, it was a post held mutually with the Ministry of Housing and Local Government.

The Labor Party finally to make a Secretary of State for Wales in its 1959 race manifesto, but it needed to hold up until its triumph in the 1964 UK general decision to formally do the job. At first, the Secretary of State just had duty regarding lodging, neighborhood governments, and streets. Over the years, other areas of responsibility were added, such as health, trade and domestic industry, nature and farming gradually included throughout the years.

Devolution Referendum: 1979

The primary vote on devolution in Wales took place on 1 March 1979. It pursued a Royal Commission on the Constitution in 1973. It detailed the selection of bodies for both Scotland and Wales. The proposition for the output of a Welsh Assembly in 1979 was dismissed by the Welsh Open, who cast a ballot four to one against the UK Labor Government's recommendations.

In the aftermath of the 1979 decision, devolution turned into somewhat of a lethargic political issue in Wales. Be that as it may, the arrangements of the UK Conservative Government during the difficult monetary states of the 1980s, combined with the Conservative Party's moderately low dimensions of constituent help in Wales (in contrast with the UK), prompted restored calls for Wales to have its very own majority rule establishment.

Devolution Referendum: 1997

In May 1997, when Labor suddenly returned to power, its manifesto incorporated a promise to hold a vote on the creation of a Welsh Meeting. A White Paper, A Speech for Wales, was distributed in July 1997. It delineated the UK Government's recommendations and, on September 18, a vote was held.

As the results were announced, constituency by constituency, Wales had to wait for the very last declaration before knowing the final result. Of the individuals who cast a ballot, 50.3 per cent supported devolution – a narrow majority in favor of 6,721 votes.

Welsh devolution – "a procedure not an occasion."

Following the decision, the UK Parliament passed the Government of Wales Act 1998. The Act built up the National Assembly as a corporate body – with the official (the administration) and the lawmaking body (the Assembly itself) working as one.

The first decisions in the Assembly were held on 6 May 1999.

In contrast to the essential law-making powers given to the Scottish Parliament, the Act restricted the National Assembly to the making of auxiliary enactment in specified areas, including horticulture, fisheries, instruction, lodging, and thruways. Such powers were extensively identical to those recently held by the Secretary of State for Wales.

The primary decade, and a changing structure

While there were numerous positives about the Assembly regarding community and a progressively comprehensive and consensual style of political issues, the single corporate body structure proved to be problematic. The difficulties experienced by the minority Labor organization in verifying predictable understanding from different gatherings in the Assembly. The substitution of the First Secretary in February 2000, featured the need for established change and strength.

Because of increased calls for change, the Assembly concurred goals in 2002 to isolate the two jobs as much as conceivable inside the structure of the 1998 Act. It accomplished by presenting the term Welsh Assembly Government to depict the arrangements. Activities of the Cabinet as unmistakable from crafted by the National Assembly, which had more prominent freedom to give counsel, research and backing to singular Members and advisory groups of the Meeting.

The Welsh Government's choices and activities held within proper limits by the National Assembly (an assortment of 60 members which holds its ministers to account. The National Assembly makes laws and speaks to the interests of the general population of Wales.

2011 Referendum Onwards

Following a submission in 2011, the Assembly increased essential lawmaking powers in connection to specific subjects without inclusion from Westminster or Whitehall. The UK Government set up the Silk Commission to consider the eventual fate of the devolution settlement in Wales.

In 2012, the Silk Commission distributed Part I of its report, making suggestions on the money-related forces of the Assembly.

Silk Commission published Part II of its report in 2014, making recommendations on the Assembly's future legislative powers and arrangements.

The UK Government distributed Powers for a Purpose in 2015, providing the basis for the development of a reserved powers model of devolution for Wales.

The assembly passed the Tax Collection and Management (Wales) Act 2016, in anticipation of practicing the tax assessment and getting powers declined by the Wales Act 2014. It saw the beginning of Assembly's job in directing the UK's exchanges for leaving the EU, investigating enactment, and characterizing Wales' place in the post-Brexit UK.

2018 saw the beginning of held forces model of devolution under the Wales Act 2017. The first Welsh taxes came on stream.

In 2019, income tax-varying powers will come on stream, as provided by the Wales Act 2014.

Welsh devolution – the long view

c. 940 Welsh laws united as one code under Hywel Dda (Hywel the Good)

1282 The Edwardian victory of Wales and the end of government by local Welsh sovereigns

1400 Owain Glyndwr's revolt begins and for a brief time builds an early Welsh state. Parliaments are held at Harlech and Machynlleth

1536 The Acts of Union, making Wales a part of England but providing for parliamentary seats for MPs from Wales.

1881 The Sunday Closing Act of 1881 was passed. This was the first law passed by the UK Parliament that pertained to Wales only.

1907 Welsh branch of the Board of Education Was created

1920 The Church of Wales turns into a free body, distinct from the state

1951 Pole of Minister of State for Wales made

1964 Welsh Office set up alongside a bureau post of Secretary of State for Wales

1979 First proposition for a Welsh Assembly turned down in a submission

1997 Wales cast a ballot for making a National Assembly for Wales in a vote.

1999 First races held. The National Assembly begins work. Government of Wales Act 1998 comes into power

2007 Government of Wales Act 2006 comes into effect; the National Assembly and Welsh Government are formally isolated, and the National Assembly picks up forces to make laws for Wales in certain areas

2011 Wales votes in favor of giving the National Assembly further law-making powers

2014 The Wales Act 2014 is passed, the National Assembly advanced law-making controls

2017 The Wales Act 2017 is passed, perceiving the permanence of the National Assembly for Wales and Welsh Government and shifting the model of devolution to an Earmarked Powers Model.

Chapter 9: Timeline of Wales

70 The Romans invade AD Wales

383   The idea of the Welsh country develops when the Picts and Celts attack the land

440   Britain, abandoned by the Romans, passes to the possession" or something of the sort.

784   The King of Mercia fabricates Offa's Dyke as a limit between England and Wales

844   844-877 the reign of Rhodri Mawr (Rhodri the Great) begins and lasts until 877. During it, he unites all of Wales.

890   Welsh lords recognize Alfred of Wessex (Alfred the Great) as their ruler

1066   1066-77 Following the annihilation of the English King Harold at the Battle of Hastings, the Normans assume responsibility for Wales

1120   1120-1129 "Historia Regum Britanniae" was composed by Geoffrey of Monmouth and details the Arthurian Legend of King Arthur. This provided the Welsh with a claim to the sovereignty of the whole island of Britain of which the Tudors took advantage

1137   The Reign of Owain Gwynedd (1137-1170) begins

1169   According to Welsh legend, Prince Madog of Gwynedd, landed in Alabama and went up to Missouri

1204   Prince Llywelyn Ap Iorwerth (1173-1240) wedded Joan, the daughter of King John of England

1240   Dafydd ap Llywelyn (c. 1208 February 25, 1246) was Prince of Gwynedd from 1240 to 1246 who had two children of Gruffydd, Llywelyn ap Gruffydd and Owain ap Gruffydd.

1277   King Edward branded Llywelyn ap Gruffydd "a rebel and disturber of the peace" and declared his lands forfeit

1278   Edward I had propelled a massive invasion of Wales, re-vanquishing South Wales and overcoming Llywelyn ap Gruffydd and North Wales. Llywelyn ap Gruffydd was compelled to agree to settle for peace of Aberconwy. Edward appointed the construction of four noteworthy castles in Wales - Flint, Rhuddlan, Builth, and Aberystwyth

1282   Llywelyn ap Gruffyd Began second Welsh rebellion with his sibling David. Llywelyn ap Gruffydd was slaughtered in a fight and his sibling David was caught and executed.

1284   Wales wound up consolidated into The Kingdom of England under the Statute of Rhuddlan

1485   The Battle of Bosworth ended the English Wars of the Roses when Henry Tudor crumpled Richard III. Henry Tudor asserted Welsh descent through Owain Tudor of Penmynedd in Anglesey. He had married Catherine, widow of King Henry V. Their child, Edmund Tudor fathered Henry Tudor, who King Henry VII of England and satisfied the old prophesy that one day a Welsh Monarch would control the entire of Britain.

Timeline

The History Timeline of Places, including the Timeline of Wales, gives fast realities and information about this favorite spot with its history. The most important occasions of the nation nitty gritty together with related chronicled occurrences which organized in sequential, or date, request giving a whole succession of times in the Timeline of Wales. The Timeline of Wales provides fast information via this time line which highlights the key dates and events of the famous place in a fast information format with concise and accurate facts and information in the order of their occurrence. The Timeline of Wales incorporates a sequence of this vital spot and its history. Specific data can be seen initially with brief and precise subtleties using the Timeline of Wales. This History course of events of a favorite spot is reasonable kids and incorporate numerous critical occasions of significant event and result which are point by point in the Timeline of Wales.

Timeline of Wales

- Fast and accurate time line details via history timelines and chronologies
- Chronology of Key Names, Key Dates, Key People and Key Events in the Timeline of Wales
- Useful time line database of history and this Timeline of Wales containing interesting chronology of facts & information
- Famous people, famous places and countries and famous events via comprehensive
- Interesting Information via the Timeline of Wales - Time line History and Chronology at a glance, for children and kids
- Chronologies of key dates, facts and info

Chapter 10: Wales History Map: Wales: First Industrial Nation

Wales has a fascinating background more than just in terms of its industrial legacy—it has numerous spots of treasure, which is perhaps why it has become such a popular destination for tourists. However, it is not simply its past that makes it significant; a modern site has garnered such significance that it has been deemed worthy of a World Heritage Marker.the core of the south Wales valleys offers various attractions including the chance to experience life as an excavator at Big Pit National Coal Museum, and as a laborer at the Blaenavon Ironworks. west is home base to the National Wool Museum, situated in the memorable Cambrian Mills, and the core of the Snowdonia mountains in north Wales is the National Slate Museum.

National Slate Museum

The National Slate Museum recounts the narrative of life in Wales' slate networks when the Welsh slate industry 'roofed the world.'

As well as chances to see the shops, fashions, sheds and the most prominent working waterwheel in the UK, talented experts also give live shows of the craft of part and dressing account.

The National Slate Museum is twinned with the Slate Valley Museum in Granville, NY, USA, strengthening the connections between Welsh people group on the two sides of the Atlantic.

National Wool Museum

What? A museum situated inside Cambrian Mills.

Where? Carmarthenshire.

Located in the core of west Wales, the National Wool Museum recounts the tale of the once flourishing-cool industry in Teifi Valley.

This pearl of a museum is housed in a unique plant building, where new apparatus and live weaving showcases can be seen which demonstrate the procedure of 'fleece to fabric.'

Did you know? The fleece business overwhelmed the Teifi zone in the late nineteenth and mid-twentieth.

Big Pit National Coal Museum

What? Industrial heritage museum.
Where? Blaenavon.

At the core of the UNESCO World Heritage landscape of Blaenavon lies Big Pit, a former working coal mine. This award-winning museum offers an experience unparalleled in the nation, and it is one of just two locales in the UK where guests can go underground in a single coal mine.

Guided by ex-diggers, guests plummet to the depths of the mine and experience what life was like for the individuals who made their living at the coal face.

There are further offices to instruct and engage all ages, including a multi-media virtual visit in the Mining Galleries and displays in the unique colliery structures.

Did you know? The open mines at Big Pit lie more than 90 meters underneath the ground.

Blaenavon Ironworks

Just under an hour's drive from Cardiff in the renowned south Wales Valleys stands Blaenavon Ironworks. The ironworks were an achievement of the Industrial Revolution.

The intensity of steam was saddled, and a method for making steel utilizing iron mineral was created, which prompted an overall blast in the steel business, taking Wales' modern way to another stature. Visitors can see the renovated Stack Square cabins, to experience how the workers, survived the ages and the reproduced organization truck shop. New, cutting-edge audio-post technology breathes life into the tale of the Ironworks.

The landscape of Blaenavon has elevated World Heritage status because of its mounting structure and capacity. From mines to prepare lines, you can now follow the courses in and out, from crude material to completed item.

Did you know? Originally built in 1790, people lived in Blaenavon Ironworks's Engine Row cottages until the 1960s.

Pontcysyllte Aqueduct

What? Nineteenth-century water channel.
Where? To Close Llangollen.

The Pontcysyllte Aqueduct directs the Llangollen Canal over the valley of the River Dee in Wrexham County Borough.

Created by Thomas Telford in 1805, it's no exaggeration to state that the systems and ideas created at Pontcysyllte helped shape the world through their impact on engineering. Taking over 10 years to build and costing £38,499 — the equivalent of £38 million today — the Pontcysyllte Aqueduct was truly one of the engineering marvels of the Industrial age. UNESCO made this masterpiece a World Heritage Site in 2009 – alongside 11 miles of waterway including Chirk Aqueduct and the Horseshoe Falls at Llantysilio, to close Llangollen.

Did you know? When Thomas Telford completed the Pontcysyllte Aqueduct in 1805, it was the tallest trench vessel crossing on the planet.

Chapter 11: Welsh Culture: Facts and Traditions

In this section, we will explore Welsh culture Investigate the way of life of land of imaginary dragons, a particular language, passionate games fans, and exciting food. In this exercise, find out about certain aspects of the Welsh culture and also look at certain customs and celebrations.

There is more to Wales than the sports and interesting cuisine. The culture of the Welsh is filled to the brim with mythological dragons and a very elvish language. Many of the cultural practices in Wales is taken from England and adopted to the Welsh lifestyle and beliefs. The little country has managed to keep its culture and traditions intact despite the large influence that its English neighbors have on it.

The nation is said to have had people possessing it for the past 30,000 years. The country was at one time a piece of the Roman Empire, and therefore, there are hints of Celtic roots still mixed in the way of life. If there is a single word to portray Wales, it's Green. Everything from backwoods, mountains, and farmlands are scattered in abundance across the entire country with quaint places for inhabitation by humans.

The Welsh culture is loaded with customs and legends. Indeed, even a dragon is the national image! This nation has embraced numerous social aspects from neighboring England, but despite everything, it keeps its national character and various unique customs.

Wales is a small country situated in the western piece of Great Britain. People are accepted to have lived around there for something like 29,000 years. The Welsh culture has Celtic roots, and the land was once part of the Roman Empire. In the Middle Ages, it governed by Norman knights and was defeated by England in 1282. When the United Kingdom was built up in 1707, Wales turned out to be a piece of it.

There are vast farmlands, mountains, and woods areas, many ensured as national parks. The populace is more than 3 million, and Cardiff is the capital city and the most significant urban region.

Welsh Culture

The Welsh culture has been influenced by England for centuries, so both share some joint aspects. However, there has always been an interest in preserving cultural elements that make the Welsh unique and significantly different from other cultures in the United Kingdom.

Language

The two official dialects are English and Welsh. There have been endeavors to save the plain Welsh language, and it is now instructed in schools as well as incorporated into printed media and television. Nonetheless, the use of Welsh has gradually decreased and now just around one-fifth of the populace can speak it.

National Symbols

Since medieval occasions, the dragon has been a critical image of Wales. This legendary animal is referenced in several legends and is part of the national flag, which features a red dragon in the middle.

Welsh Flags

Daffodils and leeks are also public images. It trusted that the leek was initially the main image and the daffodil was gradually received afterward. It was most likely because of perplexity between the two words. In Welsh, the leek is cenhinen, and daffodil is cenhinen Bedr (which deciphers as Peter's leek).

Family and Religion

Most of the populace identifies as Christian. The most significant sects in Wales are the Methodists, Presbyterians, Anglicans, and Catholics.

more distant families frequently meet once every week, usually on Sundays after going to chapel. It generally trusted that numerous neighborhood families are connected, so discussions among outsiders regularly incorporate asking about relatives in like manner.

Welsh Festivals and Traditions

Welsh customs are an intriguing blend of old folklore, legends, and religious customs. A portion of the traditional celebrations and festivities are:

- St. David's Day: Considered Wales' National Day, it is celebrated on 1 March to honor the passing of Saint David, the national benefactor holy person. Daffodils and leeks are displayed in numerous spots. Individuals frequently wear common clothing types, wave national flags, and eat typical dishes. A parade is a piece of the festival in countless urban towns.

Family Values and Cultural Communities

The whole nation has a remarkable language which is a long way from the English language that we used. There is a ton of consideration taken to safeguard the first language of the Welsh for its significance and chronicled esteem. The word itself sounds elvish, and you can see it used in numerous mysterious films as well. The quantity of individuals who speak Welsh lacks nowadays. Monsters, daffodils, and leeks are public images based on the legendary legends that structure the core of their custom.

The vast majority in Wales are Christians of different sections. Meeting with more distant families is a critical piece of the way of life and is frequently a custom. After chapel, families get together for dinner and hang out. Kids accordingly grow up to be a piece of the more distant family regardless of whether they live with only their folks. The towns are small, and a great many people know one another. When a more bizarre meets another Welsh individual, they regularly go into nitty-gritty discussion about identifying the family that they originate from, which viewed as weird in numerous traditions.

Food, Sport, and Attire

Since a great deal of Wales engaged with cultivating, their cooking is frequently, meat-based but has a ton of vegetables as well. Wales has a significant portion of long, craggy coastlines, which provides them with seafood. Their stews and soups are fantastic. The liquor delivered locally and mainly comprises of Whiskey and Beer.

The customary clothing of the Boast. The ladies occasionally wear long red and white checkered dresses covered with a frilled white apron. A tall, dark cap compliments the clothing. Some parts of Wales still have ladies who dress in conventional clothing, but the vast majority of Wales has begun wearing typical Western apparel.

If you are a sports fan, it is likely you may know about the Welsh rugby group. Passionate players play the game, and local people are equally enthusiastic about supporting them. Rugby frames an essential piece of the national character of Wales, and the Welsh invest wholeheartedly in their capacity to ace this game. Other games that are prevalent are cricket and soccer.

Food and Drink

The menu depends for the most part on locally accessible items, including beef, mutton, and vegetables such as leeks, cabbages, and potatoes. Fish and seafood are also standard items. The cawl is viewed as the national dish and is a juice of meat (Beef or mutton) and vegetables. The Welsh rarebit is another claim to fame comprising of Toasted brezd finished with a mixture of liquefied cheddar, milk, eggs, and Worcestershire sauce. Brew and bourbon are crafted locally, though on a smaller scale than in England or Scotland.

Dress

Regularly, Western garments are worn. In celebrations, notwithstanding, ladies once in a while wear the customary national clothing, which wound up prominent during the nineteenth century. It comprises of a long skirt (usually red), a checkered cover, and a tall, dark cap. In rural areas, this clothing keeps on being seen among certain ladies.

Sports

Rugby is likely the most mainstream sport, having numerous passionate fans. Multiple individuals see it as a matter of national personality and pride, and the matches against England are frequently a significant occasion. Cricket and soccer are other famous games.

Political Life

Government.

The First Minister operates from Whitehall in London, the name of the authoritative and political seat of the British government. Increasing pressure from Welsh pioneers for more self-sufficiency acquired devolution of organization May 1999, implying that progressively political power was given to the Welsh Office in Cardiff. The situation of the secretary of state for Wales, a piece of the British head administrator's bureau, was made in 1964. In a 1979 submission a proposition for the making of a non-legislating Welsh Assembly was rejected but in 1997 another choice passed by a thin margin, prompting the 1998 production of the National Assembly for Wales. The Assembly has sixty individuals and is in charge of setting arrangement and making enactment in areas in regards to training, health, farming, transportation, and social administrations. A general revamping of government all through the United Kingdom in 1974 incorporated a simplification of Welsh organization with smaller regions regrouped to frame more prominent voting public for monetary and political reasons. Grains were rearranged into eight new areas, from thirteen originally, and inside the provinces, thirty-seven new areas made.

Leadership and Political Officials.

Wales has dependably had a solid left wing and radical ideological groups and pioneers. There is also stable political mindfulness all through Wales, and voter turnout at decisions is higher than in the United Kingdom. In a large portion of the nineteenth and mid-twentieth centuries, the Liberal Party ruled Welsh legislative issues with the new areas secondary to the Socialists. In 1925 the Welsh Nationalist Party, recognized as Plaid Cymru, was popular with the goal of earning freedom for Wales as an area inside the European Economic Community. Between World Wars I and II extreme monetary depression caused just about 430,000 Welsh to move and another political activism brought into the world with an emphasis on social and financial change. After World War II the Labor Party picked up a more significant part of help. Plaid Cymru and the Conservative Gathering won places in political decisions, debilitating the Labor Party's customary

predominance of Welsh legal issues. During the 1970s and 1980s, Conservatives gained significantly more control, a pattern that was turned around during the 1990s with the arrival of Labor strength and the increased help for Plaid Cymru and Welsh patriotism. The Welsh rebel, patriot development also incorporates progressively radical gatherings who look for the making of a politically free country by social and phonetic changes. The Welsh Language Culture is one of the more unmistakable of these gatherings and has expressed its ability to use common insubordination to encourage its objectives.

Military Activity.

Wales does not have an autonomous military, and its protection falls to the army of the United Kingdom in general. However, there are three armed regiments that have strong ties to Wales: the Welsh Guards, the Royal Regiment of Wales, and the Royal Welch Fusiliers, that have strong associations with the nation.

Social Welfare and Change Programs

Health and social administrations fall under the organization and obligation of the secretary of state for Wales. The Welsh Office, which works with province and locale specialists, designs and executes matters identifying with housing, health, training, and welfare.

Horrible working and living conditions in the nineteenth century brought significant changes and new strategies concerning social welfare that continued being enhanced all through the twentieth century. Issues in regards to health care, lodging, training, and working conditions, joined with an abnormal state of political activism, have made a consciousness of and demand for social change programs in Wales.

Chapter 12: Gender Roles and Statuses

The Relative Status of Women and Men

Historically, Women had few rights, albeit many worked outside the home, and were required to satisfy the job of wife, mother, sometimes to the children of distant relatives. In agricultural areas women worked alongside male family members. When the Welsh economy started to industrialize, numerous women looked for employment in manufacturing plants that procured a solely female workforce for occupations not requiring physical effort. Women and childrens worked in mines, putting in fourteen-hour days under dangerous conditions. The enactment was passed in the mid-nineteenth century constraining the working hours for women and kids, but it was not until the start of the twentieth century that Welsh women started to demand Progressive social liberties. The Women's Institute, which currently has branches all through the United Kingdom, was established in Wales, albeit all of its exercises directed in English. During the 1960s another association, like the Women's Institute but solely Welsh in its objectives, was established. Known as the Merced y Wawr, or Women of the Dawn, it is committed to advancing the privileges of Welshwomen, the Welsh language and culture, and sorting out magnanimous undertakings.

Socialization

Tyke Rearing and Education. Children were abused in the name of work by being sent into mines in tubes that were too small for adults. Child and baby death rates were high: practically 50% of all kids did not live past the age of five, and just 50% of the individuals who lived past the age of ten were unlikely to live to their mid-twenties. Social reformers and religious associations, especially the Methodist Church, supported improved government funded training standards in the mid-nineteenth century. Conditions started to gradually improve for kids when working hours were limited and mandatory schooling established. The Education Act of 1870 was passed to implement basic standards, but also tried to oust Welsh totally from the School curriculum.

Today, essential and nursery schools in areas with a Welsh-speaking lion's share give guidance totally in Welsh and schools in zones where English is the primary language offer bilingual advice. The Welsh Language Nursery Schools Crusade, Mudiad Ysgolion Meithrin Cymraeg, originated in 1971 and has been extremely fruitful in making a system of nursery schools, or Ysgolion Meithrin, particularly in districts where English used as often as possible. Nursery, essential, and auxiliary schools are under the organization of the instruction expert of the Welsh Office. Quality government funded schooling is accessible all through Wales for understudies of any age.

Higher Education.

Most institutions of higher learning are publicly supported, but admission is competitive. The Welsh literary tradition, a high literacy rate, and political and religious factors have all contributed to shaping a culture where higher education is considered important. The primary organization of higher learning is the University of Wales, a state-funded college supported by the Universities Funding Council, with six areas in Wales: Aberystwyth, Lampeter, Cardiff, Swansea, Bangor, and the Welsh National School of Medicine. The Welsh Office is in charge of other colleges and schools, including the Polytechnic of Wales, close to Pontypridd, and the University College of Wales at Aberystwyth. The Welsh Office, employed with the Local Education Authorities and the Welsh Joint Education Committee, administers all aspects of government funded training. Grown-up proceeding with instruction courses, especially those in Welsh language and culture, are firmly advanced through local projects.

Religion

Religion has assumed a significant role in the molding of Welsh culture. Protestantism, and in particular, Anglicanism, started to accumulate more followers after Henry VIII destitute with the Roman Catholic Ecclesiastical. On the eve of the English Civil War in 1642, Puritanism, drilled by Oliver Cromwell and his supporters, was far-reaching in the fringe areas of Wales and Pembrokeshire. Welsh royalists who upheld the lord and Anglicanism were deprived of their property, acquiring disdain among non-Puritan Welsh. In 1650 the Act for the Spread of the Gospel in Wales was approved, taking over both political and spiritual life. During the period known as the Interregnum when Cromwell was in power, several non-Anglican, or Dissenting, Protestant congregations were formed which were to have significant influences on modern Welsh life. The most dutifully and informally radical of these were the Quakers, who had substantial successes in Montgomeryshire and Merioneth and finally spread their impact to areas including the Anglican fringe districts and the Welsh-speaking regions in the north and west. The Quakers, actively disliked by both other Dissenting places of worship and the Anglican Church, were severely subdued with the outcome that huge numbers were compelled to emigrate to the American states. Different areas of prayer, for example, the Baptist and Congregationalist, which were Calvinist in religious philosophy, developed and found numerous supporters in small towns. In the last part of the eighteenth century, many Welsh converted to Methodism after a restoration development in 1735. Methodism was bolstered inside the setup Anglican Church and was initially sorted out through neighborhood social orders represented by a local association. The impact of the first Dissenting holy places, joined with the profound restoration of Methodism, gradually drove Welsh society far from Anglicanism. Clashes in the initiative and constant neediness made church development difficult, but the prevalence of Methodism eventually settled as the most far-reaching section. The Methodist and other Dissenting chapels were also in charge of an increase in proficiency through chapel supported schools that advanced instruction as a method for spreading religious principle.

Today, devotees of Methodism still establish the most significant religious gathering. The Anglican Church is the additional most significant order, trailed by the Roman Catholic Church. There are also smaller quantities of Jews and Muslims. The Dissenting Protestant sects, and religion in general, played very important roles in modern Welsh society but the number of people who regularly participated in religious activities dropped significantly after World War II.

Rituals

The Cathedral of Saint David in Pembrokeshire is an essential national holy spot. David, the benefactor saint of Wales, was a religious crusader who touched base in Wales in the 6th century to spread Christianity and convert the Welsh clans. He passed on in 589 on 1 March, presently celebrated as Saint David's Day, a national occasion. His remains are buried in the cathedral.

Medication and Health Care

Health care and drug are government-financed and upheld by the National Health Service of the United Kingdom. There is an exclusive expectation of health care in Wales with roughly six medical practitioners per ten thousand people. The Welsh National School of Medicine in Cardiff offers quality therapeutic preparing and instruction.

Common Celebrations

During the nineteenth century, Welsh intellectuals began to promote the national culture and traditions, initiating a revival of Welsh folk culture. In the last century, these festivals have developed into real occasions, and Wales currently has a few internationally important music and abstract celebrations. The most critical Welsh ordinary festival is the Eisteddfod social get-together commending music, verse, and narration.

The Eisteddfod had its starting points in the twelfth century when it was mostly a gathering held by Welsh troubadours for the trading of information. Occurring unpredictably and in different areas, the Eisteddfod was attended by writers, artists, and troubadours, all of whom had essential jobs in medieval Welsh culture. By the eighteenth century, the convention had turned out to be not so much social but rather tipsy bar gatherings, but in 1789 the Gwyneddigion Society restored the Eisteddfod as a focused celebration. It was Edward Williams, also recognized as Iolo Morgannwg, in any case, who stirred Welsh enthusiasm for the Eisteddfod in the nineteenth century. Williams effectively advanced the Eisteddfod among the Welsh people living in London, regularly giving emotional addresses about the significance of Welsh culture and old Celtic customs. The nineteenth century revival of the Eisteddfod and the rise of Welsh nationalism, combined with a romantic image of ancient Welsh history, led to the creation of Welsh ceremonies and rituals that may not have any historical basis.

The Llangollen Global Musical Eisteddfod is held from 4 to 9 July, and the Royal National Eisteddfod at Llanelli, which highlights a verse and Welsh society expressions, held from 5 to 12 August, are the two most essential mainstream festivities. Other smaller, society and social celebrations are held consistently.

Chapter 13: The Arts and Humanities

Support for the Arts

The conventional significance of music and verse has energized global support for all of the expressions of the human experience. There is strong public support throughout Wales for the arts, which are considered important to the national culture. Financial support is derived from both the private and public sectors. The Welsh Arts Council gives government assistance to writing, artistry, music, and theater. The committee also offers gifts to scholars to both English-and Welsh-language productions.

Literature

Literature and verse have involve a critical position in Wales. Welsh culture is based on an oral convention of legends, fantasies, and folktales passed down from age to age. Increased knowledge, in the eighteenth century and the worry of Welsh learned people for the safeguarding of the language and culture brought forth present day composed Welsh writing. As industrialization and Anglicization compromised common Welsh culture, endeavors were made to advance the word, safeguard Welsh verse, and empower Welsh scholars. Dylan Thomas was one such Welsh writer, and possibly the most famous in the twentieth century. Artistic celebrations and rivalries help keep this custom alive. Nevertheless, the influence of other cultures combined with the ease of communication through mass media, from both inside the United Kingdom and from other parts of the world, continually undermine efforts to preserve a purely Welsh form of literature.

Performance Arts.

Singing is the most important of the performance arts in Wales and has its roots in ancient traditions. Music was both diversion and methods for recounting stories. The Welsh National Opera is one of the leading musical show organizations in Britain. Wales is celebrated for its all-male choirs, which have developed from the religious choral convention. Customary instruments, for example, the harp, are still broadly played and since 1906, the Welsh Folk Song Society has safeguarded, gathered, and distributed familiar tunes. The Welsh Theater Company is critically acclaimed, and Wales has created numerous internationally Well-known on-screen characters.

Chapter 14: Description of significant historical places

Kidwelly Castle

If you want a genuinely medieval minute, look at Kidwelly Castle in [location] enveloped in an early morning fog. Spine-tingling stuff. It is up to par with any of the other incredible castles of Wales.

The Earliest Castle on the site was Norman and made of earth and timber. The town itself is equally antiquated, built around 1115 AD. When the thirteenth century had tagged along the castle had been remade in stone, after the half-moon shape taken by the Normans. The Chaworth family assembled the reduced, but amazing internal ward and the villa was later modified by the lords (eventually dukes) of Lancaster.

Kidwelly benefited from the latest thinking in castle design. It had a concentric plan with one circuit of cautious walls set inside another to allow the castle to hold regardless of whether the external wall should fall. The construction of the large gatehouse was started late in the fourteenth century, but it wasn't finished until 1422, thanks to some degree to Owain Glyn Dwr's endeavors to stop it going up.

As with any old structure, accessibility can be a problem, but the creation of a timber-surrounded footbridge, the first passage has become wheelchair-accessible in recent years. The construction revealed an unforeseen reward: a secret underground passage!

Cyfarthfa Castle Museum and Art Gallery

Cyfarthfa Castle situated in the authentic town of Merthyr Tydfil, which set up itself as the Iron Capital of the World in the Eighteenth Century with its large Iron-Works buildings.

Cyfarthfa Castle is an incredible outing, set on the edge of the pleasant Brecon Beacons National Park, with a coffee bar offering tasty food, and an outside seating zone, which is ideal for unwinding in the late spring months.

Cyfarthfa Castle arranged in 160 acres of land of parkland with formal gardens, a lake, childrens' play region, and a model railroad. The castle was built in 1824 during the industrial revolution, and has now opened its doors to the public, hosting a spectacular museum and art gallery. Guests can observe a scope of artistry presentations and mixed Trade goods from the old world, including Egyptian grave products, Greek and Roman artifacts and Far Eastern decorative arts.

The Six Bells Miners Memorial

Finished in 2010, Guardian was dispatched to commemorate the 50th anniversary of the 1960 mining disaster in Six Bells that killed 45 men. The stunning 20-meter towers over the site of the former colliery where the catastrophe happened and is an appropriate compliment to the men whose names cut into boards folded over the commemoration plinth.

- Designed by craftsman Sebastien Boyesen, the statue is built from more than 20,000 pieces of Corten steel welded together to form a landmark that stands proudly, on a sandstone plinth. The detail that has been made utilizing this unorthodox system allows for the facial highlights, muscle definition and hair to be noticeable, and even the trousers seem delicate and streaming.
- Viewed from a distance the figure of the miner has a transparent, almost ghostly quality, allowing it to blend into the heavily wooded landscape setting. Only when viewed up close, does the figure appear solid and the true presence of Guardian can be fully appreciated.
- Guardian was devoted as a component of a Commemoration Service on the 28th June 2010 driven by the Archbishop of Canterbury Reverend Rowan Williams, and later in November 2011, HRH Prince Charles visited Guardian and Ty Ebbw Fach.
- Ty Ebbw Fach has a heritage room detailing the history of Guardian, Six Bells Colliery and the village of Six Bells. It also houses a small café serving delicious, homemade hot and cold refreshments.
- Guardian sits in Parc Arael Griffin, one of 14 environmental sites on the Ebbw Fach Trail and three of the Tyleri Trails also start from this point.

Strata Florida Abbey (Cadw)

There is much to captivate at this evocative, historically important site. Is Latin Dutch to you? Strata Florida is Latin, and can be translated to mean the Vale of Flowers. In Welsh, the name is the Cistercian priests of the Middle Ages were incredible business plural. They may have looked for wild and desolate spots to rehearse their religion but, like anxious engineers, they took the preferred standpoint of this rural area near Tregaron to amass large measures of land. They needed the space to cultivate thousands of hyphenated sheep. They also assembled streets and scaffolds which connected explorers and merchants to the nunnery — a quick move.

Strata Florida rapidly wound up not just a site of enormous religious significance in Wales but also a private home for Welsh culture. Dafydd ap Gwilym, a standout amongst the best known about Wales' medieval artists, is covered here under a yew tree.

The gigantic west entryway conveys the former glory of the building. The plan of the church can still be clearly traced and, rather remarkably, some of the original richly decorated tiles from the abbey are still intact. One of them, 'Man with the Mirror,' delineates a medieval man appreciating himself in a mirror!

Oyster Mouth Castle

With staggering views over Mumbles, Oyster Mouth Castle sits majestically on the slope sitting above Swansea Bay. It's looking especially great nowadays because of an ongoing facelift. A large amount of work has resulted in the castle being lined with an overhead shelter, protecting it for years to come. Earth has been dug under the expert eye of Glamorgan Gwent archaeologists to expose private staircases leading from vaults to previous banqueting halls. Stairs have helped by lime washing walls and made safe with rope handrails.

The Copper Kingdom Center, Amlwch

This new heritage visitor centre tells the story of Anglesey's former role as the world's leading copper producer. You can get the lowdown through intelligent presentations and exercises. In 2013, it was shortlisted for a Guardian Museum and Heritage Award for the UK's most moving museum or legacy guest fascination.

The "Copper Kingdom" alludes to the region of Amlwch on Anglesey, North Wales, which once had the biggest copper mine on the planet.

Caerphilly Castle

Caerphilly, covering 30 acres of land (12.2ha), is one of the best enduring castles in the medieval Western world. It was a highpoint in medieval protective engineering with its massive gatehouses and water highlights. It was created by Earl Gilbert de Clare, starting in 1268, to frighten Llywelyn, the last native Prince of Wales, from fighting the Normans in the southern part of Wales. It then used as a model for Edward I's castles in North Wales. Cunning Llywelyn caught it when it was half completed, but it was before long back in Norman's hands.

After Llywelyn's defeat and death, the Welsh threat substantially ended, and the castle became the administrative centre for de Clare's estates. Edward II invested energy here. Caerphilly, being uncomfortable for a family residence, eventually rotted, and the stone was taken to assemble an adjacent country house. The Victorian Bute family coal cash protected and reestablished the castle. An informative Castles of Wales exhibition is located in one tower. Working replicas of attack motors are on the grounds. There is an AV visit accessible.

Blaenavon has a pretty fantastic story

Blaenavon is a town that has throughout history been largely reliant on its coal industry. With the Great Depression and a post-war decreased need for coal, the economy was devastated. But starting with a state pledge to protect Blaenavon's Ironworks during the 1970s – the famous 18th century furnaces are attracting record visitor numbers these days. The town has appreciated a proper restoration, coming full circle in its acknowledgment as a World Heritage Site at the turn of the thousand years.

The judges had heaps of reasons to esteem Blaenavon deserving of Inclusion with the likes of the Taj Mahal and The Great Wall of China: each step taken shadows living history. The choice to give the town protection status in 1984 has paid off, keeping a significant number of the well-established niches, crevices and cobbled ways around old structures around the enchanting and suggestive Broad Street.

The pedestrianized areas make it significantly easier to sample nearby food and drink – a tempting prospect given the scope of cheddar, bread, meats and rarities created in the town.

Where mines, collieries, cable cars and prepares once overwhelmed the landscape, wildlife and vegetation have now returned in health.

Cyclists can whizz along the previous mineral railroad line, which presently frames a bicycle course driving the path to a portion of the attractions.

Huge Pit, the National Coal Mining Museum, is a standout amongst the most suggestive legacy settings on the planet, paying tribute to the sweat and effort of excavators grind of miners through a blacksmith's forge, a miners' canteen and an explosive magazine. You'll be able to imagine hard-hatters using the lockers and shower rooms, kept intact at a place which has won multiple awards and, amazingly, is free of charge.

Another must-see is the Workmen's Hall, a monumental stone building which has gone about as an active point of convergence for the nearby network since 1895. It's also well worth visiting the World Heritage Center, where a program incorporates intuitive shows and expressions and artworks exercises for the children.

Truth be told, Blaenavon is an extraordinary destination in any season, from the blossoms of spring to summer days following the Iron Mountain Trail. The yearly Winter Wonderland in December, when the Heritage Railway – moving at the greatest height of any saved household railroad, driven by a devoted group of enthusiasts – runs a Santa Special administration.

Sun-kissed or chilly, incredible undertakings await the guest.

Chapter 15: Welsh Key Figures

Roald Dahl

Roald Dahl was a well-known British essayist and author of cunning, humorous children's books. He was born 13 September, 1916 in Llandaff, Wales.

Following his graduation from Repton, an eminent British government funded school, in 1932, Dahl decided against from college and joined an undertaking to Newfoundland. He served from 1937 to 1939 in Dar es Salaam, Tanganyika (presently in Tanzania), but he enrolled in the Royal Air Force (RAF) when World War II broke out. Flying as a military pilot, he was injured in a crash landing in Libya. He presented with his squadron in Greece and then in Syria before completing a stretch (1942– 43) as assistant air attaché in Washington, D.C. (during which time he also filled in as a covert agent for the British government). There the author C.S. Forester urged him to expound on his most energizing RAF experiences, which were distributed by the Saturday Evening Post.

Dahl's first book, The Gremlins (1943), was composed for Walt Disney but was to a great extent unsuccessful. His administration in the RAF influenced his first story release, Over to You: Ten Stories of Flyers and Flying (1946), a progression of military stories that was energetically bought by critics but did not sell well. He accomplished smash hit status with Somebody Like You (1953), a gathering of grim stories for grown-ups, which was followed by Kiss, Kiss (1959), which focused on sentimental connections.

Dahl at that point swung principally to composing the children's books that would give him lasting distinction. Unlike most books that went for a youthful gathering of people, Dahl's works had an obscurely funny nature, every now and again including grisly viciousness and demise. His Characters were frequently malignant grown-ups who endangered bright and honorable tyke heroes. James and the Giant Peach (1961; film 1996), composed for his Own children, was a prominent achievement. His different works for young perusers incorporate Fantastic Mr. Fox, Charlies and the Chocolate Factory, and the Great Glass Elevator, The Enormous Crocodile, The BFG, and The Witches. One of his last such books, Matilda, was adapted as a film and as a stage show.

Dahl also composed a few contents for motion pictures, among them You Only Live Twice and Chitty Bang. His collection of memoirs, Boy: Tales of Childhood, was distributed in 1984.

Aneurin Bevan

In Tredegar, Wales, Aneurin Bevan was born in 1897, 15th November. His dad was a coal digger and the poor regular workers family in which Bevan grew up gave him direct experience to the issues of poverty and disease.

Bevan left school at 13 and started working in a neighborhood colliery. He turned into an exchanges association extremist and won a grant to examine in London. It was during this period that he wound up persuaded by the ideas of communism. During the 1926 General Strike, Bevan became one of the pioneers of the South Wales mineworkers. In 1929, Bevan was chosen as the Labor individual from parliament for Ebbw Vale.

During World War Two, Bevan was one of the leaders of the left in the House of Commons. After the landslide Labor triumph in the 1945 general decision, Bevan was selected priest of health, in charge of building up the National Health Service. On 5 July 1948, the legislature took over duty regarding all medicinal administrations, and there were free analysis and treatment for all.

Aneurin Bevan was a standout amongst the most critical pastors of the post-war Labor government and the central modeler of the National Health Service.

In 1951, Bevan was moved to become minister of labour. In an immediately afterward, he left the administration in the challenge at the presentation of remedial charges for dental consideration and displays. Bevan drove the left wing of the Labor Party, known as the 'Bevanites,' for the following five years. He arose as one of the applicants for gathering pioneer in 1955 but was defeat by Hugh Gaitskell. He consented to fill in as remote shadow secretary under Gaitskell.

In 1959, Bevan was chosen appointee pioneer of the Labor Party, although he was at that point experiencing malignant terminal cancer. He died on 6 July 1960.

Richard Burton

Richard Burton: history

In 2002, Richard Burton was incorporated into the list of the best British in history, alongside Charles Darwin, John Lennon, Sir Winston Churchill, Princess Diana, and others. The seven-time Academy Award winner, Richard Burton was the most renowned and generously compensated actor during the 1960s.

Childhood

He was born in 1925, 10th November, in the Welsh town Pontrhydyfen into large family. His father was a coal digger and his mother a [profession] married in [year] and together had thirteen children, of which Richard was the twelfth. His mother passed away in labor with his youngest sibling, when Richard was around two years old. Afterward, the family lived in poverty and could barely make ends meet.

The last on-screen character's youth can scarcely be called natural. his father spent what he earned on liquor and betting. Richard's senior sister Cecilia and her husband Elfed James, also a coalminer, took him [and his siblings] in. Afterward, Richard considered his Sister's help fortunately and stated:

> "She felt all catastrophes except her own."

Cecilia took the mother's place for the more youthful sibling. The senior sibling Ifor also contributed to the craftsman's childhood: he ingrained the affection for rugby in the child.

At five, Richard began attending the Eastern Primary School in Neath Port Talbot. After three years, he transferred to another school. The future star demonstrated the adoration for authorship in his adolescence; he had a beautiful voice and cherished the English and Welsh writing.

Motion pictures

Richard's teacher Philip Burton turned into a significant figure in Jenkins' life. It's his second name that the young fellow took as a piece of his stage name. The instructor saw the skilled understudy and supported his passion for theater. Philip helped a young Richard improve his discourse and talk without an accent.

Richard Burton in the motion picture My Cousin Rachel

In 1948, Richard Burton debuted in the motion picture The Last Days of Dolwyn. Before, the performing artist had been dealing with the radio for quite a while and also played in the theater.

The dramatization My Cousin Rachel was the artist's Hollywood debut in 1952. The motion picture turned out to be one of Henry Koster's best ventures.

Richard Burton in the motion picture The Taming of the Shrew

Richard Burton was nominated for the Academy Award multiple times, but he never got the hotly anticipated prize. In 1970, the ruler of the western John Wayne picked up his award and saw Richard had none. He murmured to Richard that Burton merited the honor.

The individual life of the gifted and handsome performing artist was as productive as his filmography. The man was married multiple times: Sybil Williams, Susan Hunt, Sally Hay, and Elizabeth Taylor (twice).

Sybil Williams Gave birth to two of Burton's Daughters, Kate and Jessica.

The undertaking between Richard and Elizabeth Taylor was a standout amongst the most scandalous and broadly examined news. The entire world was viewing the narrative of the star couple, and the actors did not keep it's a subtleties mystery.

Burton's accomplice in the motion picture Cleopatra (and twelve different works) turned into his extraordinary love. Richard got down to business on the motion picture and took his family. In any case, nothing could keep the sentiment from creating.

Elizabeth and Richard wedded in March 1964. Right then and there, Burton was the most generously compensated performer in Hollywood, and Elizabeth was the ruler of shooting.

Their life was like a fantasy: lavish yachts, relics, land property. The performing artists gave each other costly shows. Their fans viewed the passionate couple for a long time. Eventually, they separated. Even though Elizabeth and Richard remarried in some time, they lived respectively for not exactly a year. In their meetings, the stars admitted they cherished one another but couldn't exist together.

Demise

The performer passed away at an early age (58). As indicated by his biographers, Richard became liquor subordinate in his childhood, and the propensity changed into fixation later. Also, the craftsman was a smoker.

The performer was 58 when he died abruptly. It occurred in Céligny, Geneva, Switzerland, where he had a house.

Filmography

1953 – The Desert Rats

1955 – Prince of Players

1959 – Look Back in Anger

1962 – The Longest Day

1963 – Cleopatra

1964 – The Night of the Iguana

1967 – Doctor Faustus

1972 – Bluebeard

1977 – Exorcist II: The Heretic

1978 – The Wild Geese

King Arthur Biography

Lord Arthur is a semi-legendary figure, who is accepted to have been a model ruler in the early history of Britain. Much of his early legend comes from the writings of Geoffrey of Monmouth (in the Twelfth Century). His works became popular, cementing the legend of Arthur in popular folklore. All through the ages, the figure of Arthur has enthralled the enthusiasm of journalists and artists. Alfred Tennyson was instrumental in resuscitating interest for King Arthur through his ballad, "Idylls of the King."

Because of the absence of legitimate and direct chronicled proof, the life of King Arthur is available to a wide range of elucidations. A few historians question whether he truly existed at all. Notwithstanding, the most acclaimed legends incorporate the accompanying stories.

Birth to Uther Pendragon and Igraine

In one rendition, Merlin prophesized that a future king named Arthur would be born to Uther Pendragon and Igraine, the beautiful wife of Duke Gorlois of Cornwall. Knowing she would reject a man other than her husband, Uther asked Merlin to enable him to lay down with Igraine. Merlin obliged, transforming Uther's appearance to resemble the Duke for one night.

Excalibur

As indicated by legend, Arthur was ready to guarantee his rightful spot as King of Britain when he pulled Excalibur, a legendary sword, from the stone. When he obtained the sword, he fulfilled his prophecy and was crowned king. All through his rule, Arthur was advised by the slippery and mysterious figure of Merlin. Until the sixth century, it was reasonable for Welsh Kings to have an advisor, regularly called "Murthur." These guides frequently had specific data and were knowledgeable in expressions of the human experience of divination. The legend of Merlin is likely based on these court guides.

King Arthur Court

The court of Arthur kept up the most astounding standards of gallantry and ethical conduct. Furthermore, Arthur wished for his chosen knights to sit around a round table so that nobody would be superior. He tried to treat all as equal. Knights of King Arthur included:

- Sir Kay,
- Sir Gawain,
- Sir Lancelot,
- Sir Percival
- Sir Galahad,
- Sir Tristan
- Sir Bors
- Sir Geraint
- Sir Gareth
- Sir Lamorak
- Sir Gaheris
- Sir Bedivere
- Sir Agravaine
- Sir Sagramore

King Arthur and Lady Guinevere

In spite of the high requirements of honor one legend tells how one of King Arthur's most trusted and effective knights, Sir Lancelot took part in an extramarital entanglement with

Arthur's wife, Queen Guinevere. It was this betrayal that ultimately led to King Arthur's downfall.

Lord Arthur and the Holy Grail

A standout amongst the most enduring legends of King Arthur is the enchanted mission for the blessed chalice. this is a container used to catch the blood of Jesus Christ. For some, the purpose of the Holy Chalice is an allegory of the profound internal journey to find the elusive purpose of life. This fantasy has enraptured the enthusiasm of individuals through the ages and has been the subject of numerous movies including the sarcastic Monty Python and the Holy Grail.

Ruler Arthur and Mordred

All through Arthur's missions, he is opposed Morgan le Fay and Mordred. Records differ, but the most prevalent claims that Morgan le Fay was his stepsister and Mordred was his child.

T.E. Lawrence Biography

<u>Military Leader (1888– 1935)</u>

T.E. Lawrence was a British armed officer who Played the part in the Great Arab Revolt and later composed the journal The Seven Pillars of Wisdom.

<u>List</u>

T.E. Lawrence helped in the British military, getting to be Involved in Middle Eastern issues. He was a staunch promoter for Arab autonomy. later sought after a private life, changing his name. he passed on May 19, 1935.

<u>'Lawrence of Arabia'</u>

Born on August 16, 1888, in Tremadoc, Caernarvonshire, Wales, Thomas Edward Lawrence became an expert in Arab affairs as a junior archaeologist in Carchemish on the Euphrates River from 1911 to 1914, working for the British Museum on archaeological excavations. After the commencement of World War-I, he entered British knowledge.

Lawrence joined Amir Faisal al Husayn's rebel against the Turks as the political contact officer, driving a guerilla crusade that harassed the Turks behind their lines. After a significant triumph at Aqaba—a port city on the southern coast of what is presently Jordan—Lawrence's powers bolstered British General Allenby's battle to catch Jerusalem.

<u>Catch</u>

In 1917, T.E. Lawrence was caught at Dar'a and tormented and sexually abused, leaving scars that never mended. By 1918, Lawrence had been elevated to lieutenant colonel and granted the Illustrious Facility Order and the Instruction of Bath by King George V, but but politely refused the medals in support of Arab independence.

Spiritually and physically depleted, and Uneasy with his notoriety, Lawrence came back to England and began diligently working on an account of his adventures.

The Seven Pillars of Wisdom and Later Years

The Seven Pillars of Wisdom is one of his books, and it became known for its distinctive portrayals of the mind-boggling expansiveness and assortment of Lawrence's escapades in Arabia. The work accumulated universal distinction for Lawrence, who was appropriately nicknamed "Lawrence of Arabia."

After the war, Lawrence linked the Royal Air Force under an unexpected name, T.E. Shaw (as he continued looking for obscurity, he had his name officially changed).

Lawrence died in a cruiser mishap on May 19, 1935, in Clouds Hill, Dorset, England.

A movie based on his life, Lawrence of Arabia, coordinated by David Lean and featuring Peter O'Toole, was released in 1962. The film earned seven Academy Awards, plus the Oscar for best picture.

Conclusion

It seems that the progress of Welsh nationalism rallied supporters of the language, and the formation of Welsh television and radio originate a form of spectators which fortified in the retention of its Welsh. Maybe most important of all, at the end of the 20th century it became required for all schoolchildren to absorb Welsh up to age 16, and this both reinforced the language in Welsh-speaking areas and reintroduced at least a basic knowledge of it in the regions which had become more or less solely Anglophone.

The failure in the fraction of people in Wales who can express Welsh has now stopped, and there are even ciphers of a modest rescue. However, though Welsh is the daily language in many parts of Wales, English is universally understood. Additional, overall figures may be misleading, and it might argue that the mass of Welsh speakers (which, if high, leads to a flourishing Welsh philosophy) is a similarly important statistic. Put additional way, were 50,000 other Welsh speakers to be focused in areas where Welsh spoke by at least 50% of the populace, this would be much more significant to the sustainability of the Welsh language than the similar number discrete in Cardiff, Newport and Swansea cities.

With that, we have come to the end of this book. I want to thank you for choosing this book.

Now that you have come to the end of this book, we would first like to express our gratitude for choosing this particular source and taking the time to read through it. All the information here was well researched and put together in a way to help you understand the history of wales as easily as possible.

We hope you found it useful and you can now use it as a guide anytime you want. You may also want to recommend it to any family or friends that you think might find it useful as well.

Scottish History

A Concise Overview of the History of Scotland From Start to End

Eric Brown

The information in the following pages is broadly considered to be a truthful and accurate account of facts, and as such any inattention, use or misuse of the information in question by the reader will render any resulting actions solely under their purview. There are no scenarios in which the publisher or the original author of this work can be in any fashion deemed liable for any hardship or damages that may befall them after undertaking information described herein.

Additionally, the information in the following pages is intended only for informational purposes and should thus be thought of as universal.

As befitting its nature, it is presented without assurance regarding its prolonged validity or interim quality. Trademarks that are mentioned are done without written consent and can in no way be considered an endorsement from the trademark holder.

Table of Contents

Introduction

The very idea of Scottishness is inseparable from an opposition to Englishness. England's influence on its northern neighbor, after it became the most powerful political force in the British Isles by 1100 cannot be understated.

However, Scotland has long insisted on being a separate country on a shared Island. Historical fact and myth had been resolutely channeled into the creation of a distinct national identity over the centuries. For the majority of human history. However, there was no Scotland, Wales, Ireland or England to speak of. Scotland is derived from the Latin scope here, which means Land of the Scots.

The Scots were a Celtic people of Irish origins, who decided to settle on the west coast of Great Britain during the fifth century AD. The people who habit Skoda, which only meant the entire kingdom North of England during Alexander the second's rain, were certainly not monolingual or monocultural. As the Scottish language slowly became the lingua franca of the entire nation, it had to coexist with Celtic, Gaelic and Norwegian.

Before a national identity was forged through the trauma of invasion and years of painful resistance, local, regional and dynastic identities and affiliation had more meaning and relevance to everyone's daily lives. When roads and advanced technologies for communication did not exist, everyone's existence was rooted in their immediate surroundings. Identities were formed based on the specific physical geography that individuals, families and clans found themselves in.

Scotland's terrain is mostly rugged, and subject to weather extremes but this challenging landscape also possesses a striking beauty and the capacity to facilitate the evolution of a fiercely unique culture. Scottish folklore has perpetuated the idea that the Scots have never been conquered. The Scots have certainly fought bravely against conquest from various foreign powers, but they also have a mixed track record.

It is true that the Romans eventually abandon their attempts to conquer Scotland, which was then known as Caledonia. And decided to simply build walls to keep the barbaric tribes up north from attacking them. In the 10th century, the Scots managed to fend off a Danish invasion, but only with English aid. This dependency meant that the English ruler could define himself as father and Lord of the king of Scots.

Chapter 1: Early Scotland

To envision what Scotland's earliest history looked like. You must make an effort to consciously imagine a time long before there was a heavily urbanized population. There were no road networks in existence, or a string of towns and cities connected by frequent trade. The forests were all unclear, and bogs were filled to the brim, and the heavily mountainous terrain prevented easy migrations up, down and across the lands. The Highlands to the north and west, which contained most of Scotland's hills. And mountains were far less hospitable than the flatter and more fertile lowlands to the south and east. Most long distance travel and trade would have been achieved by water along Scotland's 10 major rivers, numerous forts and its extensive coastline.

The majority of Scotland's earliest inhabitants toiled in one form of agriculture or another, helping to ensure that their local area could produce all the food and goods it needed to be self-sufficient. One's wealth and happiness largely dependent on the fertility of the land that one had access to. As well as one's industriousness in extracting subsistence from it. The Scottish terrain only became inhabitable to people towards the end of the last glacial period, circa 115,000 to circa 11,700 years ago. Much of North America was blanketed by ice during this time, while the Scandinavian ice sheet extended its reach into the northern British Isles. As the ice made its final retreat northward in approximately 7000 BC Mesolithic foragers' journey northward to access the green pastures it left in its wake. Little is known about the earliest of Scotland's inhabitants, since they left little archaeological evidence behind.

A Greek Mariner left behind the first written reference to Scotland in about 320 BC. Piteous referred to the northern part of the British Isles with the name orcas. A Celtic word that was most probably derived from the name of a local tribe he encountered during his travels. It means the young boars and lives on in modern times as Orkney a rugged archipelago off Scotland's northeastern coast. It also provides evidence that Celtic speakers were present that far up north by fourth century BC. The earliest extensive historical record dates to Rome's first encounter with medieval Scotland. The feared Roman legions arrived towards the end of the first century AD, after they successfully conquered the Celtic tribes of England and Wales after three decades of subjugation. Like their Southern counterparts, the inhabitants of Scotland, or Caledonia, as the Romans referred to it then, mostly spoke a form of Celtic language. Unlike Southern Britain, however, Caledonia's fierce warrior tribes would mount an effective resistance against the mighty Roman Empire.

Roman ambitions to access Scotland's lead, silver and gold with plans to enrich it further by enslaving the Scottish tribes and forcing them to pay taxes would eventually be thwarted. By the time the Romans first encountered Scotland, a chief dumb society. Which was more hierarchical and unequal had emerged. Large underground stores, Sioux terrains were a contributor to this social inequality, allowing local chiefs to hoard surplus crops and resources they had extracted from the land. Hierarchies within Scottish settlements gave way to hierarchies between settlements as tribes, which each consisted of a few thousand members vied with each other for power and control over resources. In the presence of a foreign common enemy, the warring tribes united to defend their homeland. In 79 AD, the Roman governor led the first incursion into Caledonia. After a few campaigns, the Romans achieved a decisive victory in 83 A.D at the Battle of Mons Gropius.

General Julius Agra cola defeated the Caledonians there. They were fighting under the leadership of Cowdicas, a chieftain of the Caledonian Confederacy. When their initial vision of conquering the entire British Isles was finally at hand, however, the Roman military found that their attention was needed in other parts of their empire. To safeguard Rome's glorious conquest of Southern Britain against the fierce Scottish warriors. The Romans built Hadrian's Wall on the time Solvay line in the 120s and 130s. During the middle of the second century, a second wall, N-9 wall was built on the fourth Clyde line. This re-occupation only lasted for roughly a decade. After briefly including Southern Scotland within the Roman province of Britannia. The Romans eventually gave up their campaign against tribes, which were unsharedable described as the barbarians from the north. And relatively idealized as the last men on Earth, the last of the free.

They retreated to Hadrian's Wall. Roman presence was maintained in the southwest part of Scotland, near Hadrian's Wall until the decline of the Roman Empire. Despite Rome's aborted conquest of Scotland, its empire left behind a profound influence on the inhabitants of Caledonia. The duality was not entirely between the Imperial Roman and the oppressed native, but between those who were within and outside the mighty Empire. The inhabitants of the British Isles had the opportunity to join the Roman army for their own gain. While others undoubtedly saw the benefits of aligning themselves with the most extensive political and social entity in the West. Like all imperial powers, Rome impacted the locals through a combination of hard and soft power.

Apart from their military prowess, they came with Roman commodities, luxury items and wealth that could be used to seduce local leaders to their cause. The rivaling warrior chiefs were thus incentivized to take advantage of Roman resources to get a competitive edge over their rivals. When they came face to face with the various trade objects that circulated through Rome's international economic system. The Caledonian inevitably realized that they were isolated from an international highway of ideas, trade and cultural exchange. Room's most lasting effect on the Caledonians is undoubtedly the introduction of Christianity.

The religion of the Empire slowly extended its influence up north, reaching places and communities that the Roman military would not. Much of the evangelizing work was probably done by British and Irish missionaries, who were intent on converting the northern pagans to their cause. The new religion came with new trade links to the Irish Sea and Atlantic Gaul, which provided the foreign objects necessary for the new Christians to conduct their rituals of faith. These were pottery designed to contain wine and oil, which were inevitably accompanied by new aesthetic and intellectual conceptions.

Chapter 2: The Golden Age

The earliest evidence of mankind in Scotland, dates to the Meso lithic or Middle Stone Age after the glaciers melted. This was a period of transition between the hunting and gathering of the proceeding Old Stone Age. The agricultural development of the New Stone Age was yet to come. At this time, Scotland was mainly a woodland region. Its occupants hunted wild pigs, red and roe deer, new sources of food gathering were also found. Catching birds, fishing and gathering nuts, fruits and shellfish. Settlements during this period are found on the coast and along rivers. Tools made of bone antler, flint and stone were used. Barb's made of tiny Flint blades hafted to wooden shafts were commonly used. Bone was used to make harpoons and fish hooks. The large number of fish bones excavated suggests that boats were used in fishing even though no boats from this period had been found. There were likely dugout canoes like ones found in England.

The best known of these early excavated sites is at Morton on Tensmere north of Saint Andrew's. Other sites include Dundee and Broadly ferry on Bayside. On the isles of Rum and Orinsay, Campbeltown and Oban in Argyle along the River D. Ethan Rivers in Grampian, re-point unlock Tardan and several sites along the banks of the fourth and Clyde. The Neolithic or New Stone Age was the period the plow was developed and farming began. Scotland's woodlands were cleared and wheat and barley were planted. Sheep, goats, pigs, cattle and dogs were all domesticated. With farming came a settled way of life, which allowed for new developments like pottery. The first pots were simply built by using coils of clay. The bucket shaped elaborately decorated, grooved wear was to follow. Also, Shell and bone beads were developed during the New Stone Age.

The focus of archeological study during this period is the megalithic monuments rather than stone tools. Tombs, standing stones and stone circles all dotted the landscape. During this time, Flint tools continued to be used and were fashioned into arrowheads, knives and axes. Tools designed for woodworking were also found, as well as clothing fasteners made from jet and bone pins. Early farmers lived in farmsteads occupied by one or two families such as Nap of Hauer and

Petty Garth's field. Later small communities were found such as Skara Brae and Barn house in the Orkney Islands.

In northern Scotland. Houses were made of stone and stone built field walls have been found. Larger buildings such as Danny Dale Temple on Shetlands mainland may have been used as communal meeting places. In central and southern Scotland. Houses and fences were made of timber rather than stone. Large Neolithic timber halls have been discovered at bell Brady in Grampian and town head on the isle of Butte. Some of the larger communities may have developed a specialization of labor allowing some individuals to work solely as carpenters, fishers or stone workers. An axe factory has been identified at Killen in Perthser. Stone circles are found in all parts of Scotland with concentrations in the North East, South West, and Outer Hebrides. They were likely used as meeting places for rituals and ceremonies.

Perhaps the best known is the 12 apostles at Dumfries, which is the largest stone circle in Scotland and the fifth largest in Britain. Some stones in Scotland have other arrangements aside from circles. There is a horse shoe arrangement at Asha vantage and a fan shaped arrangement at Hill of many stains, which may have originally included 600 stones. Hinges are circular earthworks comprising a bank and a ditch. These are only found in Britain. Entry into the center is gained by a causeway across the ditch and passage through the bank.

Hinges are believed to have been gathering places for ritual ceremonies. Often hinges have stone circles within the center like the one had Karen People in West Lithion. Others like the one at Belford hinge in Fife had timber circles.

Many stone tombs from this period can be found across Scotland. There are many chambered tombs in Scotland. The grandness of these is Maize Hall on the Orkney Mainland. Some with a passage leading to a small chamber such as Univac at North West. Others are large like Midhow on Rousse, which is divided into 12 chambers. Some chambered tombs like Trevor so tweak on Rousse have double story chambers. Long Barrow Tombs are comprised of a turf and stone mound like Keapo, Kencardine. Bronze is made by melting together copper and tin. Scotland has natural copper deposits, but the tin needed to have come from elsewhere like Devon and Cornwall. Gold items in Scotland are not native, but have been thought to have come from Ireland.

The beaker culture named for their large beaker drinking vessels made their way to Scotland at this time. The beaker people first appeared in southern Britain in 2,750 BC. This was a time when the first weapons like swords and spears appeared in Scotland. Weapons have been found in hoards, deposited in rivers are locks such as the hoard found in Dunstan lock Edinburgh. Bronze items were also made for domestic use such as knives, razors, chisels, sickles, pins and cauldrons. Woven woolen cloth and leather was used to make clothes. Both men and women dressed in tunics, skirts and shirts like garments with hats commonly worn. There was a division of labor. Most people farmed, but there would have been a local Bron Smith, minors, carpenters, potters and traders. In larger communities, outstanding warriors or chieftains were free to focus on military pursuits.

Most of the population would have lived in the lowlands in circular huts, made of wood or stone. Huts like these have been excavated at green Noey and stand rip rig. At Norton on the southwest of Harris, the inhabitance lived in excavated trenches, roofed with hides and timber. In the later Bronze Age many settlements were fortified. At this time there was a change in climate, which likely brought about farming in Highland areas. Cup and ring markings made on Rock Faces and upright stones are circular indentations surrounded by one or more concentric circles. Examples of these markings can be found at temple wood and Achnabrack in Argyle and Balak Mile in Ayrshire.

The burials of the Bronze Age consisted of single grave cremations or inhumanities. Many of these graves are made insists or pits inside of hinges or stone circles, such as the stone circle at color, Lee West Hill. There are also sites like loan head of Deviat inverurie where over 30 cremations were buried in a circular enclosure.

The Iron Age is the time of the Celts who occupied central and Western Europe. The Celts were a very loose confederation of tribes who shared the same language and customs. Around 700 BC the Celts arrived in Britain bringing their language, knowledge of iron smelting and fork Construction. A few groups of Celts may have crossed the North Sea to arrive on the east coast of Scotland, but most are believed to have migrated to Scotland from England. Most of the population farmed the land and lived in round huts with large conical roofs of fache hide or turf supported in the middle by tall posts. In the south of Scotland where wood was plentiful, the dwellings were made of timber or wattle and Daub. Further north walls of the huts were made of stone.

In several parts of Scotland Larders known as sue terrains had been found. These are underground lined with stone, which would have been ideal for preserving food. Among the best examples are Cus, Aboyne and grain and Reno bester on Orkney mainland and castle law near Edinburgh. A small group of huts and a small field were fenced to create a palisaded settlement, which was common in Scotland, such as new and old canard Aboyne. Large settlements also existed such as Tappa North Riney. Where up to at 150 hut platforms have been identified inside the Fort.

Crannogs were settlements on an artificial island made of stone or timber, which were mainly found in central or southern

Scotland. A crannog has been reconstructed at the Scottish Crenoug center on locktay at Kenmore, which is based on the excavated example of Oak Bank locktay. Brocks are fortified circular stone towers that are mainly found in north and west Scotland, like Downtrodden. Glen Aog, Dones or forts are found mainly in the south and east of Scotland and are most often located on hills. One of the largest hill forts is Eildon Hill, Melrose, which had strong ramparts. Both Brocks and hill forts continued to be used after the Iron Age and into the Roman period. Several graves within the ditched area at Karen PayPal Hill, West Lothian are among the few burials identified as being from the Iron Age. Little is known about Iron Age burial.

The Roman Scotts is an Irish Celtic word that means pirate or Raiders, a name given to Raiders from Ireland by the Romans. The Scott's also settled in western Scotland in the fourth and fifth centuries A.D. Another race of people lived in Scotland who was known as the Picts. The Romans referred to all the tribes in Scotland, whether Scott or Picts as Caledonians. The Scotts inhabited Scodia and the Picts Picktavia. The Picts were an amalgam of people who were the original inhabitants of the land and little is known about them. They tattooed their foreheads and other body parts.

The Scotts lived in simply constructed round houses made of wattle and Daub with thatched roofs. They shared rooms with their animals and slept on a lump of Straw. They had wool cloaks made from sheep they kept that shielded them from the frequent rain.

They wore trousers. They had gold and silver broaches for clothes with abstract animal designs, torques, necklace of gold, swords and daggers with jeweled hilts and helmets with bronze and enamel inlay. Those who did not farm were skilled craftsmen, such as blacksmiths, coppersmiths, carpenters, stone masons, potters, weavers, fetcher's and jewelers or merchants. Julius Caesar had invaded Britain in 55 BC and the conquest continued and expanded, but did not reach Scotland.

In A.D 79 the new Roman governor of Britain, Denaze Julius Agricola, sent a fleet to survey Scotland's coast and it was on this excursion that the Romans discovered that Britain was an island. The Celts in Scotland had made some preparations for a Roman attack, but there was no dominant chief or central government. The Celts disliked central organization. The Crannogs, natural or artificial islands used for settlement in Galloway were fortified. New Dones, forts were built and older ones repaired. Some Brocks, circular stone towers in the south were strengthened.

Agricola led legions slowly northward on the first invasion of Scotland. He built roads and fortifications as he pushed further north. The Caledonians led successful guerrilla attacks. Agricola continued his advance until he reached the Caledonian stronghold in the summer of A.D 84, somewhere at a place called Mons Gropius. 30,000 Caledonians faced a Roman force only half their size. However, the untrained half naked natives were no match for the professional Roman army who killed 10,000 Caledonian during the engagement, those who were left fled into the woods. Despite his victory, the emperor Domitian recalled Agricola the following year and did not pursue the campaign. Continued raiding by southern Caledonians prompted the emperor Hadrian to begin construction of a stone wall known as Hadrian's Wall in A.D 122. 20 years later, a lesser structure known as Antonians wall was completed across the narrowest part of Scotland, from the firth of forth to the firth of Clyde.

These walls were more than just fortifications. They were boundaries of the Roman Empire. The last envision of Scotland was orchestrated by Emperor Lucy's Septimius Severus and continued by his son, Kara Kalea. Military basis from this era had been found at South Shields, Kreman and Car pile. They were estuary forts designed to provision large armies by sea. The attempt to subdue Scotland failed and by the end of the second century, the Romans abandoned Scotland. By the fourth century Raiders from Ireland, were carving out territories in southwestern Caledonia and in 4/10 Rome fell.

When the Germanic tribes migrated to Britain after the fall of Roman Britain, they pushed the Celts, who did not want to mingle with the newcomers into Wales and the Kingdom of

Cambria and Strathclyde in southern Scotland. Scotland is made up of four people's, the Picts who were the native population of Scotland. Some scholars believe that they were Celts. Others believe that they migrated from Cynthia, Modern Day Ukraine, and are the ancestors of the city and nomadic horsemen. The Scotts who migrated from Ireland around the sixth century, the Britons, the Celtic tribe that had been Romanized and occupied the territory south of Hadrian's wall and the Angles a German tribe who settled in the east of Scotland.

From 460-490 the legendary author, King of the Britons as claimed to have led a band of elite Celtic warriors against the invading Saxons. The debate about whether King Arthur was real or imagined continues today. Arthur appears in the literature of the later middle Ages. Arthur is said to have fought 12 battles. The main battle being Munns Budonicas. His victory at this battle is said to have held back the Totemic invaders for 40 years. The site of this battle remains unknown.

The two dominant Confederations of tribes that eventually merged to form Scotland were the Picts and the Celts, the Picts ruled Picktavia, also known as Caledonia by the Romans. The Picts were firstly called Caledonian. Later became known as Picts, meaning painted ones, referring to the tattoos they wore. In 600 Picktavia encompassed all of modern day Scotland except for a small kingdom in the southeast known as Dell Riata which was held by the Scotts.

There were northern Picts and southern Picts. Both apparently had sub kings but all Picts were under the rule of one king who ruled all of Picktavia. The Picts and the Scots fought against each other. King Briday of the Picts who died in 584 won a victory against the Gabbrand the king of the Scots. This brought a period of peace between the two peoples. Briday was the first Pictish king to show an interest in Christianity. He was ministered to by Saint Columbia who had arrived from Ireland on the isle of Iona in 565 on the southeast coast of Scotland where he established a monastery. St Columbia is often credited with the conversion of the Scots, but this had occurred prior to his arrival.

In 658 King Osby of North Umbria, one of the seven kingdoms of Anglo Saxon England extended the territory of North Umbria into Picktavia. This territory was held for 30 years and this resulted in close associations between the Picts and North Umbria's. In 685 Briday defeated the North Umbrian's at the battle of Nextel's mirror. The Norwegian Vikings raided Scotland in 787 for the first time. Lindisfarne monastery was destroyed in 793. Iona was raided three times between 795 and 806. By the ninth century the Vikings were seeking new land and were beginning to settle in northern Scotland in the Hebrides, the Orkneys and in the Shetlands. At the same time, they were settling the northeast coast of England. The Vikings intermarried with the Picts and Scots with the intention of conquering all of Scotland.

Kenneth McClain, King of the Scots was threatened by the Vikings as were the Picts. In 836 he received the assistance of Godfrey Mac Fergus, lard of Oreille in Ireland. In fighting against the Vikings. In 839 the Picts suffered a defeat at the hands of the Vikings. Kenneth took advantage of the situation and marched against the Picts and united the two kingdoms in 843. He was the first king of the clans who took the name of their chief. For example, Mac or Mick means son of, so the clan Mac Donald's means son of Donald.

In 934 Athelstan King of all England invaded the Scottish king Constantine the second and defeated him. He recognized Athelstan as is overlord, but in 943 he abdicated his throne and his brother Malcolm the first who took the throne and agreed to accept Edmund the first Afilestand successor as this overlord. In 973 Edgar King of England took a fleet through Scottish waters to frighten Kenneth the second into subservience to England. These events are the basis of England's claim to sovereignty over Scotland. However, in 1018 Malcolm the second king of Scotland fought to Annex Lothian in Roxboro.

In 1034 Duncan the first became king of Scotland. He is the monarch portrayed by Shakespeare in Macbeth. He is the first of the house of Canmore. The Celtic system of succession was known as Tenistry, succession through the male line. No female succession or male succession via female lines was allowed. This led to many successions which resulted in the killing of one's predecessor. Thus dunkin the first was killed by his cousin Macbeth in 1040 and in 1057 Malcolm Kenmore killed Macbeth.

In 1070 William the conqueror extended empire to include Western and northern England. He rappelled the English and bought off Danish forces that were aiding English. The last to resist was Edgar, the Ethylene who fled to King Malcolm of Scotland. Malcolm had married Margaret, Edgar's sister, which allied him with the Anglo Saxons. Much to the displeasure of the Vikings. Traditional allies of the Scots. In 1072 William marched into Scotland to demand that Malcolm stop aiding Edgar. Malcolm agreed and with the piece of Abernethy, Malcolm recognized William as his overlord, who was content to leave Scotland alone as his conquest of England was complete.

In 1092 King Malcolm, the third of Scotland, regained the Scottish lands of Lothian in North Umbria. Rufus established a stronghold at Carlyle on the Scottish border. Rebuffed Malcolm and reestablished the piece of Abernathy in which Malcolm recognized Rufus as his overlord. This was the period in Scotland when feudalism was established first in the lowlands and later in the highlands, which continued to adhere to the clan system of rule Norman's in North Umbria Killed Malcolm. Malcolm's Brother Donald Bayne claimed the throne and resisted the Normans. Rufus supported dunkin the second and then Edgar, two of Malcolm's sons who reigned over Scotland and recognized Rufus as overlord. Henry the first of England remained at peace with Scotland, who King's has recognized him as overlord. Henry married Edith, who took the name Matilda, daughter of Malcolm the third former king of Scotland.

Henry married one of his many illegitimate daughters, Savilla to Alexander, who later became Alexander the first king of Scotland. David, the first 1124 to 1153 is credited with introducing Norman feudalism to Scotland. However, his two predecessors, Edgar and Alexander the first had also done their part to introduce feudalism, but it was David the first who opened the way for feudalism to spread into the lowlands. England's first civil war began when King David the first of Scotland, Matilda's uncle took advantage of the situation and reasserted old territorial claims on border lands including Cambria and Carlyle.

David the first invaded England and was defeated at the battle of the standard in 1138 but gained most of North Umbria not in battle, but as a result of the second treaty of Durham in 1139. David the first continued to establish feudalism in Scotland.

Malcolm the fourth had taken the throne in 1153 just shortly before Henry the second assumed his throne. He was the grandson of King David. His father, Prince Henry had died unexpectedly, leaving Malcolm to assume the throne at the tender age of 12. Malcolm was surrounded by Norman advisers, which prompted two revolts at Moray and Lulac early in his reign. Henry the second assisted with these revolts and took advantage of the situation to press Malcolm the fourth to give up his claim to North Umbria, which he did. Malcolm did not marry or have children and was succeeded by his brother William, who attacked Henry the second in 1173 and 1174 in attempts to regain North Umbria.

He was unsuccessful and was captured during the 1174 attack. Henry the second forced William to swear an oath of allegiance as Henry's feudal superior and had him evacuates forces at several of his castles, which were handed over to English garrisons. Scotland was to benefit from the rule of English King Richard the first. Richard needed money for his crusade and in 1189 he canceled the obligation of the Scottish king to pay homage to England in exchange for 10,000 silver marks. Scotland again became independent and the surrounding castles were returned to their owners. William King of Scott's tried to get his claim to the northern counties recognized before John, as William had tried to do with Richard. William failed a second time. In 1209 John entered a treaty with

William and paid him 15,000 marks for his goodwill. He handed two of his daughters to be married to English princess.

In 1214 his son Alexander the second succeeded William and invaded England in pursuit of the northern counties. He was unsuccessful and John, who was busy with the rebellious barons who would soon force him to sign the Magna Carta was in no position to exact anything from Alexander the second. In 1237 Henry the third King of England came to terms with Alexander the second, king of Scotland, granting him lands in Northumberland and Cumberland. His son Alexander the third succeeded Alexander the Second. Alexander the third successfully defended Scotland from Norwegian Vikings under King Hauntcon who died sailing home from battle. His successor Magnus, surrendered the Western islands to Scotland while the Orkneys and Shetlands remained Norwegian. It was a time of great prosperity in Scotland. The influences that Scotland had felt from the Vikings were gradually changing the economy, from bartering goods to the use of currency.

Boroughs developed, which were small towns surrounded by a rampart and wooden fence. The first borough was Berwick upon tweed, now in England. Others were sterling, Dumbfirline, Perth, scone and Edinburgh. While the highlands still accepted the law of the clan chiefs, the laws of the lowlands were administered through the sheriffs who ruled Shires for the king. The sheriff collected taxes and rents for the king, heard lawsuits, criminal cases, and summoned levies on men when they were needed to bear arms for the King. Alexander the third, the Scottish king had chosen to attend Edwards's coronation. The opportunity for Edward to tightened his grip on Scotland arose when Alexander was unexpectedly killed in a riding accident in 1286, leaving no male heir to the throne. His air was Margaret, a girl of four who was the daughter of Eric of Norway, and his wife Margaret Alexander's daughter. Edward arranged that she be betrothed to the first Prince of Wales. However, the infant Queen Margaret, the made of Norway as she was known, died in 1290 in Orkney on her way to Scotland. The cause of her death is unknown.

Now there were several claimants for the Scottish thrown, the two main ones being John Bailio representing the senior survivor of the House of Canmore and Robert Bruce, who based his claim on being the son of Isabella the second daughter, and had already been recognized as heir. Edward came north to decide which should be king in order to prevent a civil war. Edward at first tried to press a claim that he should be the Scottish king, but he failed to offer a good claim. Edward Chose Bailio and it is often said that he chose Bailio because he would act in Edwards's interest. However Bailio was the choice of the Scottish people. Edward had all claimants pay homage to him prior to the appointment. John Bailio was known as Tomb tabard or empty coat for his weakness in complying with

Edwards demands. The final Straw came in 1294 when Edward was preparing to fight Phillip the fourth of France who had taken possession of Gascony. The last plant [28:54 inaudible] land in France.

Bailio was called to London to supply men to fight in France. The Scottish Bishops Berles and Barons could not endure this, and Bailio did not report to London. Furthermore, he entered into a treaty with France, known as the Halled alliance. Edward viewed this as an act of war and responded in April of 1296 by sending more troops to Scotland than he had sent to whales. The result was that by July, Bailio yielded his crown to Edward. As always, Edward attack the cultural identity of those he conquered. This was done by carrying the stone of scone on which all Scottish kings had been crowned back to Westminster in London. English officials took over the Scottish government.

Now we come to a great Scottish Patriot William Wallace, immortalized by the movie Brave heart, the son of a knight and one of the few Scots who never paid homage to Edward. Wallace led guerrilla attacks in the south with great success. However, William was not alone in the north. Andrew Demori was also leading a guerrilla attacks with even greater success. When Morei March to south and Wallace marched north to meet him at Sterling. They joined forces for a major military attack. On September, 11, 1297 the battle of Sterling Bridge was fought. The Scots won by using a guerrilla tactic of letting the English start crossing a wooden bridge. Then while the English were bottlenecked, the Scots attacked. Morei was fatally wounded and Wallace who had never had the ambition of being Scotland's king was declared guardian of Scotland.

For the next year Wallace issued Ritz and made appointments in the name of the deposed Bailio. On July 22nd, 1298 the inevitable battle between Wallace and Edward took place at Fallkirk. The Scots suffered a slaughter due to the developing technology of the Longbow. English archers cut down the Scots. Had it not been for the English Longbow?

The history of Scotland might have been far different. Wallace survived traveling abroad to France and other countries trying to gain support for the cause of independence in Scotland. Years later in 1305 he was betrayed in Glasgow. He was given a mock trial and suffered a live disownment. Wallace was a Scottish Patriot to the end. Robert, the Bruce had helped in the cause of Scottish independence, but there were times when his political ambition to become king of Scotland led him to avoid conflict. With Wallace gone the Bruce killed his main rival, John Coleman, by stabbing him at the altar at Greyfriars church in Dumfries. Then in 1306 he declared himself king of Scotland. This caused so much division in Scotland that The Bruce had to leave the country for a few months.

Upon his return, he engaged in guerrilla warfare as Wallace had done, The Bruce was said to have observed a spider in a cave reweaving its web against the weather, which is said to have caused him to resolve, to keep up his efforts against England. Edward died while on the march against the Bruce. Edward the second came to the English throne after his father's death. He did not possess the same leadership qualities as Edward the first. Bruce engaged in skirmishes, avoiding pitched battles and possessed a swift moving cavalry. Unlike the heavy, slow moving cavalry of the English. One by one, the English strongholds fell. Forfar, Brechin, Dundee, Perth, Dumfries, Linlithgow, Roxboro, and Edinburgh. Sterling was now the only English held castle in Scotland. This led up to Bruce's famous victory at the battle of Bannockburn where he was greatly outnumbered.

In 1314 Edward the second made a truce with Scotland for 13 years. By that time, Scotland had formally gained her independence. In 1327 Edward the third made an unsuccessful attempt to subdue Scotland, which ended with the treaty of Northampton. Bruce was recognized as king of an independent Scotland and his son was betrothed to Edwards's sister. David the second succeeded his father, Robert the Bruce, but was nothing like him. David almost lost everything during a time when Scotland's resources were depleted by war. What Scotland needed most was peace and time to rebuild. However, David Rashly invaded England, suffering a great defeat and being taken captive from 1346 to 1357. David would have agreed to have had the Scottish crown past to Edward or one of his sons if he died childless. And if parliament had agreed to the proposal, which they rejected. Parliament came to the rescue of Scotland again in 1363 when David agreed to pass the crown to England, if he remained childless. This time parliament had to pay England a ransom to get out of the arrangement. Under David's reign the people of Scotland suffered from increased taxes and the Black Death.

Chapter 3: The Emergence of the Scottish Nation State

The rising presence of foreign influence in the north can be traced back to Malcolm Canmore, who became the king of Alba as Malcolm The third in 1058, after Macbeth's death the previous year. His first wife Ingeborg had been the daughter of a Norse Earl of Orkney, but his second wife Margaret, was a descendant of England's Saxon Royal House. As a queen consort and patroness of the church, Margaret ushered in a climate of receptiveness to southern cultural influences, I. E. The Anglicization of Scotland. By influencing her husband and his court, she advanced the causes of the Gregorian reform, which was mainly preoccupied with the clergy's independence from the state and the conquered English population. Margaret also relocated Benedictine Monks from Canterbury England, to her new foundation at Dumbfermline establishing the precedent for non-Gaelic speaking, clergymen to influence Scottish culture.

During Macbeth's relatively long and peaceful rain, Southerners who were loyal to him migrated northwards opting to resettle in the south west and northeast of modern day Scotland. They brought with them a more international outlook and culture, sowing the seeds of foreign influence in predominantly Gaelic society. Gaelic traditions and customs prevailed in everyday life, the church and the Royal Courts as well as the institutions of law and education. This was set to change throughout the 11th and 12th centuries. When Malcolm the third died during his final English raid in 1093 however, there were concerted attempts to prevent the replacement of Tenistry with Primogeniture. This southern custom privileged, the legitimate firstborn son above everyone else. Younger brothers, older or younger, illegitimate sons and collateral relatives when it came to inheriting his parents throne, his State or wealth. Under Tenistry the heir to the king could be the eldest son, but this was not necessarily the case.

A council of family heads could opt to elect a brother, nephew, or cousin of the previous chieftain. Anyone who is linked by blood and deemed most worthy of the position. Malcolm the thirds, brother and son from his first marriage, each briefly occupied the throne after his death. In time however, it was Malcolm the thirds three sons with the assistance of Margaret who secured their control over the throne. Edgar was king from 1097 to 1107, followed by Alexander the first 1107 to 1124 and David the first 1124 to 1153. With the help of the English they defied Celtic opposition and claims from the descendants of their father's first marriage. Their rise to power was accompanied by the increasing practice of Primogeniture, which finally replaced Tenistry permanently during the late 13th century. The presence of Latin in Scotland had linked it to the international culture of the Christian Church over the previous decades, which paved the way for the impact of other influences from continental Europe.

Throughout the 12th and 13th centuries the Europeanization of Europe was underway, as the modern western European state began developing in England, France, Norway, and Germany. They were categorized by clearly defined borders, national sovereignty, a commercial economy, parliamentary representation, thoroughly institutionalized administrative and legal systems, and a shared idea of nationhood. The arrival of immigrants from Normandy, Brittany and Flanders accelerated the disruption of Gaelic norms and traditions, ringing in new influences, ideas and practices that could be repurposed for Scottish ends. David the first, the youngest of Malcolm the thirds six sons with Margaret, played a major role in Scotland's evolution into a modern nation state. He eventually proved himself to be one of the most powerful and influential Scottish kings. Unlike his mother, who did not interfere much with the inner workings of the church. He actively reorganized Scottish Christianity to align it with its counterparts in England and continental Europe. This meant that there was a clear division between the secular and regular clergy, as well as a complete system of parishes and diocese.

He also founded several religious communities, mainly for Cistercian Monks and Augustinian cannons. On the political front, David the first introduced an Anglo French Norman aristocracy that would go on to play a significant role in Scottish history. Much of his early life had been spent at the court of his brother-in-law, King Henry the first of England, like his father before him, his marriage to a prominent English woman, a daughter of Walty of Earl of North Umbria, earned him significant political clout in England. Through his wife, he became the Earl of Huntington, a title that came with large swathes of land in Northampton shire. His Anglo Norman connections helped him secure the right to rule Cambria, Strathclyde and part of Lothian before he succeeded the throne from his older brother Alexander the first. Despite his English connections, David the first remained an independent king who was intent on drawing from English, culture and bureaucracy to empower Scotland.

He paved the way for the arrival of other Anglo Norman Families to migrate northward by providing generous rewards of offices and lands. These included Debruises in Annandale, the Fitsilence in Erindale and the Demoravilles in Ayrshire. They were given control of large estates in peripheral areas where David the first regal authority could not be easily enforced. This decentralized form of government, thus introduced a form of feudalism in Scotland. A four tier hierarchy developed with the king at the apex, followed by the Nobles, kings and surfs. The nobles possessed Lens from the crown for their military services, which were provided through the training and recruitment of knights. These knights also protected the peasants on their lords lands who provided their labor and a share of their crops in exchange for this protection. Similar feudal arrangements had existed amongst the clan systems of the Scottish highlands, but these were mainly based on family bonds instead of written charters and legal contracts.

David the first rule over the Scottish kingdom was also consolidated through the creation of a more sophisticated government administration. He introduced the office of Sheriff, vice cops, a royal judge, and an administrator for each area of the kingdom, who was based within a royal castle. Central government officials such as the chancellor, the Chamberlain, and the just sure were introduced to the royal court. The royal court began playing the role of Supreme Court of law and parliament, maintaining an efficient government that facilitated piece and the flourishing of a medieval economy and society. There are four main characteristics which clearly differentiated David the first kingship from the traditional Celtic style kingship that his predecessors had practiced. Firstly, he extended royal power into practically every aspect of life, mainly the religious and the economic. He reformed the Scottish church and extended its religious orders across the land while also introducing an English type market economy.

This included the introduction of formal markets and fairs that required trading licenses that were administered by the crown. He minted the first Scottish coinage and founded the kingdoms four royal burrows, Berwick, Edinburgh, Perth, and Aberdeen. His trusted nobles established firm local lordships centered on well-defended castles. They also sent their nights to serve in his army, which allowed him to experiment with the various tools and policies of an English style administrative kingship. Secondly, he established a more totalizing and monopolistic royal lordship across a greater Scotland, a tradition that greatly benefited his successors. The older tradition of Tenistry, which nearly always engendered great chaos and uncertainty, was abandoned in favor of a strict order for royal succession. This left the regional kings with little opportunity to compete for the throne. Succession was now a matter of direct lineage. True to his centralizing ambitions. David preemptively elected his only son Henry as a co ruler in 1135. After Henry's unexpected early demise in 1152 David appointed his oldest grandson, as is apparent heir.

Malcolm the forth thus became king in 1153 at the previously implausible age of 12 when his grandfather died, a regent nevertheless safeguarded the throne until he was old enough to rule on his own. A strict adherence to primogeniture thus helped to spare the Scottish kingdom from disruptive upheavals and violent competition for the throne. Thirdly, David the first and his government sought to empower the Scottish kingship to be on equal footing with the English kingship. The objective was to thwart to the English monarchies, imperial aspirations, and to foster a greater sense of identity and status as a decidedly independent kingdom. The Scottish Church thus lobbied the pope for PayPal approval of the Scottish kingship. An effort that was thwarted until 1329 by rigorous English lobbying. This concept of a divine and semi sacred kingship was also a potent means for David the first to consolidate his rule.

In the meantime, the Scottish church insisted on remaining independent from the influence of its counterparts in Canterbury or York.

Finally, the Scottish King's began to seek a stronger footing on an international stage. They embraced European courtly fashions and began participating in international diplomacy. David the first succeeded in winning respect and admiration from his continental European peers. The first Scottish monarch to do so. He even envisioned himself as a potential leader of the second crusade. His court embraced English and French, which were both Delingua Franca of political society to such an extent that an Englishman commented that the Scots regarded themselves as Frenchmen in race, manners, language, and culture. Scottish princesses began marrying continental princes with greater frequency while their male counterparts married English, French, and Norwegian princesses, or high born women. From here on the Scottish King's insisted on being viewed as equals to the western European monarchs.

Chapter 4: The Wars of Independence

As in Wales, resistance to Edward the first had led to conquest and direct English rule. But unlike the Welsh, the Scots had not faced heavy losses in their defeat. Even the Battle of Dunbar was not a large engagement, and though it was demoralizing, it did little long term damage to Scotland's military resources. The country might look beaten, but many Scots didn't yet feel that way. Moreover, once he conquered the Scots, Edward the first returned south, the Scottish campaign had drawn time and resources away from his war with the French, and he was determined to waste no more time. However, without the English King keeping them beneath his boot heel. And with much of his armed might draw away to another war, the Scots found the will to resist.

Locked away in England, John Balliol was in no place to lead a fight back against the English, but he remained a figurehead to rally behind and the Scots nobility began appointing sheriffs and other officials in his name, establishing their own resistance government. While a new government and administration was being pulled together, armed forces were being recruited to throw off the English yoke. This took place on three different fronts under different leaders. It had the most politically prominent and therefore legitimate leadership in the southwest, where a group of important lords and churchmen started gathering troops. Among them was Robert the Bruce, a grandson of the contender for the throne, who would also eventually make his reputation fighting the English. In the Northeast Andrew Murray, having escaped English imprisonment after Dunbar led the fight. Between them in the center of the country, forces were gathered by the man who became the most famous leader of this period, William Wallace.

Contrary to popular myth, Wallace was not a peasant or common man an obscure member of a minor noble family. His social status was always likely to lead him to the life of a man at arms, the battlefield role of the upper classes. He had deeper Scottish connections than the more prominent nobles. Having been raised speaking Scots in a Scottish community, rather than in the French speaking cross border Anglo Scottish upper nobility. Still, Wallace would likely have remained an obscure figure long forgotten by history, if not for his loyal adherence to the Balliol cause. Even in Scotland's Darkest Hour, he stood by the absent King rallying armed forces in support of his claim to the throne. Whatever mixture of charisma and local influence allowed him to do it, Wallace gathered troops around him and led a series of successful hit and run raids against the occupiers. His adherence was vital to keeping the Bailio cause alive but that cause was also vital to him and provided a status he would otherwise have lacked.

As the flames of revolt spread across Scotland. Wallace entered the fray, and though hard facts about his initial war efforts are difficult to source. What is clear is that he emerged from obscurity in May 1297 by murdering the English Sheriff of Lanark, William Dehesslerig. Hesslerig was part of the English administration Edward had imposed on Scotland following his conquest the previous year. And at the head of this administration was John de Warren, sixth Earl of Surrey, who had been Edwards chief Lieutenant during the Battle of Dunbar. Assisting Warren was Hugh of Cresingham, who served as treasurer. Wallace's slaying of Hesslerig in May marked an important turning point in the unrest as what had previously been destroyed resistance turned into full blown rebellion. As Sheriff Hesslerig was a symbol of the repressive English authority. And at the time of his murder, he was in Lanark to hold an [04:11 inaudible], a court session for the trial of civil or criminal cases. It would seem that Wallace chose his target in the occasion carefully as the murder of an English official while he was exercising the Kings legal authority over the Scots, would have sent a powerful message to both the occupiers and the occupied. Precisely what Wallace was doing in Lanark in central Scotland in May 1297 is unknown, but popular tradition claims he was there to seek personal revenge against Hesslerig.

The legend stemming from blind Harry's account of Wallace holds that Hesslerig had murdered Wallace's beloved Marion Braid foot. The Eris of Leamington, a village not far from Lanark. It is not clear whether braid foot was Wallace's wife or Mistress but most historians treat the story of Wallace's hot blooded, vengeful murder of Hesslerig as myth and Marion Braid foot as part of this legend, since no evidence supports the personal vengeance claim. It is far more likely than Wallace's brutal murder of Hesslerig was intended to send a chilling message to the English that no one, not even officials would be spared in the mounting rebellion. The English declared Wallace an outlaw, but many Scots were inspired by his actions and joined his campaign. Immediately after Lanark Wallace's forces grew, spurred on perhaps by the rumor that Edward was looking to suppress Midland Scotland in order to force the men of that region into his army to fight against France.

In August 1297, Edward the first headed off to fight in Flanders, leaving Surrey and his associates to deal with the supposedly beaten Scots. He could not afford to abandon his adherents north of the border to the rebels, or allow his recent conquest to be undone. But he also could not abandon his existing plans against the French to deal with the growing revolt, as this would make the rebels look more credible. Thus he left the war to his lieutenants this time, confident that they could crush the Scots without him. In June 1297, the English led by Henry Percy and Robert Clifford, crossed into Annandale from Cumberland and burnt lock maiden on their way to Irvine. A Scottish army under the leadership of Douglas Robert Wishart, the Bishop of Glasgow, James Stewart, one of the former guardians of Scotland, and a recent convert to the patriotic cause Robert the Bruce gathered to face the English threat. Not long after the English cavalry advanced against them. The Scots sought to negotiate terms of surrender, but the negotiations were unusually lengthy. A fact that has led some historians to argue that the negotiated surrender was merely a ruse to give Wallace more time to assemble an army.

Cresingham Edwards's treasure distrusted the Scots and raised an army to fight Wallace. But he was stopped by Percy and Clifford, who believed they had successfully pacified Scotland south of Lanark. As it turned out, the English military leaders had underestimated their opponents. Following the capitulation at Irvine in July 1297, the Scots failed to surrender the hostages they had promised the English and Stewart and Bruce rejoined the Scottish forces only a short time later.

Wallace had since left the forest of Selkirk to head north, where according to blind Harry, he burned 100 English ships. Historian Andrew Fisher believes that was more likely the work of Andrew Murray. But either way, Wallace went on to push out the English from Fife and Perthsure.

By August he was laying siege to Dundee. And according to the chronicler Walter of Guisborough Wallace had attained a large and diverse following. The common folk of the land followed Him as their leader and ruler, the retainers of the great Lords adhere to him. And even though the Lords themselves were present with the English king in body at heart, they were on the opposite side. By uniting their forces in a single army, Murray and Wallace signal to the world that they believe they could beat the odds that in the right circumstances, and with the right leadership, they could defeat the English in a pitched battle, striking a decisive blow for Scottish freedom. The authority King Edward had reclaimed over Scotland the previous year was all but gone by the late summer of 1297. At the time, his Cresingham sent to his monarch the following assessment of the situation. By far the greater part of your counties of the realm of Scotland is still un-provided with keepers. Some have given up their bailiwicks and others neither will nor dare return.

And in some counties the Scots have established and place the bailiffs and ministers so that no counties in proper order, excepting Berwick and Rocks Borough and this only lately. Finally acknowledging that the Scottish rebellion was strong and growing, the English at last aimed to take firm action. Warren Edwards chief Lieutenant, who had succeeded at Dunbar in 1296 left Berwick and headed for Sterling with a sizable army, accompanied by Cresingham they, arrived near Sterling in early September. Meanwhile, Wallace left the siege of the castle at Dundee to the town's inhabitants, and also headed to Sterling. Having joined forces with Andrew Murray, whose successful rebellion in the north of Scotland had severely weakened the English there. Together the two headed what the English called a very large body of rogues. And in early September, they took up positions on the southward looking slope of the abbey Craig, about a mile north of a narrow wooden bridge stretching across the river forth. This bridge situated near Sterling castle was highly strategic because the river was too deep and wide to cross below Sterling, and to the West Lake Flanders moss, Marsh land that was impossible to cross with an army. Furthermore, Sterling Bridge tied the north and south of Scotland together. So whoever controlled this site would hold a strategic advantage over the opponent.

Wallace and Murray even with their entire Scottish army in the field, were about to face a test of strength. The English army with its heavy cavalry outnumbers the Scots by a comfortable margin. A fact that might have caused Warren to expect another easy victory like at Dunbar. He and Cresingham also had the advantage of experience on their side. Since neither Wallace nor Murray could claim extensive military practice, and neither had ever before commanded a large force. However, despite these clear advantages, Warren did not seem bent on engaging in battle. In the days before the battle, he sent representatives to negotiate the surrender of the Scots and when that failed, he sent two Dominican friars, as envoys to speak with Wallace and Murray in order to procure from them terms of surrender. Much to Warren's surprise, he received in response, not a capitulation. But Wallace is well known rebuff. Go back and tell your people that we have not come here for peace. We are ready rather to fight to avenge ourselves and to free our country. Let them come up to us as soon as they like, and they will find us prepared to prove the same in their beards. Hearing Wallace's slight Warren ordered an attack.

Earlier on the morning of September 11, 1297 the English army led by Cresingham began to cross a sterling bridge at a painstakingly slow pace, as the bridge was wide enough for only two horsemen to stand abreast. However, even after some 5000 made it across, Warren, who had overslept that morning and arrived late to the site, promptly recalled all of them. Warren convened a council of war, but he ignored the wise advice of a former Scottish Knight, Richard Lundy, who had suggested crossing the river with his cavalry at a nearby Ford were 60 horsemen could traverse together in order to outflank the Scots. Cresingham preferred the bridge crossing and Warren differed to his opinion. As a result, the army again began a slow crossing of the bridge. Wallace and Marie observed the enemy's maneuvers from the abbey Craig and waited until a certain number of the enemy had reached their side of the river. Once satisfied, they ordered their infantry down the slope along the narrow Causeway to the bridge.

The English cavalry whose horses were unable to gain solid ground on the marshy terrain floundered as the Scots seized the northern end of the bridge, there by cutting off the advancing force from the rest of the army and from the hope of reinforcements. While the rest of the English army watched, the Scots annihilated or let drown some 5000 infantry and 100 knights, including Cresingham, whose body was flayed and made into trophies. Tradition holds that Cresingham skin was used to make Wallace's sword belt. The Lennar coast Chronicle reported that Wallace had a broad strip taken from the head to the heel, to make a baldric for his sword. While Cresingham and the men on the other side of the bridge suffered their grisly fates, Warren never crossed the bridge. As he witnessed the slaughter of his men from afar. He now had to worry about preventing the Scots from crossing the river in pursuit of what remained of the English army. So Warren ordered the bridges destruction and then promptly fled back to Berwick.

Naturally, the battle is best remembered for the way in which blind Harry described it, even as his fantastical account is filled with inaccuracies. On Saturday, they Murray and Wallace Road onto the bridge, which was a good plane board well-made and jointed, having placed watches to see that none past from the army. Taking a right the most able workmen there, he Wallace ordered him to saw the plank in two at the mid straight, middle stretch, so that no one might walk over it. He then nailed it up quickly with hinges and dirtied it with clay to cause it to appear that nothing had been done. The other end he so arranged that it would lie on three wooden rollers which were so placed that when one was out, the rest would fall down. The right himself, he ordered to sit there underneath in a cradle bound on a beam to lose the pin when Wallace let him know, by blowing a horn when the time came. No one in all the army should be allowed to blow but he, the day of the great battle approached. For power the English would not fail. They were ever six to one against Wallace. 50,000 made for the place of battle. The remainder abiding at the castle, both field and Castle they thoughts to conquer at their will.

The worthy the Scots upon the other side of the river took the Plainfield on foot. Hugh Cresingham leads on the Vanguard with 20,000 likely men to sea. 30,000 the Earl of Warren had, but he did then as wisdom did direct. All the first army being sent over before him. Some Scottish men, who well knew this manner of attack Bade Wallace sound, saying they were now enough, then the remainder fled, not able to abide longer, seeking suckler in many directions, some East, some West and some fled to the North. 7000 full at once floated in the fourth, plunged into the deep and drowned without mercy. None were left alive of all that fell army.

Regardless of the subsequent embellishments, Wallace and Marie's achievement at Sterling Bridge was nothing less than remarkable. Despite their inferior numbers, and an army composed of a ragtag host of peasants, farmers and Burgess's, the two leaders exploited the terrain and outwitted and outmaneuver the far more experienced Warren and his heavy cavalry. The effects of this resoundingly victory were felt immediately too. Dundee and Sterling's castles surrendered. While the town's Edinburgh and Berwick also fell to the Scots, though their castles remained in English hands. When the towns of Headington and Rocks Borough were burnt. English hold over Scotland had been all but eliminated.

While the victory at Sterling Bridge decisively swung the wars momentum behind the Scots. It came at a cost. Andrew Murray was grievously injured during the battle and died in early November. Despite his injuries over the two months between Sterling Bridge and his death, Marie and Wallace work together as leaders not only of the Scottish army, but of the country as a whole. In October, the two sent Mrs. to the mayors and communes of Hamburg, and Lubec in an attempt to restore trading relations with Germany. And in early November, Wallace followed up this attempt at diplomacy by securing the election of William Lumberton, who turned out to be staunchly anti-English, as the Bishop of St Andrews. Around that time, Murray passed away from the wounds he had sustained at Sterling Bridge, leaving the burden of defending Scotland solely on Wallace's shoulders.

For the next year, Wallace would hold the highest rank of power and authority in Scotland. The Scottish victory at Sterling bridge came as a huge shock to the English and doubtless to summon Scotland as well. With Surrey defeated and his army in tatters Men all across Scotland joined the rebel cause. Nobles who had previously sworn fealty to Edward turned coat and raised bands of soldiers to fight against him. With momentum on his side, Wallace went on the offensive against England, and by the end of October 1297, he had invaded English territory by marching his growing army into Northumberland and taking its inhabitants by surprise. From Northumberland Wallace led his men across the northwest of England, arriving as far as Cocermouth. While it sounds particularly bold, Wallace was at least partly forced to march into England, because Scotland was stricken by famine and his army which had grown markedly in size needed more resources. It was during this period that Wallace earned the reputation among the English as a ruthless and violent brute.

Without siege machines, the Scottish army could not take any English cities of consequence, so they resorted to raiding and pillaging less protected towns. According to Walter of Guisborough, the services of God totally ceased in all the monasteries and churches between Newcastle and Carlisle. For all the cannons, monks and priests fled before the face of the Scots as did nearly all the people. The reputation for ferocity and barbarity that Wallace had gained at this time, remained with him for centuries after his death, even though as Andrew Fisher claims the cruel acts he ordered were, like those ordered by Edward the first at Berwick, and were of a kind often repeated by both sides. By late November after a failed attempt to raid the bishop brick of Durham, the severe weather forced the end of the invasion of England. Wallace and his troops returned north. Using his title of guardian of the realm. Wallace tried to reestablish order in Scotland in the name of john the first. But despite a growing mass of popular support, he was undermined by a lack of support from the nobility.

Many Scottish nobles resented Wallace's quick rise to power. And according to some contemporaries, Wallace didn't hesitate to use harsh measures against his detractors at home. Stories of imprisonment and hangings made the rounds in both Scotland and England, confirming in the eyes of the English Wallace's status as a violent Biggent. In fact, it was a shared sentiment that Wallace should be defeated that brought the English people together in support of their monarchs renewed campaign in Scotland. In the winter of 1297 to 1298. Edward had been in Flanders overseen his campaign against France, and he did not return to England until my march 1298 after a truce was negotiated with the French. Almost immediately, he said about preparing for war with the Scots and even transferred the seat of government north to York in order to be closer to his target. In April, he convened a war Council in York to plan a campaign, but the Scottish magnates ordered to attend ignored his directive. In retaliation, Edward announced the forfeiture of their lands.

On June 25, the king's army assembled at Rocks Borough, and Edward joined them by early July. Edward headed a strong force composed of roughly 2000 to 3000 horseman, and about 14,000 infantry, many of whom were Welsh, but as he led the army north and advanced into Scotland through Lauderdale, he found the land devastated and empty of inhabitants, which deprived him of the opportunity to gain intelligence about the Scottish army's whereabouts. While Edwards's preparations for war are well known, Wallace's own actions during this time are far less understood. In fact, it is impossible to place in between his return to Scotland in November 1297, following the raid of Northern England and March 1298, when documents show his presence at Porfican in Linlithgowsure on March 29. However, these documents also revealed that by March 1298, Wallace had two new titles, knight and guardian of the kingdom, both in addition to his already established role as leader of the army.

He was the first Scott to be the sole holder of the second title, guardian of the kingdom. The dates he received those titles are unknown, but it's safe to assume the military prowess he exhibited throughout 1297 was the reason they were bestowed on him. Of course, to Edward Wallace's titles meant nothing.

By the summer of 1298 Edwards's sole aim was to locate and subsequently annihilate Sir William and his motley army. But Wallace was not eager to engage in battle with the English and thus engaged in a shrewd strategy of withdraw, heading ever farther north and leaving nothing but scorched earth behind him. Edward took the bait and continued advancing deeper into Scotland, overstretching his lines of communication and supplies just as well as had hoped. Unable to locate the enemy or live off the land. His army was soon starving and in disarray. On July 19, when the army was at Temple Liston, a large supply of wine reaches them, and Edward promptly distributed it. The Welsh soldiers became drunk and ended up rioting, killing several priests. Edward unleashed his cavalry on them and at 80 Welsh soldiers were killed. Many others threatened to change sides before the outbreak was finally quelled. Following this clash, Edward decided to retire to Edinburgh. Wallace's strategy was working, and he was yet again outwitting King Edward. Edward was on the verge of retreat, when fortune finally smiled on him on July 21.

Two Earls had a messenger convey intelligence to the king, that Wallace and his men were stationed at Fall Kirk, less than 20 miles away. The messenger also informed Edward of Wallace's intention to attack the retreating English army by night. Edward acted at once and immediately directed his army toward fall Kirk. That night they camped near the Scottish forces, and the king ordered his men to sleep with their horses beside them in case the Scots attacked. Chaos soon ensued when Edward himself was injured by his horse and the soldiers panicked, and it was only by mounting his horse to display his strength that the king was able to calm his men. At sunrise The next morning, he led his army toward Fall Kirk. Edward came upon Wallace in a strongly entrenched position, protected by a morass which was hidden from the English. Though Wallace had attempted to avoid battle, he at least found himself in a strong position when Edward surprised him with his men arranged to fight.

When the English spotted them, the Scots were divided into four shield drums. The core Scottish battle strategy. A shield drum, was the formation of as many as 2000 men brandishing 12 foot long spears, and gathered in either huge circles or rectangles to look something like a lethal hedgehog. The ranks of the shield drum were to be packed tightly to be nearly impenetrable. With this formation, the Scottish infantry could face off against mounted cavalry men, England's strongest weapon. Between the shield drums Wallace had station his archers, and behind everyone stood the modest side Scottish cavalry under the command of John Commen. Despite having a clear advantage, as well as the benefit of the element of surprise, Edward preferred not to engage immediately and instructed his army to rest. However, several men, including the Earls of Norfolk, Hereford and Lincoln, refused to follow his order and lead a unit forward toward the Scots. They were blocked from advancing further by the morass, and had to shift westward splitting into two wings. Once passed the marshland, the English Vanguard clashed with the shield drums, which held their positions and managed to inflict heavy damage on the English cavalry.

In response, Edward called up his archers to weaken the Scottish ranks. When Edward called up the archers, the Scottish cavalry fled, leaving the shield drums and the Scottish archers with no rear support. But even with a barrage of arrows falling on them, the shield drums managed to keep their discipline while they were suffering heavy losses. They also killed more than 100 English horsemen. But Wallace was severely weakened without his cavalry, which became even more evident once Edward withdrew his cavalry and advanced his long Bowman and cross Bowman. The Scottish infantry was massacred by both the hail of arrows and a series of renewed cavalry assaults. Wallace left the field with a small force before the battle was over. But while the English charged him with cowardice, he was apparently working to ensure the escape of

Scottish survivors, many of whom fled into the nearby woods. Wallace headed towards Sterling and burnt the town and the castle once he arrived. Though Edward had wanted Fall Kirk, his army was too depleted to carry on the campaign or to pursue Wallace. So he began to withdraw his troops and was back in Carlisle by September 9. With that, Edwards fight for Scotland was temporarily suspended and the same could be said for Wallace.

Sometime between the Battle of Fall Kirk and the following December, Wallace resigned the guardianship, which was taken over by Robert the Bruce and john Coleman. He traveled to the European continent, where he presented Scotland's case of freedom to various courts. As it turned out, diplomacy proved to be nearly as dangerous as warfare. It is difficult to know for certain where Wallace went first, and some believe he visited Norway before arriving in France in early November 1299, to lobby for King Philip the fourth support. What is clear, though, is that rather than listening to Wallace's case, Philip had him arrested and offered to hand him over to the English. The cause of the king's sudden loyalty to the English his former enemies was Edwards's marriage to his sister Margaret only two months earlier. However, when Edward learned that Wallace was in French captivity, he responded with a surprising lack of interest and urgency. He Merely thanked Philip and requested that he keep Wallace in France until further notice.

There's no clear explanation for Edwards apparent apathy, and speculation suggests that the English King was not bent on Wallace's destruction. Perhaps he considered the Scots to removed and far from the Scottish cause and thus no longer a real threat. But whatever Edwards thinking he made absolutely no attempt to have Wallace brought to England for justice. After a year of watching over Wallace, Philip grew fond of him and released him to carry on his diplomatic campaigns elsewhere. Though Edward had broken the Scottish army, the result was not the total conquest he hoped for. Political opposition from a group of English magnates forced him to withdraw from the job half done. The English now controlled large swathes of Scotland mostly centered on castles in the south and east. But just like the Scottish kings before them, they had a harder time controlling the highlands and Ireland. Scotland was conquered in theory, but the flames of rebellion burned on.

Wallace's army was broken, and with it any claim he had to political authority. In his place, the Scots appointed a pair of Guardians, Robert the Bruce and John Coleman, Lord of Badenoch, who had supported Bailio in the disputed succession. William Lumberton, the Bishop of St. Andrews, was later added as a third guardian to mediate between the two men who seldom saw eye to eye. Under this new leadership, the Scots returned to a strategy of raids and ambushes, rather than trying to engage the English in a pitched battle. There followed several years of small struggles and minor engagements, in which the future of Scotland remained uncertain. In England, the elderly Edward was facing a range of political challenges. Asking for money to fund his wars always created some resistance from the nobles and clergy on whom the burden of payment mostly rested. And Edwards authoritarian leadership style was also leading to some resentment and calls for the reassertion of noble rights.

Like many English monarchs, he had troubles with senior clergyman, the English church and its priests might owe some allegiance as Englishman to the king. But they also owed allegiances to the Pope, and had a duty to defend the church against royal encroachments. Churchmen sometimes resisted Edwards's demands of Taxis or appointed priests to new positions in line with people rather than royal policy. When Archbishop Corbridge of York did this in 1304, it led to an angry confrontation. The king letting no man put a foreign Pope ahead of him. Arguments with the church subsided with political changes in Europe, and the appointment of the pro English Pope Clements the fifth in 1305. But the conflict between how churchmen saw their loyalties and how their monarchs did would remain a constant throughout the Middle Ages. The greatest source of conflict between Edward and the papacy became Scotland. Pressure from the French led him to release the deposed John Bailio into the Pope's custody in 1299. But this was not the end of church intervention.

The papa bull Shemosfely condemned the English occupation of Scotland, and demanded that the English withdraw, a demand that Edward completely ignored. While Edward was occupied with affairs at home, the Scots blockaded Sterling castle, forcing the English Garrison's to surrender after they ran out of food. In May 1300, Edward launched yet another campaign in Scotland to bring the country under his permanent control. He focused in particular on securing the castles and after invading Galloway, he laid siege to Carelaborock castle, near the southern coast of Dumfries. Siege engines were transferred from Lock Maven and surrounding castles in order to force out the 60 Scott's trying to defend the stronghold against the much larger English army. And once Edward finally broke through the defenses, he hanged several of the Scottish fighters from the castles battlements.

However, aside from a few other minor skirmishes, the English campaign of 1300 achieved little else of significance besides rebuke from outsiders. That August the Papacy sent a letter imploring Edward to withdraw from Scotland. Over the spring and summer of the next four years 1301 to 1304. Edward continued to lead campaigns north into Scotland, with the view of bringing the territory definitively under his control. And in 1302, his authority increased when Robert the Bruce submitted to him. Later the same year, even the papacy softened its stance on his place in Scottish affairs as Pope Boniface, the eighth wrote to the Scottish bishops, encouraging them to reconcile with Edward. As his hold over Scotland grew more secure Edward resurrected old practices, such as demanding that the Scottish nobles pay homage to him. He also reestablished an English administration, including English sheriff's in all strategic localities to run several aspects of Scotland's political and legal systems.

During Edwards operations in 1303 however, he experienced difficulties early on due to sustained opposition posed by Wallace, who repeatedly hindered both divisions of the English army from advancing. The king and his men eventually made his way across most of Scotland, before settling for the winter near Dumbfirline, and by early 1304 the tides turned in Edwards favor. On February nine, John Coleman submitted to him, followed by all of the leading and influential Scots except Wallace and a few others. Perhaps one of the reasons Wallace didn't submit is because it wasn't a palatable option. Had Wallace chosen to submit to Edward, he would not have enjoyed the same lenient terms granted to both Bruce and Coleman, because Edward all but excluded him from this option. As for Sir William Wallace, it is agreed that he may render himself up to the will and mercy of our sovereign Lord the king, if it shall seem good to him. In other words, if Wallace surrendered, no clemency was guaranteed.

The invasion of 1303 to 1304 was to be Edward the first last successful act of conquest. Now in his 60s, he was very old by the standards of the time, but still determined to lead his forces in the field, marching in strength through Dundee, Brechin and Aberdeen, the English drove into the heartland of Scotland, proving the inability of the Scots to hold against a large English force. Having advanced as far north as Murray, they returned to Dumbfirline for the winter. Coleman as guardian of Scotland could not muster enough forces to match them. In January 1304, the Scottish nobility, led by Coleman surrendered to Edward. As part of the surrender, Edward agreed that the country's laws and the rights of the nobles would be as they had been under King Alexander. This was a very different surrender from the one that had come before. Edward was diplomatic rather than menacing, returning lands to the Lords who surrender to his rule, and agreeing to the formation of a new committee of both English and Scottish members who would decide how Scotland would be governed. Perhaps having learned a lesson from responses to his previous harshness, or perhaps seeing that his son would need a different approach to keep the Scots in line. Edward used the carrat as well as the stick. With nearly all of the powerful Scott's in his back pocket and Sterling castle now in his possession, Edward intensified his efforts to capture the elusive Wallace.

In March 1304 he had sent a large force, which included Robert the Bruce to fight against the Scottish hero, but it failed to capture him. Pope Boniface the eighth, who had fallen out with Philip the fourth of France, and now needed the English kings backing supported Edwards's occupation. He ordered the Scottish bishops, many of whom had been among the Lord's leading the revolt, to join in obedience to the conquering king. The last bastion of Scottish resistance was at Sterling castle, where the garrison refused to accept the new order. From April to July 1304 Edward laid siege to the castle. In one of the most spectacular pieces of showboating in medieval warfare. Gunpowder a rarity at the time was used to make Greek fire. Massive siege machines were ordered, including the colossal tribute shih war Wolf, a masterpiece of the siege engineer's art that earned its creator Thomas Greenfield the substantial sum of 40 pounds.

A viewing gallery was constructed so that ladies of the English court could watch the siege as it played out. The English combined bombardment with cutting off Scottish supply lines, leaving the castles garrison starving and shaken. Always looking to lead from the front. Edward took part in the siege, and his life was twice put in jeopardy. Once when a crossbow bolt pierced his clothes, and once when a stone from a manganell scared his horse into throwing him. Gray haired but still determined, the aging King responded to the locals resistance by having the lead stripped from church roofs for the counterweights of his siege machines. Short of supplies and without hope of relief the Sterling garrison eventually asked to surrender. Edward did not allow them to do so until war wolf had been completed and tested against their walls. That done and despite earlier threats, he let the 30 men of the garrison leave with their lives. Only their leader Sir William Olyphant was sent to the Tower of London, and only an Englishman who had given the castle to the Scots was executed.

During a skirmish in September 1304 Wallace again managed to escape the English army, but only after inflicting considerable casualties on the army. In response, Edward increased the stakes with bribery and coercion by promising several Scots who had submitted to him, including Coleman to commute their sentences of exile in return for Wallace's capture. Despite the intense pressure on Wallace, it would take Edward nearly another full year to find and detain him. How he lived at large until then, is unknown. As no documents make reference to his movements or actions. But on August 3, 1305 Edward finally got his wish when Wallace was taken by one of his fellow Scots John Menteith, the keeper of Dumbarton castle. Menteith was rewarded with land for his compliance. Edward refused to meet with Wallace following his arrest, and they had him transported to London on August 22. In the early morning of the next day, Wallace arrived and was taken on horseback in a procession of judicial and legal authorities to Westminster Hall. There was frenzy of excitement on the streets, as many Londoners came out to catch a glimpse of the notorious Scottish warrior.

Inside the hall Wallace was accompanied onto a scaffold, where officials placed a laurel crown on his head, in an apparent attempt to humiliate him by deeming him merely a king of outlaws, and it was the only crown they believed he merited. The Justice presiding over the trial presented the indictment, accusing Wallace of treason and engaging in war crimes by spearing neither age nor sex, monk nor nun. While admitting to the other allegations, Wallace denied the charges of treason, replying, I could not be a trader to Edward, for I was never his subject. No examination of evidence took place, nor was any testimony of witnesses heard. Wallace was not permitted to defend himself because his legal status was that of an outlawed thief. Obviously, the proceedings were a mere formality, and the judgment was given on the same day, William Wallace was found guilty of treason against the English King for taking up arms against him in Scotland, and for making an alliance with France, and he received the standard sentence for treason.

He was to be drawn to the gallows on a hurdle by horses through the streets of London, where he would be hanged for the crimes of murder and robbery. As a desecrater of churches he was to be cut down from the gallows while not quite dead, in order that his internal organs and genitals be removed and burned. Finally as an outlaw, his head was cut off and placed on London Bridge, while the remainder of his body was to be cut into quarters to be displayed in Newcastle, Berwick, Sterling and Perth. As historian John Reuben Davies put it,

Wallace's execution is a classic scene from one of history's great tragedies the death of a national hero, a bloodthirsty judicial killing the demonstrative and exemplary justice of an English King. A plaque now documents the spot near where he was executed on August 23 1305. After the Treaty of Edinburgh Northampton in 1328, Scotland began the 1330s in a fairly good position.

Almost three decades of civil war and war with England had severely sapped the country's resources and morale. However, Robert the Bruce had for the time being secured a peaceful end to the English coveting of Scotland. Bruce's Death On the seventh of June 1329, left behind a four year old son, David the second. David the second was crowned King of Scotland on 24 Nov.1329. And a guardianship was assumed by Thomas Randolph, who was then Earl of Murray. In England Edward the third was determined to avenge the humiliation of England by the Scots. Despite having signed the Treaty of Edinburgh, North Hampton, Edward the third was not the same man as his father, and though he was young, he had a similarly ambitious nature to that of his grandfather, Edward the first. Edward had not acted under his own initiative, having instead been pressured by Roger Mortimer, his Regent, as well as his mother, Isabella of France.

The peace of North Hampton, dubbed by the English as the shameful piece had failed to account for Reparations to a group of nobles, who held land and estates in both England and Scotland. Their properties and titles had been given to Bruce's allies, an act that still sat sourly with both the English nobility and Edward the third. England was suffering from a depleted Treasury following the wars waged against Scotland. Yet the outraged English people and its King were in no position to attempt any further action against Scotland by them. In 1330, the year following the coronation of David the second saw two events occur, which would prove to be significant for both Edward and the future of Scotland. Edward the third had his regent Roger Mortimer executed, thus taking full control of his crown and country. Secondly, Edward Bailio made an appeal to the now unbridled English King. The previous King of Scotland, John Bailio, who after the English invasion of Scotland in 1296, had been forced to abdicate his throne had left behind a son, Edward Bailio. Edward Bailio approach the King of England, wanting the return of ancestral lands that he claimed was rightfully his.

Before the end of the year, Edward the third sent demands to young King David's Regent Thomas Randolph, Randolph delayed responding, despite Edward the third pressing the matter, with the second request on 22 April 1332. Meanwhile Bailio and his followers began to prepare for an invasion of Scotland. The Battle of Duplinmore was to be the opening skirmish in what would become known as the second war of Scottish independence. The battle was a significant opener to the war, one which was won by Edward Bailio and Commander Henry DE Beaumont. To circumvent the terms of the Treaty of North Hampton, the Scottish rebels and their English allies sailed from several ports in Yorkshire to the king horn in Fife, on the 31st of July 1332. The terms of the treaty did not permit English forces to cross the tweed. From King Horn they eventually marched to Perth. On the 10th of August, the army was camped at For Teviot, a few miles short of the much stronger force led by Donald the Earl of Mar, which was positioned on the heights of Duplinmore.

A second Scottish force led by Patrick Earl of Dunbar was fast approaching Bailio's army from the rear. The predicament led to no courage to the smaller army, and morale and Bailio's camp began to shrink. Henry Beaumont, the commander of Bailio's army, was accused by the other disinherited lords, claiming he had betrayed them through false promises of Scottish support for Bailio once they had entered Scotland. Beaumont, by far the most experienced soldier on either side, reacted with cool precision, ordering his troops to risk crossing the river earn at night and launching a surprise attack on the enemy before they could link with the approaching second force. Overconfident of his superior force, Donald the Earl of Mar, ordered his army to settle down on the night of 10 August, not bothering to set a watch. At midnight under the cover of darkness, and with no guard present from the opposing army to raise the alarm Beaumont Bailio's force across the urn to take up a defensive position on high ground at the head of a narrow valley, outflanking Mar. With the rapid approach of the main Scottish force Beaumont knew that the time to act was now. The army formed aligns, with archers on each flank and men at arms at the center, resembling a quarter moons.

The Scots, angry that their enemy had out-maneuvered them, charged up the defensively formed English army in disorganized shieldtrins, all formation lost to the reckless charge. Mars wild charge was met with a hail of arrows, falling on the Scottish flanks. The unarmed Scottish footmen with unvisered helmets were ill prepared for the volley of arrows which fell murderously, thinning their ranks in heartbeats. The superior force however, was able to get through the storm of arrows and meet the center of the English force, where Beaumont's men at arms finally gave some ground but the unrelenting barrage of arrows thinned out the charging armies' flanks, forcing them to push into the middle to escape the reign of death. The larger force lost all ability to maneuver and the crowded middle ranks of the army were pushed into the waiting Spears of the English. The Scottish dead were piled high as the battle ended with the English surrounding the mass of bodies. The Scots losses were heavy. Mar himself was killed, as were several other key members of the Scottish army. Estimates and between two and 13,000 Scottish dead against relatively light English losses had marked the first battle of the second war for Scottish independence. And not since the Battle of Fall Kirk and the Scottish felt such a terrible defeat.

The worst casualty of all was the loss of national confidence that had grown through the successive victories of King Robert Bruce. Dunbar's army was still in the field of a similar number to Mars prior to his defeat. However, the confidence of Bailio and Beaumont's troops sword. The decimation of Mars troops was felt through the arriving army. Dunbar was reluctant to engage the force that had so thoroughly dispatched one of equal size to his. The English would learn from this battle most keenly and the formation adopted by the Bailio and Beaumont would become a standard battle order one which would provide England with many future victories. The decisive victory granted valuable time to Edward Bailio's invasion, also leaving him well placed in Scotland to gather supporters and swell his ranks. Bailio saw particularly strong support from the residents of Fife and Straightern. Not long after his victory at Dunbar, Bailio was crowned the king of Scots, a title he used to gain further support as his army marched across the country, eventually settling in Rocks Borough. While at Rocks Borough, with his forces swelling due to the spreading news of his victory against the usurpers and claim to the throne. Bailio offered his loyalty to Edward the third, pledging to support all of Edwards's future battles as well as offering to wed David the second sister. A move that would further legitimize his claim to the throne and expand his lands and fortunes.

Bailio then left Rocks Borough moving on to Anand, which would be the site of the chemist's aid of Anand, a battle between the supporters of Bailio and the loyalist troops of David the second led by Sir Archibald Douglas and John Randolph, third Earl of Murray. Bailio would lose this battle to the Bruce loyalists, but managed to escape fleeing Scotland to return to Edward in England. Meanwhile, David the second own resistance had been thrown into turmoil at the death of Thomas Randolph his regent. Thomas had been a constant companion to Robert to Bruce in his final years and taken over management of Bruce's household. Robert had decreed before his death that Randolph would serve as David's Regent, a role he performed wisely and with honor before his unfortunate death at Muscle Borough. Randolph had been on his way to engage Edward Bailio and his supporters when he died. Many believed it to be the result of English poison, but the most likely culprit was a kidney stone.

Once he had returned to England, Edward Bailio once again offered his loyalty and homage to Edward the third, requesting his aid in the combined campaign against Scotland. Bailio returned to Scotland in March 1333 to lay siege to Berwick upon tweed. Berwick upon tweed held a strategic position on the border between Scotland and England, being the main route for both invasion and trade. The town had a tumultuous past, having been sacked by Edward the first in 1296, one of the first actions which marked the beginning of the first

Scottish War of Independence. Edward the third justification of the military actions against Berwick upon tweed, and the violation of the Treaty of Northampton was due to his claims that Scotland was preparing for war.

His incursion being a response to threats from the North. Bailio cross the border first with his disinherited Scottish Lords on 10 March, accompanied by some English magnates. Edward had invested heavily in the nobles accompanying the campaign, providing grants of over 1 million pounds to the Englishman, and similar amounts to Bailio and his Scottish nobles.

Bailio's army reached Berwick in late March and immediately made moves to encircle the town and cutting off all aid by land. Edwards Navy having already done the same by Sea. Edward himself arrived at Berwick with the bulk of the English army on the ninth of May, some six weeks after Bailio had arrived and laid siege. Bailio had not been idle, unleashing a scorched earth policy upon the surrounding lands, ensuring that there was little to no sustenance in the region to resupply the town if the opportunity arose. The town's water supply had already been cut, trenches dug, and all communication out of Berwick was made impossible while Edwards accompanying craftsmen began work on the siege engines required to take the town.

A large Scottish army was gathering just north of the border under the leadership of Sir Archibald Douglas. He concentrated his energy on swelling the ranks of the army, rather than utilizing the troops he already had, except for carrying out some minor rating into Cumberland. Unfortunately, these raids had little effect in drawing the English away from Berwick and instead provided Edward with justification for his military campaign. By the end of June with the full support of the English army, it's tribuchais and catapults and also Edwards Navy Berwick was close to falling. With its garrison exhausted and half the town destroyed a truce was requested by the defending commander Alexander Seton.

Edward agreed to the truce on the condition that Seton surrenders by 11 July. Douglas was now without options, and the army that had gathered north of the border was compelled into action. Douglas had approximately 13,000 troops, significantly more than Edwards 9000. On the last day of Seton's truce, the army entered England marching to the port of tweed mouth. The little port had been destroyed. Having been an obstacle for the large Scottish army, who were eager to provide the relief required by the truce set down by Edward? A few hundred Scottish cavalry were able to navigate their way across the ruins of the old bridge, and then force their way to Berwick. In their minds and in those of the Scottish garrison at Berwick. The terms of the truce had been satisfied. Edward argued that the relief was to have come from Scotland, or rather the direction of Scotland. While the few hundred Scottish cavalry had entered Berwick from the English side.

After much arguing a fresh truce was agreed to on the provision of relief before the 20th of July.

Douglas knew that a foray against England in his current defensive position would be disastrous, even with a superior numbers. To draw the English army out to more favorable terrain Douglas Marched the Scottish army south towards Bambra, threatening to besieged the town where Edwards Queen was currently in residence. However, Edward was confident in Bambra' defenses, and the Scots had not the time to construct the type of machinery needed to breach the fortress. Instead, the Scottish army ravaged the countryside. Edward ignored this, positioning his army on Haledon Hill, a highly defensive position on a rise of some 600 feet. Douglas out of options had little choice but to engage Edward on the ground of his choosing. To engage the English army the Scots descended downhill to the marshy ground that covered the area before Haledon Hill. Once over the marshy ground, they still had the hill to climb before reaching the English forces. The journey left the Scottish Spearman vulnerable to English arrows for a long period of time without cover. Casualties were heavy. However, the survivors made it to the crest of the hill, climbing towards the waiting Spears of the English. The Scottish army broke. Their casualties were in the thousands including Douglas himself. Edwards's casualties were numbered at just 14.

The next day Berwick's truce expired, and the towns surrendered to Edwards's terms. The loss of Douglas and the troops at Haledon Hill was a tremendous blow to the supporters of David the second. The Scottish King would soon be exiled to France, where he would remain until 1341. Edward Bailio was crowned and quickly fulfilled his promises to Edward. Acknowledging fealty and subjection to Edward, Bailio surrendered Berwick as an inalienable possession of the English crown. Following Later that year, Bailio also yielded Rocks Pearl, Edinburgh, Pebels, Dumfries, Linlithgow and Headington and though Edward did not remove Scottish laws, he did replace the men in charge with his own. While David the second was removed, and Edward the third attended to the issues of his own kingdom, Bailio was troubled by unrest among both the Scottish nationalists and his own allies. While Bailio's allies seemed to be deserting him, his enemies were only growing in number. He retired to Berwick, managing to convince Edward the third that the situation was under control. Though In the meantime, more and more of his men were defecting to join those loyal to David the second.

French and English relations were already tense but Philip the second to France offered shelter to David the second. A mutual defensive pact had been signed between Scotland and France in 1295 under the then King John Bailio, Edward Bailio's father. After a plea for aid from David's new co regions, Philip sent an ambassador to England to discuss the recent events between Scotland and England. Unfortunately, not much would be gained by the ambassadors, who failing to make headway with the disorganized members of Edward the second loyalist's supporters only succeeded in unwittingly allowing England time to recover their finances. In March 1335, having lost confidence in Bailio's ability to hold sway over the Scottish nobleman, Edward began mustering his forces, Scotland was aware of the growing mobilization of English forces and began to quietly prepare. Edward raised his largest army to date, number 13,000 men. His strategy a three pronged invasion of Scotland. Bailio would take troops west from Berwick. While Edward led his troops north from Carlyle and a naval force near the Clyde would form the third front of the invasion. The armies encountered little resistance, meeting up at Glasgow and eventually settling in the area of Perth.

In France, an army of 6000 soldiers was openly assembled to aid the Scottish troops. Edward was informed that these troops would be deployed if he did not submit to arbitration by France and the Pope. Edward refused. Meanwhile, Scottish loyalist forces were not faring well. Andrew Murray agreed to a truce with Edward lasting from October until Christmas. However Bailio and his followers were not included in the terms. Bailio through the support of David the third Streth Boogie, laid siege against Kildromi Castle.

Murray sent troops after him routing his force and killing

Streth Boogie. Bailio would see many more defeats in the coming years that would force him to rely more and more heavily on the English King.

In May 1336, Edward pushed on with his invasion plans despite the threat from the French. He received reports of the massing forces of Philip and intended to block the most likely port of arrival, Aberdeen. Edward moved from Newcastle, with the force of 400 men swelling his ranks as he marched on Lockingdorm ending Scottish sieges and destroying everything he encountered before burning Aberdeen to the ground. The English embassy had been attempting to negotiate with Philip the sixth and David the second. However, in August, they received final word from Philip. His invasion of England would proceed. French privateers attacked the town of Oxford also capturing several royal ships. Edward received word of French actions by September. He abandoned his immediate plans in Scotland and returned to England. However, he was too late to strike back at French ships. He raised funds before returning to Scotland, settling down to winter at the fortress in Clyde after a series of wins and losses. Scotland was under heavy strain, with both English and Scottish forces ravaging the countryside, each trying to eliminate any advantage the other force might acquire.

Disease and hunger were rampant among the people. The Scottish loyalists used the French distractions to their advantage, and by the end of March, they had reclaimed most of Scotland north of the fourth and had dealt serious blows to lands owned by Edward Bailio. Edward the third was forced to focus on France vowing to return to Scotland once they had been taken care of. In the meantime France had also continued to pour supplies into Scotland to aid the Scottish loyalists. The newly provisioned Scottish forces were able to progress further south and into northern England, laying waste to Cumberland and forcing Edward to split his efforts between both French and Scottish threats. Early winter of 1338 was seen as a turning point for the Scots and though the ruthless actions of Murray had left such devastation in his own lands that thousands of Scottish people were left without a means to feed themselves. He had effectively ended the possibility for Edward the third to establish a stable lordship over southern Scotland.

Chapter 5: The Black Death

After killing millions as it spread westward from China and throughout the Mediterranean. The Black Death devastated England between 1348 and 1349. Deaths were caused by a combination of fatal airborne diseases. The bubonic plague during the summer months, the pneumonic plague during winter and possibly anthrax. Modern scientific studies attribute the infection to the bacterium you're Sinia pesto. This strain is ancestral to all currently existing why pesto strains, but there is also evidence to indicate that it may have had viral origins. The inhabitance of medieval Europe believed that the plague was airborne, but scientists believe that it actually spread on the backs of Rodin's, primarily rats, which were surreptitiously infested with plague carrying fleas. London was hit in September, 1348 with the entirety of East Anglia affected the following year. Whales and the Midlands were infected by the spring of 1349. That summer it spread across the Irish Sea and penetrated northward into Scotland.

Historians believed that the Scots had been infected because they chose to attack various English towns as they were succumbing to the plague, believing that the disease was retribution from God. Nearly 5,000 Scottish soldiers fielded a botched attempt to invade England. Scotland did not suffer as much as it's Western European counterparts because of its cooler climate and more dispersed population. Even so, the plague was capable of wiping out the majority of the urban populations based in cities like Glasgow and Edinburgh. An English account of the pandemic reveals that even small villages were not fully spared from its deadly embrace. Sometimes it came by road, passing from village to village, sometimes by river as in the East Midlands or by ship, from the Low Countries or from other infected areas. On the villas of the bishop of [02:13 inaudible] states in the West Midlands, they, the death rates ranged between 19% of manorial tenants at Whortleberry and Hanbury to no less than 80% at Aston.

It is very difficult for us to imagine the impact of plague on these small rural communities. Where a village might have no more than 400 or 500 inhabitants. From the world upside down in Black Death in England, J Bolton. Apart from the mystery of its origins and how it spread, the Black Death was so terrifying because of the speed in which it struck and the scale of its activity. Entire villages could be wiped out in a matter of days. While large urban areas could easily lose between 80 to 90% of their populations. The exact number of Scottish people that died due to the plague is unknown, but historians estimate that about a fifth of Scotland's population was lost during this time. Approximately 1 million people. Even this conservative estimate is enough to make it the most fatal calamity in the history of the kingdom. The very small minority who survived an infection had to live the rest of their lives with crippling mental and physical disabilities.

The first signs that someone had been infected were usually the emergence of lumps in the armpits or groin. After that, angry black spots began to appear on the thighs, arms, and other parts of the body. This was typically a death sentence within three days. The colder Scottish climate deterred the bubonic form of the plague, but it allowed the pneumonic or septicemia plague to achieve a high death toll. The nobles were often spared by virtue of their isolation in the castles, but the middle and lower classes were mostly unable to escape its ravages. To make matters worse, the plague was not a one off phenomenon. Instead it returned to haunt Scotland multiple times throughout the subsequent centuries. The final outbreak occurred in the 1640s. It stifled all aspects of life from the economic to the political, to the cultural. Children whose parents were dying from the plague, refused to visit their death beds out of fear of becoming infected themselves.

There was a shortage of labor leaving many farms, unmanned for years. Many fields were allowed to rot, reversing all the agricultural and manufacturing progress that had been achieved after the wars of independence finally came to an end. Wars were halted as were much of international and international trade. Combating the plague certainly took its toll on Scotland. In the 17th century. It finally managed to return to pre plague population levels. This was achieved by the implementation of strict health controls whenever an outbreak occurred, people were prohibited from gathering, and those believed to be infected, were placed in quarantine. The foul cleansers were widely employed in Edinburgh and other Scottish towns by this time. Their job was to relocate plague victims far away from human settlements to die and to burn all their homes, clothes, and possessions to the ground.

Chapter 6: How Scotland Was Built Into An Industrial Economy By Inventors, Explorers, And Missionaries

In the early 1700s, Scotland was mostly a rural and agricultural economy. It had only a population of 1 million people with a relatively small portion based in its modern urban townships. Within the course of a single lifetime, everything changed. By the 1820s the effects of the Industrial Revolution were unmistakable. The scientific theories that had been conceptualized during the Scottish Enlightenment swiftly turned into practical applications that could be turned into hardy profits in a capitalist world. Scotland's population rose dramatically, people left the countryside and traditional farm life for manufacturing towns, which eventually became bustling cities.

There were approximately 1.5 million people in Scotland during the start of the 19th century. By the end of the 20th century, this number had tripled to over 4.5 million people. A significant portion of this rise can be attributed to immigrants, particularly Irish immigrants, who were fleeing the prospect of starvation during the Irish Potato Famine 1845 to 1849. This population rise was also partly the byproduct of crucial advancements in medicine, health care and public health standards. These improvements reduced the mortality rate in the face of previously fatal epidemic diseases. Meanwhile, the scientific innovations that were assimilated into traditional agricultural practices allowed fewer farmers to produce enough produce to feed a larger population. South Eastern farmers were praised for their efficiency. Northeastern farmers for their cattle and beef and Airsher a county in the southwest for the large quantities of quality milk their cows produced.

Innovations in chemistry, for example, the use of chlorine to bleach linen, helped make the Scottish textile industry surpass agriculture. Linen production became more efficient than ever before, with the use of newly discovered chemicals and the adoption of English inventions, like Hargreaves, spinning jenny, argrites water frame, and Crompton's mule. These inventions transformed the weaving process, radically increasing output, productivity and competitiveness. Instead of relying on human power alone, these new spinning machines were powered by massive water wheels. The old tradition of men working on hand blooms was replaced by an efficient factory system. Women and children were roped into the workforce spending long hours toiling for relatively low wages.

During the 1830s heavy Industry replaced textiles as the most important component of the Scottish economy. The production of coal and iron rose tremendously, facilitating the popularization of railways, steam locomotives and ships. The use of canals and horses as the dominant form of transportation slowly became obsolete. If the first phase of the Industrial Revolution mainly consisted of old industries becoming more efficient through the adoption of new technologies. The second phase was driven by Scottish innovations themselves. Henry Bell 1767 to 1830 built the comet, the first successful passenger steamship in 1812. It catalyzed the birth of the Scottish shipbuilding industry and the railway industry. James Watt 1736 to 1819 did not invent the steam engine as commonly believed. It had existed since the early 18th century, but he did invent the separate condenser, which reduced the amount of water steam engines needed while allowing them to produce more power.

The introduction of an extensive railway network helped Scotland to make significant economic progress during the

Victorian era. When Queen Victoria assumed the throne in 1827, there were only a few Scottish railway lines in existence. These were mainly used to transport coal and other industrial raw materials between the bustling urban hubs of Glasgow, Edinburgh and Dundee. In 1843 the Edinburgh Glasgow railway line opened, catalyzing a national obsession with railways. Within a single generation practically all of Scotland's railways were built, constituting some of the world's most ambitious engineering projects at the time. Railway tracks were built between small villages and major towns stretching across all directions. Thanks to the advent of efficient steam engines, journeys that would have taken days on horse drawn carriages were now completed in a matter of hours. There was, of course, a dark side to all this intellectual, economic and technological progress. The extensive railway network effectively bridge the distance between the urban centers and the countryside, allowing tourism in rural Scotland to boom.

Urban growth during the Victorian era had created dirty, overcrowded and polluted cities. With Glasgow being the primary example. The lack of adequate housing for the large influx of migrants had led to the sprawl of slums with dire standards of living. With over 20,000 people forced to live in shabby housing and practically no sanitation. One can only imagine the effect of such conditions on the body and mind. These dismal living conditions were incredibly conducive to disease. Glasgow soon became a hotbed for typhus and typhoid. Scotland's participation in the global British Empire also led to a deadly outbreak of cholera. In 1832 the first cholera outbreak in Scotland killed 3000 people in Glasgow alone. All the public health advances that had been achieved since the black plague were temporarily reversed as death rates soared to 17th century heights. It appears obvious now, but the link between dirt and disease was not immediately apparent then. It was only after the subsequent color epidemics of 1848 and 1853 that the medical community identified the filthy living conditions as a problem that had to be solved.

The introduction of an expensive sewage system and a clean water supply from Lock Katrine from 1850 and 1875 was crucial in improving sanitation and public health standards in Glasgow. Eager to escape the grimness of city life, many wealthier Scots took the opportunity to breathe in the fresh air and enjoy the stunning vistas of the Scottish countryside. They also developed appetites for hunting deer, shooting birds and fishing. By the 1890s there were widespread concerns that urban rural tourism was devastating the countryside and causing various species of bird and deer to tether towards extinction. Apart from the rising pollution levels, and the desecration of nature for the extraction of raw materials, Scotland's relentless appetite for wealth and progress incurred heavy ethical costs. As Scotland looked beyond its traditional trading relationships with France and the Low Countries, Netherlands, Belgium and Western Germany, it became complicit in the impure exploitation of countries and populations outside of Europe.

The Scottish textile industry developed a dependence on imported cotton from India, England's prized colonial possession as well as the slave plantations of America. Scottish capitalists also proved to be adept at extracting profits from the Atlantic trade of tobacco. There were no tobacco plantations in Scotland. But Glasgow's infamous tobacco Lords were able to gain a firm grip on the trade through their strategic position. Glasgow was closer to the transatlantic shipping routes than London or Bristol and Saby use of capital. Their agents sailed out to North Carolina and Virginia to trade with the owners of small tobacco plantations. They provided credit and loaned them tools brought from Scottish iron and Scottish made linen, which would be repaid with takings from their future crops.

As these plantations grew in size and scale with the help of their funding, so did the amount of tobacco that made its way to Glasgow's warehouses.

No ship that sailed into Glasgow needed to wait very long to be fully loaded with tobacco. Tobacco was only one component of Scotland's three way trade, with the rapidly evolving American economy. Ships from Scotland would sail to Africa to be filled with slaves. These slaves would then be taken to either tobacco plantations in America or sugar plantations in the West Indies. The ships would return to Scottish ports with the products of this exploitative labor system, primarily sugar and tobacco. This arrangement also brought in large amounts of profits into Scotland, which could then be reinvested into the Scottish Industrial Revolution. In 1747, the tobacco Lords became even wealthier when the French government gave Glasgow a lucrative monopoly over the supply of tobacco to France. The huge influx of money into Scotland's rising number of banks facilitated the growth of a financial industry and newfangled forms of credit.

Chapter 7: Problems Facing Scotland Today

The powers in question involve matters of broad national concern, such as food safety laws, public service recruitment and environmental laws. The Scottish Parliament is concerned that Westminster may compromise Scottish interests in its desperation to strike up a trade deal with United States President Donald Trump. A prospect that could easily materialize if Westminster can sideline the Scottish Parliament from the decision making table. This situation also exemplifies the fact that the Westminster Parliament only holds its sovereignty as a matter of principle. The interest of the Scottish, the Welsh and the Northern Irish are purely secondary. Scottish First Minister Nicola Sturgeon has noted that her government would in good faith and a spirit of compromise. Seek to identify a solution that might enable Scotland's voice to be heard and mitigate the risks that Brexit poses to our interests within the UK.

Sturgeon has pointed out that the majority of Scottish voters opted to remain in the EU, and that access to the European single market was crucial. If Scotland cannot remain as a full member of the EU post Brexit, then the option may be to seek full independence. One option in my view, the best option, is to become a full member of the EU as an independent country. Indeed, independence would resolve the fundamental cause of the position Scotland currently finds itself in. Westminster governments that Scotland doesn't vote for imposing policies that the majority in Scotland does not support. This is undoubtedly the boldest of options, especially since the United Kingdom is a far more significant trade partner than the EU.

In 2016, exports to the rest of the UK accounted for 61%, 45.8 billion pounds of total Scottish exports, while exports to the EU only accounted for 17% of total exports, 12.7 billion pounds. Scotland's interests in maintaining ties with Europe are thus not purely materialistic. Sturgeon diplomatically contrasts the attractiveness of European ideals in contrast to Westminster's historical heavy handedness in dealing with Scotland. Europe is about more than economics. The European ideal is one of peaceful coexistence, mutual solidarity and support and prosperity built on cooperation. There is much still to achieve, but a Europe which encourages openness and civic dialogue and which welcomes difference is one from which Scotland has gained much into which it still wants to contribute.

His history and endless cycle or a series of progressions and regressions. The dilemma that sturgeon's government faces would certainly be familiar to many of Scotland's medieval kings, many of whom have actively sought fraternity with their counterparts in Europe as a means to neutralize the threat of their dominant southern neighbor. Sturgeon's emphasis on

Europe welcoming difference hints at inalienable rights that the EU accords to its smaller members, beneath its countless rules and treaties, there is an acceptance of cultural and historical differences between its members. A reflection of the post-World War Two striving to avoid further conflicts between European nations. This acceptance of heterogeneity stands in contrast to the general pressure to conform and Anglicized according to English norms within the United Kingdom. The pragmatic benefits of a continued relationship with England and the United Kingdom as a whole remain. But this relationship is predicated on Scottish interests playing second fiddle to Westminster's.

Sturgeon herself has made it clear that she wishes for Scotland to finally wrestle its rights to complete autonomy. A desire to be free of Westminster that is akin to Westminster's own desire to be free of influence from Brussels, once and for all. Her patients indicate that she has a long term strategy in mind. After calling for a second referendum in 2016 after Brexit, which Theresa May denied, she obtained a good sense of Scotland's appetite for independence in the light of an impending loss of EU membership. A second referendum on Scottish independence after May has ironed out all the Brexit details with Brussels is imminent. In the meantime, Scotland looks inwards towards its various problems, social and economic inequality divisions between the Catholics and Protestants. Its economic prospects in the near future before contemplating her place in a politically volatile world.

Conclusion

With that, we have come to the end of this book. I want to thank you for choosing this book.

Now that you have come to the end of this book, we would first like to express our gratitude for choosing this particular source and taking the time to read through it. All the information here was well researched and put together in a way to help you understand the history of Scotland as easily as possible.

We hope you found it useful and you can now use it as a guide anytime you want. You may also want to recommend it to any family or friends that you think might find it useful as well.

Thanks!